D0895194

Love Behind Bars

THE TRUE STORY OF AN AMERICAN PRISONER'S WIFE

JODIE SINCLAIR
PREFACE BY SISTER HELEN PREJEAN

Arcade Publishing • New York

Arcade Publishing books may be purchased in bulk at special discounts for sales promotion, corporate gifts, fund-raising, or educational purposes. Special editions can also be created to specifications. For details, contact the Special Sales Department, Arcade Publishing, 307 West 36th Street, 11th Floor, New York, NY 10018 or arcade@skyhorsepublishing.com.

Arcade Publishing® is a registered trademark of Skyhorse Publishing, Inc.®, a Delaware corporation.

Visit our website at www.arcadepub.com.

10 9 8 7 6 5 4 3 2 1

Library of Congress Cataloging-in-Publication Data is available on file.
Library of Congress Control Number: 2020931616

Cover design by Brian Peterson

Print ISBN: 978-1-948924-84-9
Ebook ISBN: 978-1-948924-85-6

Printed in the United States of America

This memoir is written with deep appreciation for:

Sister Helen Prejean and her inspiring fight against the death penalty,

All who stand by loved ones in prison despite the hardship and pain,

My children, my family, and my friends who stood with me for twenty-five years as I fought to free my husband from one of the most vicious prison systems in the United States of America.

CONTENTS

PREFACE

IN 1984, I WITNESSED THE executions of two men at Angola, Elmo Patrick Sonnier and Robert Lee Willie. I was their spiritual adviser during their last months on death row, the last hours of their lives, and their executions.

They began my thirty-four-year fight against the death penalty.

Dead Man Walking tells their stories. My book, and the movie it inspired, shows they were not beyond redemption. They were children of God, despite their crimes.

In His infinite wisdom, God gave us the power to protect ourselves from the hate so many feel toward those on death row. Forgiveness illuminates the path to redemption.

Forgiveness is the path to heaven on Earth, the sense of community that comes when we live according to the greatest theme in Christendom: Loving our neighbors as ourselves.

It shows us there is value in every human being. When forgiveness fills our hearts, we live in the peace that God intended for us. We are protected from hate's temptation and the awful state it can create in those who succumb to its appeal.

This book tells the story of a woman's journey through a quarter century of hatred that threatened her soul until the sight of the Cross on her mother's church saved her early one morning.

Her love for her convict husband—a man who was once on death row—teaches us the soul can endure when it is filled with love.

Sister Helen Prejean
New Orleans, Louisiana
2018

FOREWORD

"From the first moment I set eyes on you, I became a complete man—a man with purpose and hope. I loved you then. I love you now. And I will love you until the last breath leaves my body."

HE WROTE THOSE WORDS IN 2005 as hope began to fade that he would ever come home.

Therein lies a story of pain so deep that I could not write it for twenty-five years. But I swear no other man could have given me so much life.

Jodie Sinclair
December 2019

THE FATEFUL DAY

"Crime, like virtue, has its degrees."
—Jean Racine, French playwright, 1639–1699

THE SWEET SCENES OF EARLY spring rolled by one after another as my photographer and I headed up a country road on March 17, 1981, toward the Louisiana State Penitentiary at Angola. Known as the Alcatraz of the South, the state penitentiary was preparing to carry out its first execution in decades. I was assigned to do a five-part series on the death penalty for WAFB Channel 9, the CBS affiliate in Baton Rouge where I was the capital correspondent.

An inmate on Angola's death row had kicked off a media frenzy when he persuaded a local court to set a death date in his case. In 1978, Colin Clark was sentenced to death for the brutal after-hours killing of a Baton Rouge restaurant manager. When he told a local court that dying in the electric chair was better than spending years waiting for his appeals to work their way through the court system, the judge obliged him with a date in late April for his execution.

The series was a prime assignment. Interest in the death penalty was at an all-time high. No reporter had been allowed to interview death row inmates in Louisiana or get video of their highly restricted cell block in a decade. My stories would bring viewers face-to-face with the electric chair in Angola's death house. Every element was fascinating—how the chair kills, what happens during a man's final hours, what his family feels, what victims' families feel, and the religious, moral, and ethical questions that surround the calculated taking of human life.

Executions had resumed nationwide in 1977 after states rewrote their death penalty laws in the wake of the US Supreme Court decision in 1972 in *Furman v. Georgia,* which declared the death penalty unconstitutional as it was then being applied. The high court upheld these rewritten state laws in 1976 in a series of decisions—*Gregg v. Georgia, Roberts v. Louisiana, Jurek v. Texas, Profitt v. Florida,* and *Woodson v. North Carolina*. Now, Louisiana would have its first opportunity to carry out the ultimate sentence under its new law: death in the embrace of "Gruesome Gertie," as the state's electric chair was popularly known.

The road ended abruptly at the Angola front gate. We stopped the car and waited for approval to enter. Spring sunshine lay across the prison's vast fields, stretching on their alluvial plain as far as the eye could see—eighteen thousand acres of continental soil, silt the Mississippi River had deposited there for a thousand years. A soft March wind blew across its fields and an azure sky belied the prison's infamous past.

Angola is a stain on Louisiana's history. More than two hundred graves a year had been dug at the prison for convicts treated like slaves in the 1880s: men, women, and children dying under the whip and worse at the height of a callous prison operation on a plantation named Angola.

The road into the prison slanted down from the surrounding hills, their woods the last trees for miles. To the right of the front gate, hard up against the hills, stood a separate building—Angola's death house—its bunker-like concrete covered with flaking green paint. Beds of rosebushes dotted the lawn inside its razor-wire enclosure.

Far inside the prison, crops pushed up sturdy shoots. Convicts in work gangs moved among them in the humid heat; rags tied around their heads kept steady streams of sweat from their eyes. Guards armed with shotguns rode on horses beside them through the fields as the inmates tended the crops.

I knew little of Angola's history. Crime was not my usual beat. When I wasn't covering the governor and the legislature, I was a general-assignment reporter covering fast-breaking news. I loved its pace, urgent demands, and excitement.

I had followed the usual pattern for middle-class women growing up in the 1950s. I married at nineteen and had my first child nine months later, followed by two more children by the time I was twenty-six. At night, in my early thirties, as I watched the evening news on a small TV set in my kitchen on Camp Street in New Orleans while I fixed family dinners, I began to picture myself in place of every woman reporter I saw.

Feminism was in full flower in the 1960s and 1970s. Marching and burning bras, women were raising hell all over the country for equal rights, demanding political, economic, and social opportunities. Millions of women benefited. We became people in our own right. We could have credit cards in our own names even if we were married. We could have careers instead of secretarial jobs. We could look forward to college degrees and titles instead of the usual Miss or Mrs. in front of our names.

When I was thirty-six, I swallowed the fear that I wasn't smart enough to earn a college degree and became a freshman at Loyola University in New Orleans. I majored in communications and loaded my curriculum with courses in history and economics to make sure I had the background to be a good reporter. I graduated magna cum laude in May 1979. But no TV station in New Orleans would hire me. Neither would any other station in Louisiana.

I was a misfit, a forty-one-year-old woman hoping for a job in TV news despite its emphasis on youth. That fall, after searching all summer for a job at TV stations across the state, I was hired at a small station in Cheyenne, Wyoming. I spent four months there during the fall of 1979, thousands of miles from my family. In January 1980, I was hired at Channel 9 in Baton Rouge, just eighty miles from New Orleans, an easy ride home for weekends. Now I had the best assignment of my budding career—a series on the death penalty.

A prison guard at Angola's front gate approached us to search our car. Everyone, coming or going, was subject to a mandatory search. Drugs and other contraband were often smuggled into the prison, sometimes in the hands of the most unlikely carriers.

The illicit drug trade that had formed the basis of the inmate warlords' power, and their unholy alliance with corrupt prison officials, was still too much of Angola's recent past for anyone to escape a check. My photographer, Susan Jackson, smiled and raised the trunk of our news car to allow a look at the camera, lights, and other equipment we carried. The guard was polite.

"Drive down to the main administration building, and there'll be an escort waiting to take you to Camp F. Know where the main building is?"

Five miles of flat green fields separated us from the death house at Camp F. Our drive ended at a cinderblock complex not unlike the prison's other out-camps. Outside, flags snapped in the breeze as the wind rippled across a small lake and birds circled and wheeled above newly plowed fields. A sign at the entrance of one of the building's wings warned that only those on official business could enter.

We unloaded our equipment and stepped into a large, sunlit room. Inside, a lush green fern stood in a pot by the door. A small caged-in office faced us across the room's broad expanse. Adjacent to it, one after another, lining a short hall to the right, were holding cells where prisoners were taken to wait out the final hours of their lives.

At our escort's direction, Susan and I lugged our heavy equipment toward the opposite end of the big room, away from the cage and the cells, toward the door of a small room with the electric chair. Just inside the death chamber, I knelt and placed the heavy lights I carried on the floor, glad to be rid of their awkward burden, and glanced up at the people I was told would be there: a TV crew from Lafayette, the warden, and two award-winning prison inmate writers, Wilbert Rideau, an African American inmate from Lake Charles in South Louisiana, and Billy Sinclair, a white prisoner from Rayville, a small town in rural northeast Louisiana.

Nothing in my life prepared me for what happened then. At the sight of Billy Sinclair, time stopped. I stared, fascinated, and knew I would never forget him. In that one moment, he became part of a special catalog in my mind filled with sights that touched my soul: tall yellow grass blowing on Wyoming hills, wind in South Texas pine trees, the sun glinting on the water off Mexico's Pacific coast as I watched whales play in the ocean from Acapulco's cliffs when I was twelve. Now, there would be Billy Sinclair.

He stood next to the electric chair, like the reincarnation of some mythical Western figure, one long booted leg stretched out in front, the other bent at the knee, braced against the wall behind him, his lanky frame at ease in the small room with Angola's electric chair. He was impeccably dressed in pressed Levi's, a starched blue jean jacket, and a denim work shirt. His boots were polished to a military shine.

Why did I immediately feel like I knew him?

His face held my attention. Its high cheekbones and dark mustache awakened something lost in memory. Inchoate half thoughts swirled to the top of my head, illusions drifting up like smoke from somewhere deep inside my brain. He was an archetype, a throwback to Old West outlaws who rode backcountry trails too rough for lawmen to follow. I could picture him on horseback, a bedroll and rifle lashed to his saddle.

A wild response to him rushed up inside me, the urge like nothing I had ever felt. I wanted to press myself against the hard muscles beneath his jeans, the sudden desire as natural as the need to breathe. For a moment it played within me, wild and unfettered, a reckless response to the stranger standing before me.

The attraction was instant, compelling, and unavoidable, a magnetic force that pulled me out of orbit. It was as natural as the genetically ordered shape of my face or the color of my eyes.

"Jodie Bell, meet Billy Sinclair."

At the sound of the warden's voice, I broke free of my strange fascination with Sinclair. We shook hands by the electric chair as Warden Frank Blackburn stepped forward to introduce us. Warden Blackburn was a short, round, pleasant man, a psychologist and a minister. There had been no inmate killings during his four years at Angola's helm, a miracle in a prison famous for its inmate-on-inmate violence. But Blackburn had managed to maintain peace under a humane rule.

Coolly, I reached out to Billy Sinclair's hand. Protocol protected me. Our first words were merely the pleasantries polite society reserves for such occasions.

I knew almost nothing about him when we met, so it was not his reputation that stunned me. It was the power of his physical presence. If his years at Angola had scarred him, I couldn't tell. There was no fawning, subservient quality about him. His level gaze met mine like any professional peer.

There was no sign he noted my sex. His manners were studied and correct. His demeanor, I would later learn, was a carefully practiced art, necessary camouflage in Angola's dangerous environment.

I had no plans to use Sinclair's interview, or Rideau's, in my death penalty series. The warden had simply told me that they were prisoners who once had been sentenced to death and that their views might add perspective. He did not tell me they were national award-winning prison writers. But Rideau and Sinclair were coeditors of the *Angolite,* the only uncensored prison magazine in the United States.

The *Angolite*'s rise to prominence began with a federal court order that deposed the corrupt regime governing the prison. No longer would abusive guards and wardens share their power with drug lords. Prison families—tight cliques of inmates bound together for protection and profit—were broken up. Homosexual slavery rings and the illicit drug trade that formed the basis of the inmate drug lords' power were smashed. To stifle conjecture and stave off violence, as inmate suspicions about the changes grew, the administration unshackled the *Angolite,* giving its coeditors the unheard-of freedom to publish prisoners' stories and their complaints.

The license to write, to move freely around the prison, to question administrators, to quote inmate leaders, to examine documents and report on meetings, to criticize and editorialize, helped defuse inmate tension. With the most savage prisoners locked away, and the *Angolite* providing moderate inmate leaders with a voice, a new order gained traction in the prison community.

Stories by the two self-taught inmate editors exposed the truth at Angola, shattering conventional beliefs about keeper and kept. They wrote of cell madness and the scalding shame of homosexual rape, of guards turned pimp and drug runner, midnight suicides, cell-block bitches, self-mutilation, and the paranoia necessary for survival in prison. The inmate editors' lack of formal education was no obstacle. They worked at carefully crafting their words and tempering their bitterness. They were insiders exposing the truth about Angola. The impact of their journalism was stunning.

Between 1979 and 1982, Rideau and Sinclair won seven national journalism awards between them: five for Sinclair, two for Rideau. They included the profession's highest honors: the Robert F. Kennedy Special Interest Journalism Award to both editors for separate articles; an American Bar Association Silver Gavel to Wilbert

Rideau in 1979 for his "Conversation With The Dead"; a George Polk Award in 1980 to Billy Sinclair for his treatise on the death penalty, "The Other Side of Murder"; another Polk to Rideau that same year for "The Sexual Jungle," his savage account of prison rape and homosexual slavery at Angola; a Silver Gavel in 1980 to Billy Sinclair for his article "A Prison Tragedy," about the murder of an African American inmate leader trying to protect young prisoners from rape; an ABA Certificate of Merit to Sinclair for his story of a prison suicide; and the Sidney Hillman Award in 1981 to Sinclair for his article "Louisiana Death Watch," about the state's last execution in 1961.

Susan started shooting video inside the death chamber—the red phone on the wall in case there was a last-minute stay, the huge fan to suck out the stench of burnt human flesh after an execution, the small window in a half wall behind the chair that let the executioner see the warden's signal to throw the switch, and the big window into the death chamber for the witnesses to watch. When she finished getting the video I would need, I interviewed Warden Blackburn about sending the signal that would kill a man.

Then we moved out of the death chamber to set up my interviews with Rideau and Sinclair. Susan grabbed two straight-back chairs and placed one facing the other. They were close enough for me to hold the microphone, just below camera range, near Sinclair's mouth. Then, she stood behind me, her camera aimed at Sinclair's face, ready to tape the interview.

As I sat down, my left knee brushed Sinclair's leg. I sucked in a deep breath at the physical response in my body and tried to concentrate on the interview as he described the different methods of execution he had studied during his six years on death row.

He said it could take up to four minutes to die in the electric chair, twenty-seven minutes in the gas chamber, and twenty minutes by hanging, if the neck doesn't break. Death by firing squad was usually instantaneous.

I listened to his timetable of death, unaffected by his laundry list of dying. Instead, it was his down-home drawl and Southern slur that captivated me. Deep creases at the corners of his eyes spoke of his birthright—a life in the sun, hard rider over fields, and hunter on horseback. He was instead one of the living dead, a man with a perpetual life sentence. Near enough to lean against him, I watched the breath rise and fall across his broad, powerful chest, knowing how close he had come to death, going rigid in the electric chair.

It had been sixteen years since he shot a convenience store clerk and nine since the US Supreme Court's decision in *Furman v. Georgia* overturned his death sentence. He was resentenced to life without parole, releasing him from death row into the general inmate population at Angola. He was a thirty-six-year-old with a life sentence that would never end. In his mind, it was worse than dying in the electric chair. The year before, he said, Louisiana's pardon board had recommended commuting his sentence from life to forty-five years, a decision that would have made parole possible had Governor Edwin Edwards signed the recommendation. The Cajun governor was noted for his liberal attitude toward clemency, but he refused to approve the pardon board's recommendation.

Sinclair had to begin the two-year clemency process again, this time under the state's first Republican governor in over a century, Dave Treen, an ardent political conservative. For months, the new governor had refused to discuss the clemency process with reporters who questioned him about his policies concerning Louisiana's large and growing number of lifers.

From 1972 to 1980, Governor Edwin Edwards had released twenty-four murderers during his two consecutive terms in office. None had served as much time as Sinclair or had as good a prison record. Some, Sinclair said, had been freed despite criminal records and crimes far worse than his. I was braced for the appeal I felt he would inevitably make. I made a mental note to investigate what he said. If it was true, it seemed strange, but I wanted to trust him.

In the background, the warden's two-way radio crackled out a message. Somewhere a cell door slammed shut. The background noise threatened to drown out Sinclair's voice on the tape. I reached out to tap him lightly on the knee to silence him, as I had done in other interviews when noise threatened to interfere. Instinctively, I stopped. My hand might betray me, conveying more in its touch than I wanted him to know. My photographer caught my hesitation.

"Don't worry, Jodie, we got it. The interview's fine."

I turned my attention to Sinclair's coeditor, Wilbert Rideau, an equally valuable source, the warden had said. He was a smaller man, but more intense in starched, pressed jeans like Sinclair's. He riveted the viewer with a steady gaze, one round black pupil clearly visible, the other half-hidden by a drooping eyelid.

A slight smile played at the corner of his lips. Mercy was a Johnny-come-lately in his world. There was a bitter irony in what he said: his victim had begged for mercy, but he ignored her pleas. Living on death row made him realize the stark fear and despair she must have felt before he cut her throat. He would never be released, he said. An African American man cannot kill a white woman in the South and expect to be freed. His crime was still infamous in Lake Charles, where it had occurred in 1961.

He held up a Lake Charles bank next door to the Singer Sewing Company store where he had worked as a janitor for months when he was nineteen. He took three hostages, two women and a man, all of whom worked at the bank, all of whom he knew. Later, in a wooded area outside town, he tried to kill all three. The man managed to run away. He shot the two women. He thought he had killed one of them. He turned on the other one.

"Why did you cut her throat?" I asked, recoiling at the thought.

"I think I ran out of bullets," he said in complete candor.

It was a crime of passion, he said, against white oppressors. He went on to other remarks then, about crime and the ultimate punishment, these more in the vein of a general assessment. Our interview concluded, I shook his hand and rose to make way for the reporter from Lafayette in case he had questions.

I stood in the hall near the complex door as my photographer packed our equipment, surprised to find Sinclair suddenly by my side. We began trading stories about our beats, mine at the state capitol, his at the prison, and he gave me no sense of being different from other reporters I knew. Our conversation flowed as if we had known each other for years. I basked in the friendly repartee, hoping it would last as he leaned against the adjacent wall, much as he had when I had first seen him with one foot braced behind him, thumbs hooked in his jeans. The others began to drift toward us. It was time for lunch and the trip home.

Quickly, I shook his hand as I realized he and Rideau were not allowed to eat with visiting reporters. I wasn't finished with our conversation, nor was I ready to say goodbye. Resentment pricked at me as I was ushered off to the out-camp dining room with the warden. The abrupt end to our meeting left me with no appetite. I picked at the prison food, wondering all the while where he had been taken. It was a relief when lunch and its social demands came to an end. I looked forward to the trip back to the station. On the drive, I could lose myself in a mental review of meeting Billy Sinclair. I knew he would stay on my mind.

THE NEXT MORNING, I WAS late for the 9:00 a.m. news meeting. The news director's voice boomed across the room at me as I opened the door to the newsroom.

"Hello, little woman."

I dumped my purse on my desk and headed over to the conference table.

"How are you this morning?" Carlton Cremeens asked in an exaggeratedly polite voice, as though he were greeting a visiting movie star. Carlton was an easygoing news director who knew the business inside and out. He patted me on the shoulder and pulled a chair up to the table for me. Every woman in the newsroom knew his comments were jokes.

The newsroom's TV monitor was off. We sat around the table: Carlton; reporters Chris McDaniel, Jeff Simon, Frances Hutchins, and John Voinche; Paul Gates, the assignment editor; and me.

Maxine Crump sat at an adjacent desk. She was a morning show anchor.

"Hey Carlton," she jibed, "you better lay off those biscuits."

His tie looked like it was sticking out at a forty-five-degree angle. He fixed her with an amazed stare.

"Now, Maxine . . ." he scolded.

Carlton's sincere blue eyes looked out on the world like a child in permanent surprise and disbelief. But there was a cunning behind them that belied an "Arkansas bumpkin come to town." Carlton was an accomplished news director. He had more than twenty years in the business. Leaning back in his chair, his more-than-ample belly straining against his dress shirt, he looked over us like we were his grandchildren.

"Well, Miss Frances, you look lovely this morning."

"Thank you, Carlton," she said, waiting like everyone else for the pleasantries to cease.

Paul cleared his throat. He ran the desk and handed out assignments.

"Now if you all don't mind," he said, his voice rising like that of a Southern preacher, "we'll proceed with the formalities."

Paul sat on a stool, his heels hooked over the edge like a schoolboy. He had a smooth quality, an easygoing, melted-butter manner that attracted viewers and helped grease the newsroom's wheels. In a position easily disliked by independent-minded reporters, he had the cooperation of every member of the staff. It was a gift. He smiled at Carlton.

"Now," he said, "let's get on with it."

He thumbed through the newspaper clips in the day file.

"Voinche, see what you can do with this," he said. "The city says it hasn't got the bucks to upgrade the sewer system. Get some video of lines in a poor neighborhood and grab a few sound bites at city hall. You know, like when the hell is it gonna be fixed? Try to take a little bit different angle from the paper. Humanize it a bit more. People don't give a damn about the money. They just don't want to be knee deep in crap."

"They already are," Jeff pronounced from his side of the table, "just living with this city government is enough."

Jeff bit into his biscuit and bacon. I glanced at Carlton. For once we would apparently be free of the don't-eat-your-breakfast-at-the-morning-meeting lecture. Paul turned to Frances.

"Tougaloo . . ." he said, looking at her.

Tougaloo College in Mississippi was her alma mater and Paul's favorite nickname for her. "There's a hearing at natural resources. I think it's already in session. Lyle's gonna be in early. Grey is already on a fire," he said, referring to two dayside photographers. "Take Lyle when he gets in. You all go over to natural resources. Get me some good stuff. You know, people with all that shit in jars from chemical dump sites. I want some of that Lord-God-we're-all-gonna-die sound."

Frances smiled and folded her hands.

"Oh, Paul, those little people are really scared," she said.

"I know, Miss Frances. Just get me that shit on camera. It'll help them out." Across the newsroom, the side door swung open. Lyle had arrived. Paul was ready with a directive.

"Hey, Lyle, get your gear and get on over to natural resources with Frances."

Lyle sauntered over to the assignment board to see what else Paul had listed.

"Lemme get my equipment loaded." He started for the equipment room to get freshly charged batteries.

"Just hang in, Lyle, I'll cut you free for something later," Paul promised.

"Need any help, Lyle?" Frances asked.

"Naw, I'll get it loaded OK," he said.

Paul turned his attention back to the rest of us. Chris sat some distance from the table, long legs stuck in harness boots, hooded eyes staring through his cigarette's smoke. A worn tan corduroy jacket covered his brown plaid shirt. He suffered through the morning meetings. As Channel 9's investigative reporter, he dug up his own stories.

"Come on, Paul, let's get it rolling. You people are wasting Paul's time," he scolded us. Paul continued handing out assignments.

"Jeff, there's a school board meeting this afternoon. See if you can get a sound bite with that woman who always shows up carrying a sign. I think she's trying to get herself arrested to prove her point. Just be there and be ready. You got all morning to set it up and get your sidebar stuff."

Paul handed Jeff a newspaper clipping with the story about the woman's fight with the school board. Jeff held a cigarette, his morning breakfast half-finished, scraps of biscuit and bacon scattered on the small paper plate in front of him.

"Finished down there, Jeff?' Carlton couldn't resist a dig.

"You want the leftovers?" Jeff said, a hint of sarcasm in his voice.

"Watch it, Carlton, you ain't gonna be able to sit down at the table if you keep it up," Maxine crowed.

"Let's get settled down here," Paul interjected. I could see the grin in Chris's eyes. He loved a good fight. I glanced back at the assignments board, waiting to hear what Paul wanted me to do.

"Jodie, head over to the capitol. See if any of those committee hearings are worth it." The immediate assignments handed out, Paul shifted his attention down the table. "Jeff, if you got any of that stuff left over . . ." Paul started to say. Chris unfolded his long body and grabbed Jeff's plate.

"I'll eat the motherfucker," he whooped. "It ain't kosher anyway, Jeff."

Jeff stared back at him, meticulously flicking his ashes in a Coke bottle.

"Dearly beloved, we are gathered here," Paul intoned, "to try and get this show on the road. Amen. Anybody has questions, see me at the assignment desk. Max, I'm going across the street to get a biscuit."

"Here," Chris said, fishing Jeff's half-eaten biscuit out of the garbage where he had tossed it. "Try this. It's kosher bacon all the way from New York City."

"You could do worse," Jeff laughed. "It has my blessing."

"Well, I think this meeting is over," Carlton said, mildly stating the obvious. He had an appointment upstairs with the station manager.

"Better hump it, Carlton," Maxine warned.

"Hey, Chris." John lobbed a wad of paper across the newsroom at Chris, whipping off a fancy shot, underhand, from behind his back.

"Listen, Max, I'm gonna need some video from that last school board story," Jeff said, rising from the table. "I think the last piece I did was a couple of months ago. It should be easy to find in the file."

"When have I ever failed you, Jeff?" Maxine clapped her beautifully manicured hands together. "Tell me when," she said.

The door pushed open. Grey Hammett walked in, carrying the tapes he'd just shot of the fire. I could tell he was on a roll.

"Hey, Boudreaux," he called out to Van, another photographer. "Why'd you drown Mobile four yesterday?

"Well," I said, interjecting myself into the conversation. "You know Cajuns, Grey. They just love the hell out of water."

"Yeah," he agreed. "But to drive past a road barrier, jump the median, and sink the sucker in three feet of water ain't too bright. Hell, it ain't a pirogue," he teased Van.

The Cajun's eyes lit up.

"Shit, man. Everything in Louisiana is amphibious. If it ain't, it oughta be."

I loved the newsroom's banter and its fly-by-the-seat-of-your-pants environment. I belonged there, more than anywhere else I had been in my life.

THREE DAYS LATER, LIFE IN the newsroom was hitting its usual frantic pace late in the afternoon. Voices, ringing telephones, and the steady clack of typewriters filled the air as the tension grew. The newscast would hit the air in an hour. The reporter next to me sat hunched over, staring into space, the earplugs of a tape recorder jammed in her ears as she listened to a crucial interview over and over, the lead story still working in her typewriter. Next to her, another reporter grappled with a final task: subtitles for his story, a perennial cigarette burning in the ashtray on his desk.

My story was finished. I sat with my back against the room's cinder-block walls, feet up on my desk, skirt folded modestly around my legs. Across the aisle, the station's anchor perfected his delivery of the evening news, reading and rereading his scripts out loud, the newsroom's chaos tuned out as he prepared his nightly performance when I heard Paul Gates yelling at me over the din.

"Hey, Jodie, you got a letter."

I wondered what sort of press release it might contain. Aside from my legislative stories, I covered breaking news, not the consumer issues or investigative reports that prompted viewers to write.

The letter was from Angola. But it wasn't from a prisoner. There was no disclaimer on the back. Prison authorities stamped it in big letters on all inmate mail leaving the prison. UNCENSORED, NOT RESPONSIBLE FOR CONTENTS the disclaimer warned. But this envelope bore a set of scrawled initials I didn't recognize above the prison's return address. I decided it must be from an administrator and wasn't an embarrassing declaration of love from a prisoner striving to make some midnight fantasy real. Female reporters in Baton Rouge had a justifiable dread of such letters. Letters like that made them the butt of newsroom jokes. Angola was in the station's viewing area, and sudden declarations of love arriving in the mail weren't unusual. The letters were often passed around the newsroom, from reporter to reporter, convulsing each in turn with laughter at the trite sentiments written in pencil on lined paper in the prisoners' usually childish scrawl. But I had nothing to fear. Confidently, I opened the envelope and pulled the letter out.

A large ball, chain, and leg iron filled the upper right-hand comer of the page. It was the *Angolite*'s letterhead. The bottom of the page listed the magazine's awards. They were a parade of the highest national journalism honors, firsts for prisoners. I glanced at the signature under the single short paragraph on the page. The letter was from Billy Sinclair. I flushed with pleasure. It was dated March 17, 1981, the day we met.

Dear Jodie:

It was a pleasure meeting you today and appreciate the interview. Wilbert is sending you some material under a separate cover. We will send you a copy of the issue we devote strictly to capital punishment. You've been placed on our complimentary mailing list. Take care.

Billy Sinclair

My interest in the letter was short-lived. It was merely a courteous, professional note. The lack of a personal message stung me. Only the letter's last two words—"Take care"—suggested any sense of extra regard. I put it on my desk and rubbed my fingers back and forth across the two words as though they were Braille and might reveal a hidden message. Perhaps they were all he could say given the scrutiny of a prison administrator.

I felt another flush of pleasure at the idea. It transported me back to his side, just three days before, as we stood near the door outside the death house at Camp F, talking freely, as though we had always been part of each other's lives. The feeling deepened into a crazy delight that careened around inside me. I quickly killed it with common sense. The two words that ended the letter were not unusual in casual business correspondence.

I put the letter back in its envelope and dropped it on my desk. He had only meant to be polite. Or to cultivate a reporter who could be a useful source, if not one who could be manipulated into doing favorable stories about him.

But why write to me? Famous reporters were interested in his case. The networks had covered his journalism awards. The *New York Times* and other equally prominent news outlets had done stories about the honors heaped on him. I was a small-time reporter, not a mover of mountains or conduit to his release from prison.

Sternly, I reminded myself that he was convicted of murder. But there was nothing sinister in his appearance. The word "killer" didn't fit him. Everything about him contradicted it. Yet he was still at Angola when inmates who had committed multiple serious crimes were serving less time. Politics was obviously playing a big role in his case. It wasn't unusual. Trading flesh for votes was a time-honored tradition in Louisiana.

I wrote back, thanking Billy Sinclair for helping me with my death penalty series after I called him at the prison to check some facts.

March 26, 1981

Dear Billy,

Thank you for your help today. Small inaccuracies destroy credibility. So, I called to make sure there won't be anything I use if there's a question in my head about like how far it really is from the front gate to Camp . . . and if it's called the front gate . . . or what? I'm sure I'll need help as I go along. I'm doing a lot of work at home in the evenings these days on the "Electric Chair" series. It will run in May, as I told Wilbert. Meanwhile, I am wading through Angolites *every night and spending a lot of time thinking about you all.*

Jodie Bell

DAYS LATER, AS INTENSE RAIN pelted Baton Rouge just before the 5 p.m. newscast, Paul Gates's voice suddenly jerked me upright. A tornado was slamming into Lutcher, a town south of Baton Rouge along the Mississippi River. It instantly became the lead story in the newscast at six.

"Jodie, I'm sending Joanie and Meaux down to Lutcher. Go with them. Phone me any details you can so we can update the show when it goes on the air. We can slap the video on the bottom of the show if you can get it back in time."

High-heeled sandals hampered my stride, and my thin black sweater dress offered no protection from the wind and rain. I was dressed to cover the legislature. But Paul hadn't been interested in sending me to any of the day's committee hearings. Now, I had a breaking news assignment. I jammed a notepad and pen into my purse, paused at the door to get some last instructions from Paul, hit the street, and jumped in the news car.

Rain poured out of thick black clouds above us as we drove to meet the helicopter. We hit a nearby freeway on-ramp with a thud and fought our way across three lanes of backed-up five o'clock traffic, then shot down the next off-ramp, switching from one street to the next to avoid the traffic. Every road was a rain-slicked mess.

At the helicopter pad, we raced to load the equipment. The rotors were already turning; the wind churned up from the steady beat of the propellers felt like a series of body blows as we climbed in and buckled down for the ride. The skies were clearing toward Lutcher, but black clouds were still hanging over Baton Rouge, and high winds rocked the helicopter. We put on headsets to kill the engine's noise. The chopper lifted off, tilting slightly toward the front as we began to rise, and headed toward the I-10 freeway. I smiled, heady with the feeling, pleasure singing in my veins. The experience was everything I had dreamed of as I'd stood in the kitchen cooking dinner, watching other women cover the news. I had made it. I was part of that special world.

Rain pounded across the helicopter's nose. The rivulets formed a pattern as they coursed backward toward its sides. I was above the world, plugged into a different sphere, on the front row, where I belonged. We flew due south, marshlands below, cars on the freeway, swamp shacks visible from the air. The pilot's voice cut through my thoughts.

"We'll be on scene in about five minutes."

Below us, traffic on the highway was backed up for a quarter of a mile. Sheriff's deputies directed each car in turn out of the congestion. We descended slowly, like gods dropping out of the sky into a lush field. Wind from the helicopter's rotors flattened the grass. I slipped off my headset and fished a pen and pad from my purse as Joanie and Meaux slid out of their seats. I dropped out of the chopper and felt my heels dig into the mud. We all ran for the highway to get the video, interviews, and official information we needed. Across the road, we could see several houses off their foundations. Shards of timber littered their yards. I stopped when I reached a sheriff's deputy directing traffic by the side of the road.

"Anybody dead?" I asked.

"Negative. Three houses wiped out and a mobile home off the foundation. That's the major stuff."

"Any estimates on the damage?"

"Naw, you'll want to talk to the sheriff. He's over there in that house trailer. Gonna have it added up in a little while. Man, it was fast. It tore everything all to hell in seconds."

Bits of wet grass clung to my shoes and mud was splattered across my dress. A woman let me into her house to use her phone. It was ten minutes to six. I called Paul with details for the top of the show.

"Get me the video as fast as you can, Jodie. How far out are you?"

"About twenty to twenty-five minutes," I answered.

"OK, land on the levee at the bottom of Government Street. We'll stand by for your call."

The levee was just a few blocks from the station. Outside the woman's house, I stopped short. The helicopter was gone.

"He moved it across the road," some kids called out. "You Channel 9?"

"Yeah," I answered as I edged away from them toward the road.

"Which one are you?" they demanded.

"Jodie Bell," I called out.

"Jodie Bell. We gonna watch for you, Jodie Bell."

Back in the newsroom, Paul was holding up an envelope.

"Look who made an impression at Angola."

He laughed as he announced to the newsroom that another letter from Billy Sinclair had arrived for me.

I had written him with more questions about the prison and the officials I was regularly encountering as I covered stories who talked openly of their opposition to his release. They were bitter that he hadn't died in the electric chair.

That night, I sent him my home address along with a brief note to avoid another incident. I had more questions about my death-penalty series, and I didn't want to be confronted with newsroom jokes about sick inmates courting a free woman's love. I thought he deserved more than that. He was an award-winning journalist and an expert on matters at the prison. Sharing perspectives and information would give me valid insight into the shocking world confronting me.

"CHRIST, IT'S HOT."

My photographer looked at me and laughed.

"Hell, you know better than that, Jodie. Why don't you save your breath?"

Van Boudreaux was full of common sense, a trademark of Cajuns. We would suffer with the heat on assignments until October. Then the rains would start, and outdoor assignments would go from hot to sloppy.

"Bitch and moan," he went on teasing me. As we drove toward our assignment, I sassed him back.

"Come on, Boudreaux, since when are you the epitome of patience? If I weren't shooting my mouth off, you would be. We gotta spread this bitch-and-moan privilege around. Or didn't you hear of women's lib?"

"Well, I tried not to as long as I could."

We were well on our way then, rolling down the freeway, off to interview Louisiana's ex-governor, Edwin Edwards.

"Boudreaux, you got any idea where the hell this place is?"

"I was there once. It's somewhere off Jefferson Highway."

"Come on, Van. Photographers drive, photographers leave with directions. That's the way the equation goes, baby. I don't do windows."

I looked at the speedometer as we shot down the freeway.

"Boudreaux, you're doing seventy and you're not sure where you're going?"

"It's hot!"

"That's a piss-poor excuse. If you don't get this air-conditioning fixed, I'm not gonna ride with you anymore, darlin'."

"Promise me, Jodie?"

I laughed. He blew smoke at me and picked up the two-way. "Mobile four to base two, I put our ETA at about five minutes. Mobile four, clear."

He knew where we were going all along. We took the next exit and headed toward an unpretentious looking suburban bungalow. A small wooden sign hung out front, one word stenciled in capital letters on both sides: EDWARDS.

He was the most popular governor in Louisiana history, despite a reputation for corruption that dogged his sixteen years in office, longer than any other governor had ever served. During a successful election campaign in 1991 for his unprecedented fourth term, against David Duke, Grand Wizard of the Ku Klux Klan, Edwards's bumper stickers put the voters' choice in blunt terms: "Vote for the Crook."

Scandals dogged Edwards's political career. In a 1976 scandal known as Koreagate, Edwards was one of the one hundred US congressmen who allegedly took bribes from a South Korean businessman named Tongsun Park. Edwards admitted taking ten thousand dollars from Park in 1971 but said it was just a gift. He escaped indictment, but his former North Louisiana congressional colleague Otto Passman was not so lucky. He was indicted in 1978 for conspiracy, bribery, accepting illegal gratuity, and income tax evasion. It took a Monroe, Louisiana, jury less than ninety minutes to acquit the popular Passman. Louisiana juries saw nothing wrong with their representatives accepting a little gratuity.

Edwards's first eight years in office, from 1972 to 1980, were blighted by charges of selling positions in state agencies. An ex-bodyguard wrote a book detailing the governor's frequent extramarital affairs and gambling trips to Las Vegas. He left office in 1980, after serving two back-to-back terms, only because he could not succeed himself. He spent the next four years preparing to run for governor again in 1983 against Dave Treen, an election he would easily win. As we headed to interview Edwards that April, he was doing all he could to undermine Treen. There were whispers in political circles that Edwards had actually run a covert campaign to help Treen get elected in 1980 because he believed the Republican would be the easiest candidate to beat when he ran again in 1984.

"Come on, Van, let's get this sleazo interview out of the way."

His eyes lit up.

"Hey, you talkin' about my governor. What's wrong with a little here and a little there as long as it's for a good cause?"

Edwards's intense brown eyes never left my face as we sat down on a small sofa for the interview. I had been told his memory was legendary. His face was remarkably unwrinkled for a man of fifty-three.

"Rolling."

Van was framed up on Edwards's face. I lifted the microphone and started the interview, my voice at its professional pitch.

"Governor, Lieutenant Governor Bobby Freeman said today he'd like to be your running mate in '83. But the governor's race is still two years off. Will you commit to a choice like that this early?"

His legendary charm was evident. He was at home in front of a camera. He photographed well, and he knew it.

"Well, I am flattered he would want to run with me. It's well known he has a personality conflict with Governor Treen. I feel sorry for him that the governor won't give him anything to do."

Edwards was a master at deflection and flattery. No early public promise would mar his reelection campaign. I admired the gambit and tried again to get a newsworthy statement free of deflection.

"Are you taking a potshot at our good Republican governor?"

"I only state the facts," he said.

I expected a courteous dodge. Edwards only told reporters what he wanted them to know, no matter how many times they queried him about a pressing issue. That night, he would get what he wanted. He would be the lead story in Baton Rouge on Channel 9, in an exclusive interview. I thanked him and rose to help Van take down the lights.

"My, you certainly keep yourself trim," Edwards said as he watched me from the sofa. I had expected an intimate remark. He was well known for flirting.

"Thank you, Governor." I smiled and moved away from the couch to help break down the equipment. He smiled and sat back on the sofa. He understood my message. Any interest I had in him was purely professional.

"Don't mess with my lights."

Van had a particular way of wrapping their cords. His mock-tough warning was a reminder. I turned back to ask Edwards an off-camera question.

"Governor, I was at Angola on a story recently and I met this inmate, Billy Sinclair. He's an *Angolite* editor. Your secretary of corrections and Angola's warden are both on the record saying he's rehabilitated. And your last pardon board recommended a time cut of his life sentence to forty-five years. How come you didn't sign his clemency recommendation?"

"Well," he said, "the Baton Rouge district attorney called me up ten days in a row and asked me not to sign it."

I wasn't surprised. No doubt it was politics. As soon as I started reporting at Channel 9 in January 1980, politics confronted me on assignments in almost every facet of life in Louisiana. It was the only reason I could think of why Edwards had pardoned twenty-four murderers but refused to sign a clemency recommendation for Billy Sinclair.

I SAW BILLY SINCLAIR FOR the second time in late March. I was headed back to Angola to interview two men who had the death penalty for my series. There, I came face-to-face with impending death.

I watched as they were brought to a holding area near death row one at a time, their legs chained together at the ankles, their hands in cuffs secured to a chain around their waists. I looked in their eyes, as the camera rolled, and saw their terrible fear and resignation. There was no way to escape the sentence the state would soon carry out as payback for their crimes.

Robert Wayne Williams hobbled into the interview room and sat directly across the table from me. The African American inmate was plainly terrified of the electric chair.

"Some bionic thing just holding you down and killing you," was how he described it, his intense fear showing in his eyes.

Williams was sentenced to be executed on December 14, 1981, five years after killing an African American security guard with a shotgun during a grocery store robbery in Baton Rouge in 1979. A weapons expert testified at his trial that Williams's gun could have discharged accidentally, as his defense lawyer claimed. Williams's mother defended him.

"Killing is killing; no matter if you say you are doing it in the name of the law," she said.

Williams was polite and composed when his head and one of his legs were shaved so the electrical charge would encounter no resistance. It was "please" and "thank you" when he was given Pampers to wear for his execution. (The involuntary discharge of body waste is an inevitable outcome of electrocution.)

Williams's mother was denied permission to accompany her son to the death house the night he was executed. She told reporters in a quiet voice, after waiting for hours in the December cold at Angola's front gate for word of his death, "They used my son and they've abused my family."

I asked Benjamin Berry, a twenty-five-year-old bank robber, cigarette smoke wreathing up around his face from hands chained to his waist, what he thought about the death penalty and if he would ask for drugs to make his execution easier when his time came.

"Naw," the young Charles Manson look-alike said as he looked calmly into my eyes. "That old man didn't have nothin' when I shot him."

In January 1978, Berry went into a branch bank in a bedroom community of New Orleans, armed with a 9-millimeter automatic pistol. He was wounded in a shoot-out with an off-duty deputy sheriff who was moonlighting as a bank guard. The guard died from three bullets to the neck and shoulder. Witnesses claimed drug use by Berry's lawyer, before and during the trial, prevented him from effectively investigating the case and representing Berry at trial.

But courts at the state and federal level rejected the argument. The Fifth Circuit Court of Appeals ruled that "the fact an attorney used drugs, in and of itself, is not relevant to an ineffective assistance claim." Berry was electrocuted on June 7, 1987.

After my interviews with Williams and Berry, I was escorted to the *Angolite*'s office in the main prison to see Sinclair and Rideau to check facts for the article I was writing about them for the *Gambit Weekly,* titled "Angolites in the Death House."

The sight of Billy Sinclair took my breath away. The thought of him waiting to die like Williams and Berry shot across my brain. Billy was only twenty-one when he was sentenced to death. I wondered how a man barely out of his teens had dealt with his death sentence. What keys, if any, might that hold to his character?

As I sat across from him that late March afternoon in the *Angolite*'s office, there was no sign he thought more of me than any other reporter. The gulf between us was far wider than I knew. The *Angolite*'s editors had orders to obey a strict prison policy when "free people" were present. It prevented anything but polite reserve. It also protected inmates from the jolting pain of a "Dear John" letter. A "free woman," enticed by an inmate's behavior, might profess her love for him and then suddenly end contact. It was better not to invite that pain. But Billy's measured reserve had deeper roots.

"Don't ever get above your raisin'," his mother would say, as she smoked cigarette after cigarette at the cheap kitchen table where she ordered him to sit and listen to her weekly tirade about the indignities inflicted on the lower classes by the elites.

"High-class people will always turn on you," she'd warned, her eyes glittering with hatred. She told him they had snobbish, indecipherable ways.

"I'm telling you, Billy Wayne, they will hurt you if you get above your raisin'." His mind rejected the message. But his soul absorbed it.

When I looked at him, I saw an accomplished journalist and paralegal whose soft-spoken reserve negated the label that society applied to him. When he looked at me, he saw a woman he wasn't meant to have.

"You have class," he would later tell me in reverential tones, as he touched my hair or gently patted my face, all the physical contact the prison allowed.

His childhood left scars that took years to heal. His father beat him with switches, branches, electrical cords, fists, and feet, and had tried to drown him in a washtub when he was eighteen months old. His collarbone broke before his hysterical mother could pull the hulking six-footer away. It was only the first time his father tried to kill him. John Sinclair believed that Billy—his second-born son—was a bastard, conceived by a cheating wife while he was away in the army during World War II. His mother escaped her abusive husband after a final, brutal beating that left her nearly senseless, lying in a bloody heap by the front door of a house in New Orleans his parents were buying.

Bessie Jewel Patrick Sinclair divorced her husband and returned to Rayville, the small farming town in northeast Louisiana where Billy Sinclair had been born in 1945.

She rented a "shanty" Billy named "the green house" on the "colored" side of town. Its leaking roof, broken windows, and peeling paint were symbols of the social stigma Billy Sinclair would feel most of his life. In the racist South of the era, the few whites forced by circumstances to live in black neighborhoods were lower on the social ladder than local blacks.

Ranting about "class" was a staple as Bessie Sinclair struggled to provide for her five children on a rural Louisiana waitress's pay. Water in the green house bathroom froze during the winter. The family heated the house with the kitchen stove's burners and a small gas heater in the one large bedroom—the only sources of warmth in the house. The whole family slept together in that one room and bathed in a washtub with water heated from the gas heater. Often, there was little or nothing to eat.

They eventually moved into a better house on the white side of town. Extra money came from men that his mother invited home from the truck stop where she worked to subsidize the life change.

She'd send Billy and his brothers and sister out to roam when "visitors" came to see her, as she looked for love and extra sustenance to feed her family.

The children's clothes came from the Salvation Army. The shoes Billy was given one year in junior high school year were too large. Most of the stitches holding the leather tops to the soles had worn away. He wore three sets of socks to keep them on his feet and sewed the uppers to the soles with thin silver wire to keep them from flapping when he walked.

One day, during a lecture on hygiene, his seventh-grade teacher made him take off his shoes. She held them up for his classmates to see. They laughed and jeered. He ran out of the class sobbing and vowed never to return. A truant officer rounded him up for the trip back to school.

I grew up in one of Houston's most affluent neighborhoods. I was the eldest of four sisters, the granddaughter of a Houston real-estate developer, the daughter of an independent oil operator, and the cousin of a US congressman. In 1956, when I flew to Europe to attend the Mont-Olivet—an exclusive Catholic boarding school in Lausanne, Switzerland, where I went to learn to speak French—the *Houston Post* carried a story about me with my picture on the society pages. I spoke fluent Spanish at eleven years old after living in upscale neighborhoods in Mexico City and Acapulco for two years when my father had moved us from Fort Worth to "broaden our cultural horizons."

When I lived in Fort Worth, I took ballet, art, and drama classes on Saturdays at the Reeder School. It was an extraordinary nonprofit aimed at teaching young children the fine arts. Each spring, the school staged a classical play with imaginative props made by local artists on outdoor stages created on the palatial grounds of a local philanthropist we called "Sanny Sue." Children were cast in every role. In the fall we took dance classes, learned to paint, and practiced portraying characters in mock dramas. From January to June, we memorized the roles we were assigned in classical plays.

I played Titania, the queen of the fairies, in Shakespeare's *A Midsummer Night's Dream*, Miranda, the daughter of an exiled magician who falls in love with a shipwrecked prince, in Shakespeare's *The Tempest*, and Aucassin in *Aucassin and Nicolette*, a French play derived from a twelfth- or thirteenth-century *chantefable*, a medieval love story written by an anonymous French troubadour. I had books of literature and poetry. But I was no stranger to child abuse.

Billy Sinclair and I lived on opposite sides of an impossible divide. Except for the abuse we suffered as children, stark differences in class and his life sentence separated us.

But desire sprouted in me like a hothouse flower as I sat across from him in the *Angolite*'s sparse office after my death row interviews that day. Smiling, I boldly dropped a note on his desk as my photographer and I left after taping interviews with the *Angolite* editors:

> *I know that I should leave this feeling at the front gate . . . But it makes me want to touch you.*

And then I waited for word from him, wondering if I had gone too far, venturing into emotional territory I should have avoided, fearing that friendship was all he wanted.

Meanwhile, I was struggling with my death penalty series. I sifted, weighed, and calibrated each word and camera shot to be fair as I wrote the scripts. I rolled the tape back and forth in the editing bay, looking for the best shots and sound bites. I carefully selected video of the men and their victims to balance the series. The faces of the condemned men stared back at me. I looked again and again in the eyes of the state trooper's mother and listened to her death wish for the man who had killed her son.

"I am living for the day they put him in the electric chair," she said of Dalton Prejean, her son's mentally incapacitated killer.

The moral battlefield I faced in writing the series was littered with arguments both for and against capital punishment. An interview with Baton Rouge's coroner assured me that condemned men felt no pain when they were electrocuted. Why, then, I wondered, did the death house have a fan to suck out the stench of burning flesh and excrement?

Once a criminal, always a criminal, my thoughts warned me as I struggled to write the script.

But there was more to the problem. If killing is wrong, how could executions be right? But didn't murder deserve the death penalty? Perhaps natural law gave the state the right to kill to protect society. But what about the French Revolution and its incessant, bloody guillotine? What about Russian purges, and the ovens at Dachau and Auschwitz? Where were the limits on popular will? Could a constitution that guaranteed life promote death?

Friends advised me. From a law professor about legal history: "Avenging blood by taking blood is as old as mankind in all civilizations in all times," to a counterargument from an informal logic class: "Just because everybody is doing it doesn't make it right."

Can evil protect good without defiling it? What about the insane and the mentally incapacitated on death row? Or the innocent who were exonerated after being sentenced to death, or those sentenced to die for acts they committed as children? Perhaps there was no logical way to think about the death penalty. Either a person approved of efficient, state-run killing to avenge society or they were appalled at the idea. The debate raged on as I wrote my death penalty series:

"Thou shalt not kill."

"Live by the sword, die by the sword."

"I am my brother's keeper."

"Eye for eye, tooth for tooth."

"Forgive them, Father, they know not what they do."

After two years as a reporter, I knew life was fragile. I recoiled at the swift decay in corpses I saw on assignment: the flies crawling on a dead man's blackening tongue less than an hour after alcoholism killed him in the woods one bright summer afternoon off Hooshatoo Road, or the barely congealed blood covering the face of a nineteen-year-old driver after a deadly 1980 Easter Sunday collision on Highway 1, near White Castle, Louisiana, his body hanging like a piece of meat in a butcher shop over the steering wheel.

The facts that I amassed for the death penalty series convinced me the death penalty was nothing more than murder masquerading as justice. But my series drew no such conclusion. My job was to cover facts and opinions from each side, not to insert my own. Stories had to be distilled into ninety seconds on average, written in easily understood language, relating facts in the right sequence, providing details about images viewers were seeing, emphasizing the most important without bias. I loved the art and the challenge of TV news reporting. But my death penalty series was taking me far beyond the everyday stories I usually covered.

Carlton Cremeens and Paul Gates, the news director and assignment editor, read my scripts, reviewed the edited stories, and found no bias in my series. It aired in early May, just as I wrote it. The final shot was a close-up of the electric chair. I had Susan reverse the color and make it look iridescent, like electricity was surging through the chair.

I ended the series with a question that scrolled silently across the chair just before the screen slowly faded to black:

"The death penalty: Is it justice or state-sanctioned murder?"

Then I waited anxiously for the series to air. How would viewers react? Would it reveal my bias against the death penalty, or had I successfully camouflaged it with both sides of the story? I waited in the newsroom as the first story in the series began to air, holding my breath, fingers crossed that it would explore all sides of the death penalty without betraying my personal feelings about the death penalty and Billy Sinclair.

A morning show host, angered by the final question that scrolled mid-screen over the glowing electric chair, accosted me just outside the newsroom.

"Convicts sentenced to death should die, no questions asked," he declared.

I turned to face his outrage.

"I did my job. I wrote that series while my mother was unconscious, dying in a Houston hospital. I stayed here and finished it anyway because it was already being promoted on the air. The news director and the assignments editor approved every word. Take it up with them."

BY THEN, BILLY SINCLAIR AND I were writing each other frequently. His letters inserted him into my life as though he had moved into my apartment. I was living in a small apartment complex on Cezanne Street on the north side of Florida Boulevard, several blocks from Baton Rouge's affluent Goodwood neighborhood. While the letters I got from him continued their professional tone, personal observations began slipping in. He wrote of his love for country music, Thomas Wolfe's novels, and memories of his childhood.

I wrote of my love for mountains in the nation's national parks and the Las Lomas section of Mexico City, an upscale neighborhood where I lived for a year as a child, the volcano Popocatépetl framed perfectly in my bedroom window.

Each night, I drove home from the station hoping to find a letter from him in my mailbox. When it was empty, I reread others, listening to tapes of Chopin's etudes and barcaroles, the crystal-clear notes falling, one by one, on the evening air in my apartment as my mind marked ballet exercises in time to the music—a plié here, a tilt of the head there—as I imagined a brutal world where no grace note was ever heard.

April 15, 1981
Dear Billy—

Tonight . . . I am dreaming of Sunlight Basin, on the north fork of the Clark River . . . north of Cody, Wyoming, the most beautiful place in the world and the fish in the stream at Dead Indian Pass . . . and the sapphire blue sky and the smell of my tent in the noon day sun and the sound of the tent's zipper that shuts out the night's cold. Have you ever been camping? In Wyoming, you can count every star in the sky at night . . . every night.

Once on the way to Laramie, I passed a roundup that could have been one hundred years ago. It was October. The snow was late. The sky was so blue, a color you never see here. And the forest was dark against the mountains. On the hills, there were cowboys, rifles in their saddles, many horses in the remuda, and at least two hundred head of cattle moving toward a pen. I pulled over and watched for a long time before I began the descent into Laramie through the Medicine Bow National Forest, and I hoped they knew how lucky they were.

April 18, 1981
Dear Jodie,

No . . . I have never been camping. There is so little from the past that I can look upon with kind memories. I'm sure Sunlight Basin is most important place in the world. It must be since your memory of it is so beautiful. I can't even imagine a place so serene, so peaceful—a place so clear you can count every star in the sky. God, how prison stifles life's beauty. . . . Count a blessing . . . thank your life for pleasant memories of Wyoming. I'd give a right arm for a few. Time slips by us here. . . . All I have to do is look across the room at Wilbert and see the desperation in his stare, and I wonder if we'll ever have other memories than death and dull grey cinder blocks to reach back and touch. You take care and be good.

One evening, shortly after I received Billy Sinclair's April 18 letter, I found a large brown envelope from the *Times-Picayune* in the mailbox. It was full of newspaper articles from the New Orleans daily about Billy Sinclair that I had requested from the newspaper's archives. Instinct and training had prompted my search for stories about the *Angolite* editor. The clips that tumbled out of the envelope left me reeling.

Newsprint from the 1960s jumped out at me in a jumble of headlines about sex and murder. Billy Sinclair was no first offender. J. C. Bodden's killer had a record of four felony convictions. At the least, he was an armed robber and a sex offender. The sex charge hit me like a blow in the stomach—carnal knowledge of a juvenile, the newsprint read. I had been duped by the slickest of cons—sincere, clean-cut, straightforward Billy Wayne Sinclair. The facts stared back at me, ugly and unavoidable. There were no redeeming stories. I slumped on the bed. His illegal escapades read like a catalog of crime. Tears stung my eyes at his betrayal. Why hadn't he told me? Why had he let me believe he was a first offender?

In a burst of anger, I grabbed the phone and called Angola. A prison operator answered. I told him I was a reporter in Baton Rouge who needed to check some facts with Wilbert Rideau. He connected me to a guard deep inside the prison. Cell block noise filled the receiver until Rideau answered. I asked him to tell Sinclair never to call me again.

"Tell him I found out all about his criminal record."

"That's all?"

"That's it. And thank you for relaying the message." I hung up and went to bed.

I was done with Billy Sinclair. Trust was out the window. I had wanted to believe in him. A profound tide of understanding had seemed to flow between us in recognition of common values, as though we had held similar candles aloft in the dark for years, our hopes concentrated on their small flickering flames. I thought his remarkable rise to journalism's heights proved he was no longer criminal.

I thought he was like "Everyman," the embodiment of fifteenth-century morality plays about sinners who ultimately find their way to heaven through good deeds. With courage and a measure of God's grace, I believed a man could turn his back on crime. But it was clear from Billy Sinclair's criminal history and his lack of disclosure to me that the *Angolite* editor preferred the appearance of rehabilitation to its reality. His choice struck at the heart of my worldview.

I believed in redemption. Free will meant a man could change. Evil could never possess those who rallied against it. My belief grew out of a personal code of noblesse oblige and a Catholic upbringing.

Suddenly, the telephone rang. It was Billy Sinclair. I sat on the edge of the bed debating whether to accept the call. A conversation with him now or anytime was useless. How could it change the facts? I decided to take the call. He needed to pay for what he had done.

"Jodie." His voice had an unfamiliar husky tone. "Wilbert told me what you said. I thought you knew. So many reporters know about me. I made a dumb assumption."

"That's hard to believe."

He began stumbling over his words, leaving sentences unfinished, an edge of desperation in his voice, anger in my responses.

"You're a sex offender."

"It ain't what it sounds like."

He started a description of the night he was charged with the sex crime. She was a girlfriend, he said, a few weeks shy of her seventeenth birthday, the lawful age for consensual sex in Louisiana. He had just turned eighteen.

He had a party at his mother's house while she was at the movies. Three sisters came to the party. They were fifteen, sixteen, and nineteen years old. He had sex with his sixteen-year-old girlfriend.

A friend had sex with the nineteen-year-old girl, and Sinclair's thirteen-year-old brother, who begged to be included, had sex with the fifteen-year-old.

When his mother came back from the movies, the sex party was in full swing. Sinclair, his friend, and the three sisters ran out of the house. His thirteen-year-old brother cried, telling his mother that Billy made him have sex with the fifteen-year-old girl. She called the police. They rounded up the sex party participants and let everyone go except Sinclair. They took him to the parish jail in handcuffs.

Five months earlier, he and a friend had stolen a car and driven it on a cross-country joyride to California where they were caught. They were charged with violating the federal Dyer Act—stealing a car and driving it across state lines. They were put on juvenile probation until they were twenty-one.

Given his age, his federal probation officer and state prosecutors came up with a plea deal. In return for a guilty plea to the carnal knowledge charge, he would be sentenced to six months on the parish "pea farm." His federal probation would be revoked after he did the jail time and he would be sent to a federal reformatory with rehabilitation programs.

The deal went south fast. Judge Mack E. Barham, who later became a prominent Louisiana Supreme Court justice, was incensed when he read that Sinclair's little brother said Billy forced him to have sex at the party. He rejected the plea deal and sentenced Sinclair to three years in Angola.

I sat on the side of the bed listening in silence. Angola was a bloody hellhole in 1963. How was an eighteen-year-old supposed to defend himself in general population with hardened, violent criminals? But there were other charges he needed to answer for.

"What about the armed robbery charges?" I demanded. "What in hell were you doing walking into places with a gun?" Outrage spilled out of me like acid burning up the phone wire.

There had been a crime spree, he said, for four months after he finished serving time for stealing the car and having sex with his girlfriend. His "fall partner" was a tough young punk from Dallas he met in federal prison who said he was running from the law. He needed money to get out of the country and robberies were easier with an accomplice. The convict code, he learned at Angola, dictated his response.

"I was the lookout," he said, "Alexander went in with the gun. I waited outside."

He said they pulled off stickups in Florida, Mississippi, and Bossier City, Louisiana, but they were never charged with the robberies. They also pulled a convenience store robbery in Baton Rouge in November 1965.

He and Alexander split up in Dallas when his prison buddy threatened to kill him for being clumsy. Alexander gave him a .22 pistol he bought at a Dallas pawn shop before they split up. Billy told me he was going to use it to pull one last holdup in December at a convenience store in Baton Rouge to get money so he could buy a fake seaman's ID in Alabama, get a berth on a merchant marine ship out of Mobile, and start over. This was the robbery gone wrong that landed Billy in Angola.

"How stupid," I said.

"Yeah," he replied.

I sat for a long time holding the phone, waiting for more, unmoved by his description of the robbery spree and the fatal encounter at the convenience store in Baton Rouge. I was focused on his omission.

"Are there any others?"

"I tried to hold up a convenience store in Pine Bluff, Arkansas, when I escaped from the Baton Rouge jail in November 1966 after I got the death penalty for the December shooting. I got scared and ran out of the store in the middle of it. Nobody got hurt."

"What about the car theft in Beaumont?"

"Me and Alexander had to take a bus back from Florida after the robbery there. We needed a car. But I was never charged with it."

"So, there's other stuff on your rap sheet you never got charged with?"

"Yeah."

"How bad?"

"A car theft in Alabama, the Pine Bluff attempted robbery, and a couple of burglaries. I broke into some vending machines when I was fifteen or sixteen before I did time on the carnal knowledge charge and the Dyer Act."

"My God." My tired expletive ended the conversation again for a time.

"Jodie." He sounded spent. "Taking a car to go joy riding and then running away from home to keep from getting caught, and having sex with my girlfriend, they ain't crimes of violence. They happened when I was seventeen and eighteen years old. I spent a year in Angola and another fifteen months in the federal system. I was pretty damn bitter when I got out in July 1965. I did that year in Angola because a judge got pissed over the bullshit lie my brother told about being forced to have sex with that girl. I wasn't a criminal when I went in Angola, but I damn sure was when I came out."

I was not forgiving.

"Well, you still tried to hold up another store after you escaped."

"I know, and it was just as wrong . . . and I am just as sorry. But I ain't done nuthin' violent in sixteen years in a place where it's easy to 'strong arm' to get what you want. I spent six years on death row paying for what I did. I . . . Jodie," he begged me, "I've done all I can to make up for it. Please don't . . . don't shut me out."

"I'll think about it. I just . . . it's just very upsetting. It's a lot, a lot to get hit with."

"Just think about it, Jodie, please, for God's sake. Just think about it."

I hung up the phone with a terse goodbye.

His picture was lying faceup on top of a stack of his letters. It was taken the day we met. He was standing by the electric chair, his right hand resting on its back. The stark reality of capital punishment—the orchestrated killing of a healthy human being in the middle of the night—was embodied in the image.

I thought I was through with the death penalty. Writing my series had put me through tautological hell. But this time the hell was personal. I picked up Billy Sinclair's picture and stared at the man whose criminal record was tormenting me.

Had he deliberately lied to me? Why hadn't he told me he wasn't a first offender? I reviewed his tormented confession over the phone about his criminal record over and over again in my head. Was his regret real? Had he really thought I knew all about his rap sheet given the national stories about his crime and his accomplishments?

And then there was the murder. What should society do with a man who took chances with a gun? He had walked into a convenience store with a loaded .22 caliber pistol, and a man had lost his life. Why shouldn't he spend the rest of his life among the living dead?

"Fairness," he said the day we met.

There were precedents. Louisiana's governors had granted the clemency petitions of men convicted of murder. Why not Sinclair? Numerous corrections officials, including the head of Louisiana's department of corrections and other free people who had observed him closely for years, were on record in the *New York Times* and other publications favoring his release. His sixteen-year prison record contained no violence despite the frequency of violent crime among inmates at Angola.

I agonized over the bits and pieces of information like a piece of scrap metal caught between two magnets. Force and counterforce threatened to lock me in mental paralysis. The feeling that I was falling in love with a murderer who had lied to me was terrifying.

I thought about him in the middle of the night, on assignments, after work, over coffee at dawn. Billy Sinclair was intruding on my life as my marriage was ending. Were the robberies and stolen cars before the murder proof of a hidden instability that would overtake him if he were free? Should he have been executed? The moral battlefield was littered with arguments for and against capital punishment. But this time, it was more than philosophy. Billy Sinclair made it personal.

I thought about his rap sheet, the nature and circumstances of his offenses, the length of his prison sentence, his accomplishments, the high-ranking prison officials who vouched for his rehabilitation, the trips he made overnight around the state with Wilbert Rideau and one unarmed guard to warn high school students about a life of crime. If prison officials trusted him to that extraordinary degree, why couldn't I? With a single guard, he could have easily jumped to escape from custody. But Billy returned from those trips without incident to one of the most notorious prisons in America.

In 1977, five members of the pardon board voted unanimously to reduce his life sentence to forty-five years. But the victim's family and friends objected and the governor refused to sign the recommendation. They called him a cold-blooded killer. It was a lie.

DUE PROCESS DENIED

"There is a demand these days for men who can make wrong appear right."
—Terence, Roman Republic playwright, 195–159 BC

FOR DECADES, POWERFUL PEOPLE IN Baton Rouge made sure Billy Sinclair would stay behind bars. Two blatantly illegal efforts, deliberately designed to make him look like a cold-blooded killer, were instrumental in destroying his chances at release until 2006.

In 1966, Sargent Pitcher, the district attorney of Baton Rouge, let his lead prosecutor, Ralph Roy, suppress mitigating evidence and use perjured testimony to get the death penalty in Billy's case. Pitcher belonged to the White Citizens Council. The Ku Klux Klan and the Council virtually controlled politics in Baton Rouge at the time. Some of their members lived in Baton Rouge's "Little Dixie" neighborhood. So did people insisting on the death penalty for Billy—the victim's family and his Istrouma High School friends.

In 1979, James Patin, a young probation officer, doctored Billy's criminal record to make him look like a fourth offender instead of a second offender as his real criminal record showed. Patin's father and the victim's father were close friends. They worked together in Baton Rouge's petrochemical industry. Patin knew fourth offenders were considered far too dangerous to be paroled.

Others who fought against relief in Billy's case also held powerful positions in the state legislature, Baton Rouge city government, the department of corrections, and state and local police departments. They included prominent athletes, businessmen, evangelical ministers, legendary football coaches, members of the news media, teachers, and education administrators. Many had gone to the same high school with Billy's victim or had close friends who did.

Billy Cannon, three-time AFL Champion and Louisiana State University's first Heisman Trophy winner, was one of the most influential local opponents in Billy's case. Cannon was a national sports legend and a cultural icon in Baton Rouge by 1966 when Billy went on trial for killing Cannon's high school buddy, J. C. Bodden. Bodden had played football with Cannon at Istrouma High School, a blue-collar school also located in "Little Dixie." In 1955, its football team, the Istrouma Indians, was called the "greatest high school football team in Louisiana history."

In 2003, the *New York Times* profiled Cannon, writing about the sports legend's amazing popularity in Louisiana despite his conviction on counterfeiting charges. By the early 1980s, bad real-estate investments and gambling debts were eating up Cannon's finances. On July 9, 1983, his fans woke up to reports that Cannon had been arrested and charged with participating in the "seventh-largest" counterfeiting operation in American history. The *New York Times* reported that federal agents recovered about five million dollars in high-quality counterfeit hundred-dollar bills buried in ice chests on Cannon's Baton Rouge property.

The football legend pled guilty and was sentenced to five years in federal prison. On August 6, 1986, the *Los Angeles Times* reported he was released for good behavior after serving three years. He remained a political power to be reckoned with in Baton Rouge. After all, as the *New York Times* article said: "In a religiously and ethnically diverse state, LSU football unites the Catholic southern parishes and the Baptist north. And in a state that lags behind others in such areas as education, LSU football provides confirmation that Louisiana nonetheless measures up."

An LSU coach, quoted in the *Times* article, put it this way: "There is no question that the psyche of the people is wrapped up in the football team. In Louisiana, we rank forty-five to fifty in things that are good and in the top ten in things that are bad. But in athletics, we rank very well."

Billy had other powerful opponents with deep ties to Little Dixie's Istrouma High School. The superintendent of education in East Baton Rouge Parish, two members of the Louisiana house of representatives, an executive assistant to the president of the Louisiana senate, two ranking members of the Louisiana state police, at least four members of the Baton Rouge police department, employees in strategic jobs in Louisiana's prison system, and a Baton Rouge probation officer who became head of the Baton Rouge Division of Probation and Parole were part of the opposition in Billy's case. They were ideally positioned to maneuver behind the scenes to keep Billy behind bars.

They were joined by students of the victim's widow, a teacher at Istrouma High School, many of whom grew up to become part of the Baton Rouge power structure. They never forgot why their favorite teacher wore black every day for years.

In 1989, a Baton Rouge minister said that killing an Istrouma High School football player was "the worst crime a person could commit in Baton Rouge." In 1999, Jim Engster, a popular Baton Rouge radio personality, interviewed a man who went to high school with Billy's victim. Don Hooks told Engster on the show: "Billy Sinclair's crime was that he killed a man with a million friends."

Ralph Roy suppressed eyewitness accounts of the crime that proved Billy wasn't a cold-blooded killer. He compounded this unethical misconduct by using testimony from two witnesses he knew were lying—one of whom he coached to lie. Both witnesses testified that Billy shot the victim down in cold blood inside the store and calmly walked out the door.

Roy had a "history of overturned convictions" due to "intentionally" withholding exculpatory mitigating evidence from criminal defendants." A 2017 story in the *Advocate,* the Baton Rouge newspaper, about African American teenager Wilbert Jones, titled "State Supreme Court orders hearing for Baton Rouge man convicted in 1971 rape," listed Roy as one of the prosecutors in Jones's original trial.

In pleadings for a new trial for the now sixty-one-year old inmate, Innocence Project lawyers argued that "prosecutors withheld key police reports from his defense team" during his trial that cast doubt on his guilt. The newspaper's story cited a Louisiana Supreme Court justice who "accused Roy of systematic disregard for . . . the constitutional rights" of criminal defendants.

Billy's powerful opposition turned his crime into one of the most notorious in Louisiana history, generating hatred among people who knew little or nothing about him. For years, there was no escaping the picture painted of him by the witnesses who lied on the stand and the criminal record that the young probation officer doctored to make him look like a "career criminal."

The facts about Billy's crime finally emerged in 1979 when his mother visited a member of the pardon board, questioning Governor Edwards's recent denial of a 1979 clemency recommendation for Billy. The pardon board member said the "truth" about Billy's crime was in a 1965 police offense report in the board's file.

She left the board member's office and asked a clerk for copies of all the documents in Billy's file. The clerk complied. As Billy's mother started to leave, with the copies under her arm, a pardon board attorney burst out of his office. He ordered her to give them back, saying she wasn't legally entitled to them. She ran out of the building, clutching the documents, and left in a waiting car.

Billy's attorney mailed the copies to him. The package with the copies was protected by attorney-client privilege. Prison officials weren't allowed to open it and destroy the documents. For the first time, Billy had proof that the death-penalty trial he had questioned since he was convicted in 1966 was a fraud. He finally had the 1965 police offense report that named the four suppressed eyewitnesses and their accounts of what really happened before and after the convenience store robbery.

What the four eyewitnesses told the police destroyed the legal basis for felony murder that Roy presented at Billy's murder trial in 1966 to get the death penalty. Roy told the jury the murder was intentional and it was committed during a robbery, two arguments necessary to meet the requirements of the felony murder statute under Louisiana law. They were based on perjured testimony from two witnesses: one who said Billy shot J. C. Bodden inside the store after the clerk refused to open the cash register and then walked "coolly and calmly" to his getaway car, and another who said Billy was the man he saw in his restaurant a half hour before the crime "looking like a robber trying to find a place to rob."

But the four eyewitnesses told the police they saw Billy running away from the store with Bodden chasing him. One said Bodden was brandishing a broom above his head when Billy fired the fatal shot over his shoulder in the dark outside the store. If they had been allowed to testify, Billy would have been convicted, at worst, of murder without the death penalty and sentenced to life in prison with an automatic release after ten and a half years under Louisiana's old "10/6 law," in place at the time. Their testimony would have made it clear that Roy and his two witnesses were lying.

I bristled with anger for years every time I thought about the deliberate, cold-blooded lie that Roy concocted to secure the death sentence against Billy and the second flagrant lie Patin concocted in 1979 to keep him in prison until he died. Billy never tried to deceive me about shooting Bodden. He talked openly to me in detail about the robbery attempt and the killing that put him on death row, walking me step by step through the crime that led to Bodden's death.

It happened on a cold, drizzly Sunday night on December 5, 1965, when Billy found himself in Baton Rouge needing money to get to the Alabama coast to get a job, he hoped, on a merchant marine ship carrying goods to South America. He said he needed to "ship out," hoping that would change his life and that the police would quit hunting for him after a few years. There was a warrant out for his arrest for the robberies he and a partner, a former prison friend, had committed. Billy had been the lookout while the partner went in with the gun and robbed the stores.

The convenience store Billy picked was a Pak-A-Sak at 7925 Greenwell Springs Road. James Cleveland Bodden, called "J.C." by his friends, was a thirty-one-year-old clerk working the cash register in the store. A second, younger store employee named Ray Neyland was working outside, sweeping the store's parking lot.

Billy pulled the car he was driving into the store's parking lot. He was armed with a .22 caliber pistol. When he loaded the gun, he didn't put a bullet in the firing chamber. He didn't want to hurt anyone by accidentally firing it. He wanted to scare the clerk, grab the money, and run.

There was one customer in the store when Billy went in—an elderly woman checking out at the cash register. Billy went into the store, turned right down an aisle, and picked up several items as though he were going to buy them. He didn't want to look suspicious. As soon the customer left, Billy walked up to the counter, pulled the .22 from his waistband, and demanded the money from the store's cash register.

Bodden resisted, saying he didn't have the keys to open it. Billy knew he was lying. He had just put a payment from the elderly customer in the register. What Billy didn't know was that Bodden wasn't about to comply with a robbery demand. Several weeks earlier, the clerk had chased down a young African American kid armed with a knife, who had tried to rob the store, and pinned him down until the police arrived.

Two customers came in at that point: Grundy Sampite, an older man who was a former Louisiana state police officer, and Donald Lee Jones, a much younger man. Billy motioned with the gun for Jones to move away from the register and down an aisle to the left of the front door. Sampite moved to the right of the front door, positioning himself between Billy and the door.

Then Bodden moved down the inside of the counter away from the cash register. Billy motioned him back toward the register with another demand for money. But the clerk stopped near the end of the counter. He was on Billy's right side and Sampite was on his left, blocking the door. The stage was set for tragedy.

Suddenly, Bodden moved toward Billy. Billy pointed the pistol at the floor and pulled the trigger. The gun made a clicking sound since there was no bullet in the firing chamber. Bodden pointed across the counter toward Jones, telling him to stay put, before turning to yell at Sampite:

"He's shooting paper wads."

Bodden may have known that Sampite was a retired cop, because Sampite was a regular customer. He may have been signaling Sampite that the two of them could foil the robbery. The clerk moved a few steps closer to Billy.

"He's shooting paper wads," Bodden yelled again, trying to alert the young employee outside the store sweeping the parking lot.

Billy pointed the pistol at Jones and yelled, "Stay put." He then pointed the gun at Bodden's leg and fired a shot to stop the clerk's advance. It hit Bodden in the thigh. Billy started edging toward the door. Sampite began moving away. Hearing the shouts and the gunshot, Neyland, who had stopped sweeping the parking lot, moved cautiously toward the door.

"C'mon in here," Billy told Neyland, trying to get him to move out of the doorway so he could escape. Bodden was standing near the end of the counter, staring down at a growing red spot on his green pants leg. He had been instructed by Pak-A-Sak's corporate office not to resist a robbery. But he charged Billy.

Billy turned and ran toward the door. He fired another warning shot as he ran past Neyland, who had stepped aside, leaving his broom propped against the door. It hit an artificial snowflake can in a Christmas display near the front counter. Artificial snow filled the air, creating a bizarre, messy scene that made the police think there had been a shoot-out inside the store.

Billy ran across the parking lot toward his car with Bodden close behind. The clerk had snatched Neyland's broom as he ran outside and began swinging it over his head as he chased Billy across the parking lot in the dark. Billy fired a third warning shot over his shoulder to stop Bodden. It struck the clerk in the left armpit, traveled across his chest cavity, and hit his aorta. Bodden staggered a few more steps, clutching his chest, and sat down on the parking lot pavement in front of the door, yelling "Call the police. Call the police." He bled to death in a matter of minutes.

Statements Jones and Neyland gave to the police support this version of the events that led to Bodden's killing.

Jones told police investigators in the 1965 offense report that he got to the store shortly after 8:00 p.m. He walked to the bread area and then back toward the checkout counter.

"Look out," Bodden yelled at Jones. "He's got a gun." Jones told the investigators the "intruder" then pointed a gun at him and said, "If you don't want to get shot, get over there." Jones also told investigators that the intruder was trying to get Neyland inside the store.

"C'mon in here, boy!" Jones quoted the intruder as saying. Jones was right. Billy wanted Neyland inside the store away from the door. He was blocking Billy's only way out of the store.

"While the intruder was looking outside the store," the offense report quoted Jones as saying, "Mr. Bodden rushed him, and the intruder fired one shot, hitting an aerosol spray can. The intruder then turned and ran, with Mr. Bodden in pursuit. The intruder fired another shot. When he next saw Mr. Bodden, Jones said, Mr. Bodden was holding his left chest."

Neyland's statement to the investigating officers supported Jones's account. The official report stated:

> *Mr. Neyland said he first noticed the intruder while he was sweeping in front of the store and the intruder parked his car in the east portion of the parking lot. He said he heard Mr. Bodden whistle, and he looked up to see him talking with the intruder. He also saw Mr. Sampite and thought that Mr. Bodden was whistling to Mr. Sampite. He said he then heard two shots and looked up to see the intruder waving a revolver toward Mr. Jones and pointed his left hand at the bread rack.*

Neyland was mistaken. He might not have heard the click of the empty chamber that prompted Bodden to think Billy was shooting "paper wads." Only one live round had been fired—the one to hit Bodden's leg to stop his approach.

The offense report continued:

> *Mr. Neyland said he heard Mr. Bodden say, "Go on, we don't want any trouble," and he then heard the intruder, standing in the doorway, calling "Come on in here, boy, come here." When he [Neyland] asked the intruder what he wanted, the intruder merely repeated his command, "Come on in here," two more times. Then, he said, he saw Mr. Bodden rush up to the man with the gun, and the intruder turned and shot [hitting the aerosol snowflake can among the Christmas display]. Mr. Bodden and the gunman continued running outside the store, he said, and he started toward Mr. Bodden to assist him, when the gunman fired another shot, and Mr. Bodden held his hand to the left side of his chest and began staggering back and toward the door.*

Jones's and Neyland's statements put Bodden outside the store when the fatal warning shot struck him. Both witnesses confirmed that Bodden rushed Billy, and Billy turned and ran from the store. Two other eyewitnesses, Donald Ray Kennard and his wife, told police that Billy was running away with Bodden chasing him.

Ramona Kennard told investigators:

She and her husband were driving on Greenwell Springs Road when she saw a man chasing another man in the Pak A Sak parking lot. She said she saw the man in front turn and shoot at the man chasing him, and she said she saw the gun. She said the gunman was running east on the parking lot and got into a dark car which she could not describe further. She said she saw Mr. Bodden grab his chest on the left side but does not remember anything else.

The offense report had no statement by Donald Ray Kennard.

But in 1984, Kennard, then a Louisiana legislator, agreed to give Billy's attorney, Helen "Ginger" Berrigan, now a sitting federal judge in New Orleans, an affidavit. He made her swear she would come to his house after dark so that none of his neighbors would see her. His political career was supported by the Bodden family and the Istrouma alumni. In the affidavit he said:

On December 5, 1965 I was driving down Greenwell Springs Road, coming from Central, with my wife and child in the car. My wife reminded me that we had no matches for our heater at home and suggested we stop to get some.

I pulled into the Pak-A-Sak grocery located on Greenwell Springs. Just as the front wheels of the car touched the curb, I heard my wife exclaim "oh!" I looked up and saw two men running out of the store; the second man was chasing the first who was about four to five feet ahead of him. The second man was J. C. Bodden and he was holding a broom over his shoulder as he chased the first man. I remember hearing a gunshot and seeing smoke from the gunshot, but I did not see the actual shooting. I do not recall seeing J. C. Bodden fall. I do recall the first man continuing to run around the side of the store. The whole incident happened extremely fast—no sooner had my car wheels touched the curb when the figures burst out of the store.

Ramona Kennard also gave Ginger Berrigan a statement in a similar 1984 affidavit:

On December 5, 1965, my husband, Donald Kennard, and I were driving down Greenwell Springs Road and we intended to stop at the Pak-A-Sak at 7925 Greenwell Springs Road.

As we were pulling into the parking space, two men came running out of the store. The first man had a gun and he was being chased by the second man who, I believe, had something in his hand like a broom. They were only a few feet apart. I saw the first man fire a shot at the second man who then grabbed his chest.

I was subpoenaed by the state for trial and went to court. However, I was told I would not be needed as a witness since I could not make a positive identification of the man with the gun.

None of these witnesses were allowed to testify. In fact, Ramona Kennard was specifically told by Ralph Roy on the day of the trial that her testimony was not needed.

The defense attorney appointed to represent Billy at his trial was in his seventies. He had handled mostly civil cases during his career and had little experience in criminal trials, much less a death penalty trial. Ralph Roy never told the attorney about the four eyewitness accounts in the police report. There are more than forty pages of trial transcript of Billy's defense attorney telling the court he was totally "unprepared" to defend Billy as the trial started.

But Roy was relentless. He pushed ahead, telling the court that the trial should commence as scheduled. The trial judge, Fred S.

LeBlanc, who had a long public career as an avowed segregationist, agreed with Roy. The judge denied the defense motion for a continuance. Roy put two eyewitnesses on the stand—Sampite, the former state police officer, and his wife, Katherine. Grundy Sampite testified that Billy killed Bodden inside the store and then "casually and calmly" walked to his getaway car. Katherine, who was sitting in the Sampite vehicle outside the store, testified she heard shots from inside the store and saw Billy "casually" walk outside the store to his getaway car.

Roy also put Larry K. Sullivan on the witness stand. He testified that Billy was in his restaurant at 7:30 the night Bodden was killed, looking like a "robber trying to find a place to rob."

But two of Sullivan's waitresses, Gloria Hill and Betty Scalan, placed the suspicious-looking man they couldn't identify in the restaurant between 8:10 and 8:30 p.m.—the exact time Billy tried to rob the convenience store, according to police reports the night of the crime.

Sullivan deliberately altered the time he placed Billy in his restaurant from roughly 8:20 to 7:30 in order to support Roy's account that Billy was a cold-blooded killer looking for any place to rob before he tried to rob Bodden. Without the eyewitness testimony that Bodden was shot outside the store as Billy was running away, Roy's cold-blooded killer depiction went unchallenged. It only took the jurors forty-five minutes to decide on the death penalty while they ate a quick dinner.

The second almost insurmountable denial of due process was the 1979 clemency investigation report in which James Patin manufactured Billy's fourth felony offender status.

Louisiana law required the corrections department's parole division to conduct pre-clemency and pre-parole investigations before hearings so that pardon and parole boards could review their findings. The investigations covered an inmate's social history and criminal record, the nature and circumstances of the offense, and any law enforcement and/or victim opposition to clemency relief. Patin prepared the report in Billy's case.

Patin had a unquestioned bias in Billy's case because of his father's close friendship with J. C. Bodden's father. Both fathers bitterly opposed the 1979 clemency application Billy had pending before the pardon board that Patin was investigating.

Patin also knew Carroll DiBenedetto, an Istrouma High School teammate of J. C. Bodden who was also opposing Billy's clemency application. DiBenedetto worked in the corrections department's probation and parole division with Patin.

Against this backdrop, Patin deliberately altered Billy's criminal history to make him look like a fourth felony offender—the "career criminal" DiBenedetto and others in the opposition would repeatedly call him in pardon and parole board hearings. The false Patin fourth offender designation destroyed Billy's release efforts for the next thirty-five years.

Patin's doctored investigation report stated:

"The records of the East Baton Rouge Sheriff's Office, Baton Rouge City Police, New Orleans Police Department, Louisiana state police, and the Federal Bureau of Identification were searched to find all information concerning this individual's criminal record."

Patin's report continued:

Attached for your convenience you will find a copy of the subject's Louisiana State Police Rap Sheet concerning prior arrests and convictions. We will note that no FBI Rap Sheet is attached to our clemency report, since none was available at the time of dictation.

Subject's first felony conviction occurred when he was arrested by the U.S. Marshal's Office on 10/1/62 and charged with the Dyer Act. On 10/15/62, the accused was placed on probation for a period of minority on this charge.

The subject's second felony conviction occurred when the subject was arrested by the Sheriff's Office in Monroe, Louisiana, on 3/2/63 for the offense of simple burglary. On 3/21/63, the accused was sentenced to three years in the custody of the Louisiana State Penitentiary at Angola.

Subject's third felony offense occurred when he was sentenced on 4/8/64 by the Federal authorities for the Dyer Act to 2 years, 6 months, and 20 days.

The subject's fourth offense occurred when he was convicted of the present offense of murder and armed robbery.

Patin made deliberate false assertions in the report. Billy was also not separately convicted of "armed robbery" in connection with Bodden's murder. The 1962 Dyer Act offense (stealing the car) was a federal juvenile delinquency adjudication, not an adult criminal conviction. And Billy was not arrested or convicted for "simple burglary" in 1963. He was convicted of carnal knowledge in '63.

Billy's only two adult criminal convictions, determined years later by the corrections department's records office, were the carnal knowledge and murder convictions. It would take years of legal efforts before this second offender designation was corrected in Billy's records, although parole boards continued to use the Patin report to deny him parole.

Billy waged a twenty-year legal effort to have both these due-process violations corrected by the courts: the suppressed evidence and the false criminal history.

Between 1972 and 1984, Billy filed four post-conviction habeas corpus pleadings about the prosecutorial misconduct in his case, ranging from the state trial court to the US Supreme Court. In two of these applications, the federal courts acknowledged that Billy's rights had been violated, but said the violations were "harmless errors" because of the "overwhelming evidence of guilt" against him.

After he discovered the suppressed evidence in the 1965 Offense Report, Billy filed civil lawsuits against the clerk of court's office, the coroner's office, the city police department, the parish sheriff's office, the district attorney's office, and an individual civil lawsuit against Larry K. Sullivan.

Sullivan didn't deny the perjury. Instead, his attorney filed a motion to have Billy's lawsuit dismissed because the statute of limitations for suing him had expired.

Billy also filed an ethics complaint with the Louisiana Bar Association against Baton Rouge district attorney Ossie Brown for his opposition in Billy's case that began in 1979, because Brown had been the first attorney appointed to the case. Brown, who was a prominent criminal defense attorney in 1965, was forced off the case by the Bodden family and friends. Throughout his twelve-year tenure as district attorney (1972–1984), he vehemently opposed Billy's release efforts.

Three other prominent Baton Rouge attorneys were also pressured off the case by the Bodden family and friends before Judge LeBlanc literally forced Harris English to defend Billy at trial despite the attorney's repeated protestations to the judge that he was not prepared to proceed to trial. The lead attorney, J. St. Clair Favrot, withdrew from the case on the morning of the trial, leaving English alone to defend the case. English did not have any of Favrot's trial materials. He knew nothing about the crime, the victim, or any trial strategy Favrot had prepared.

Billy also sued the pardon board under the Treen administration, the department of corrections records office, and the Baton Rouge Division of Probation and Parole because of DiBenedetto's involvement in his opposition. Corrections employees like DiBenedetto were not supposed to be involved, one way or the other, in an inmate's pardon or parole efforts. Billy also filed a personal lawsuit against DiBenedetto.

In1984, not long after Edwin Edwards returned to the governor's mansion and had once again named C. Paul Phelps to head the corrections department, the corrections secretary visited Billy in the *Angolite* office to deliver a stern warning. "Your lawsuits are rocking the very political foundation of Baton Rouge," Phelps said. "And I cannot impress upon you the depth of the anger those lawsuits are causing some powerful and influential people in Baton Rouge. I'm afraid the anger will become so intense that it will place you beyond my means to protect you."

To defuse the political backlash based on the advice given to him by his attorney Jack Martzell, Billy decided to stand down. He began a very deliberative process of either dismissing or reaching out-of-court settlements in the lawsuits. Billy had gained a measure of satisfaction through his legal efforts. He had forced agencies to hire outside counsel with law firms as far away as Dallas and caused people like Sullivan and DiBenedetto to hire attorneys out of pocket. But at the end of the day, the lawsuits did little to change the way the justice system treated his case. Instead, they fueled the opposition's intensity.

DESPITE THE POLITICAL OPPOSITION, THE cold-blooded-murder narrative, and the doctored Patin report, Billy managed to secure five unanimous clemency recommendations from the pardon board that his life sentence be reduced to a specific number of years under three governors between 1979 and 1990, including a forty-five-year recommendation in 1979, a sixty-year recommendation in 1981 and 1984, and a seventy-five-year recommendation in 1988 and 1990.

Billy became immediately parole eligible in January 1992 when Governor Buddy Roemer commuted Billy's life sentence to ninety years. Billy now had a fixed good-time release date: April 2011. Louisiana parole boards, under two governors, would use the doctored Patin report to deny parole to Billy in 1994, 1995, 1997, 1999, 2001, and 2003, although the boards had no problem paroling brutal murderers during that time frame.

Between 1992 and 1999, the boards granted paroles to seventy-one inmates convicted of murder, including Lewis Graham and Paul "Tex" Chandler, while they repeatedly denied Billy.

Graham was a Shreveport doctor who murdered his sleeping wife with a sledgehammer in 1981. He hit her on the side of the head and then rolled her over and hit her in the face three times. He was sentenced to life in prison. He was paroled after serving eleven years.

Chandler went to a Bossier Parish barroom in 1975 to reconcile with his girlfriend. When she spurned his attempts, he went out to his car, got his shotgun, walked into the bar, and fired at the table where she was sitting with several people until the gun was empty. He reloaded and kept firing. He killed two patrons, including his best friend, and wounded two others. He was sentenced to two life terms in prison. He was paroled after serving twenty-three years.

None of the seventy-one killers released by the parole board between 1992 and 1999 had spent as much time behind bars as Billy and none could match his record of rehabilitation, including his role in blowing the whistle on the pardons-for-sale scam at Angola. But Billy would serve forty years and four months in prison—more than twice as much time as any of the seventy-one murderers—before he was finally paroled in 2006.

"CHILDHOOD DECIDES"

"Childhood decides."
—Jean-Paul Sartre, French philosopher and author, 1905–1980

OUTRAGE, BORN OUT OF THE injustice I endured as a child, shaped my life. It was no accident that I saw Billy Sinclair for what he was and not what they made of him. Life with my father, William Reynolds Archer, was a toss of the dice when I was a child. In some ways, it gave me a distinct advantage. I learned to roll with hard punches and get up again. By the time I was six years old, I knew life could be mindlessly vicious. By the time I was nine, I no longer trusted authority. By the time I was twelve, I learned to face down fear on my own.

Baby chicks taught me the first lesson—tiny, sweet balls of fluff cheeping under the warmth of a brooder's lights on my daddy's chicken farm in Brookshire, Texas, not far from Houston. Eggs were precious commodities during World War II. Rationing was a fact of life for every American family. We ended up on the farm in the 1940s as World War II raged around the world, after my great-uncle Billy somehow managed to get my father an honorable discharge from the army.

The chicken farm was little more than a tall farmhouse with a barn that held coops for hens that laid a seemingly endless number of eggs and brooders to keep baby chicks warm. At night, Daddy would climb trees to grab hens that had escaped the coops and roosted in trees near the house. Mother held up a flashlight to blind the birds, so they couldn't get away before he could grab them. He would clip their wings, so they couldn't fly, and stuff them in a bag for a trip back to the coops. I stood under the trees that surrounded the house, staring up into the darkness until mother's flashlight illuminated a pair of shiny eyes. Then, Daddy would begin his climb. It was a nightly ritual.

I loved the baby chicks. Hours old, they crowded together in the brooder like fluffy animated toys. One day, as Daddy and I bent over the side of the brooder watching a new batch of hatchlings, he pointed at a particular chick.

"See that chick?" Daddy said. "The one with the speck on its head? It will be dead in a couple of hours."

I recoiled in horror.

"Why, Daddy?"

"The other chicks will kill it. They are born to peck at spots. It's an instinct. They will peck it to death."

He said it couldn't be rescued because it would die away from the brooder's warmth. I hoped somehow it could survive. Hours later, it was dead. The other chicks had pecked at it incessantly until its little yellow body lay limp and unmoving under their feet as they crowded together, pecking at other spots on the floor of the brooder.

The brooder was a microcosm, a little universe, a merciless killing field where creatures mindlessly eliminated one of their own and then stepped over its body as though it had never been a living being like them. It taught me that groups exclude and punish those that are different, killing them if they must. Inquisitions, banishment, lynching, executions, gulags, prisons, and concentration camps are the lot for those society deems misfits.

When I was nine years old, my father almost drowned me without knowing what he was doing. He wanted to teach me to swim. I knew how to propel myself through the water facedown, whipping each arm forward in turn, but I could only last the length of one breath. I had practiced all summer, putting my face in the water where I could stand, lifting my feet off the bottom, swallowing down my fear as I tried to teach myself to swim.

Daddy stood in the water in the swimming pool at the Fort Worth Country Club where we were members, urging me to jump in. He promised a big leap would put me in his arms. I stood on the edge of the pool, shaking with fear. After a last desperate gasp for breath, I gritted my teeth, closed my eyes, and jumped into the pool. I plunged under the water and began swimming toward my father as fast as I could. Just as I was about to reach him, he moved back several feet.

I was out of breath, but my father made no move to help me. I hurled myself at him, beating my body through the water in desperation. I reached him just as I was going black. He swooped me up in the air, laughing in delight.

"See how much more you could do than you thought you could," he shouted in triumph. I sucked in breath after breath, my face turned up toward the sun. He sat me on the edge of the pool, gloating over the lesson he thought he had taught me. What I learned was far more valuable. Authority disguised as love, or shielded by law and custom, could not be trusted.

When I was twelve years old, a water tower in Fort Worth, Texas, on top of the Will Rogers Memorial Coliseum, taught me the third lesson. We lived on Watonga Street then, just off Camp Bowie Boulevard, in a neighborhood that Daddy thought was beneath us. We had moved there from a mansion in Westover Hills after he went broke.

Westover Hills was a private enclave for Fort Worth's richest families. Architects had designed most of its elegant Tudor and Mediterranean-style homes. Lawns were gracious and expansive.

The mansions were partially hidden behind rock walls on the neighborhood's winding, hilly, tree-shaded roads. Cattle barons and oil magnates headed up many of its families. When Daddy made a million dollars in his dog food canning business, he moved us to Westover Hills. In Westover Hills, our chauffeur drove us to school and the sunroom was filled at Christmas with extravagant toys from FAO Schwarz in New York.

Somehow, my father lost his business. I never knew the details. We moved to Watonga Street while he worked to rebuild the business. Christmas morning on Watonga was different. There were only four presents under the tree, one for me and one for each of my three sisters. Mine was a bathrobe. There was no money for toys. I remember my mother crying in the bathroom.

My sisters and I were happier on Watonga Street. We didn't have to make appointments to play with other children after school anymore. We were free to jump on our bikes, climb trees, and play sandlot football, "kick the can," and other games that we loved.

Our Watonga Street house was just two blocks from the Will Rogers Memorial Coliseum. There were swing sets on the side of the coliseum. I was a tomboy. I loved to ride my bike down to the coliseum, get on a swing, and pump my feet harder and harder, lost in the effort to go as high as I could, until it seemed I would be launched into a sky that I remember was always a gorgeous, unpolluted turquoise blue.

The coliseum fascinated me. I often rode my bike down to its grounds after school to see what I could discover. The coliseum was the largest building I had ever seen. It was the first domed structure of its kind in the United States. Built in 1936, its six monumental piers supported a huge, curving façade.

I discovered that one of its enormous front doors wasn't always locked. When I found it open, I slipped inside. The coliseum's silent halls had a special appeal. They were cool on the hottest of days. I would press myself against a wall, listening for janitors or anyone who might catch me, before tiptoeing upstairs. One day, I found an unlocked door on the second floor. I opened it and stepped onto the coliseum's roof.

I saw a tall water tower with a ladder on the side a few feet away. I climbed to the top of the ladder, expecting to find a platform where I could stand and gaze out over the neighborhood. It would be a secret hideaway, where I could escape the strife of my parents' tumultuous marriage and my father's frequent rages and spankings. But there was no platform when I got to the top. I glanced down and almost fainted with fear. I was at least two stories above the roof. The ladder's rungs were too far apart for a small twelve-year-old girl to easily descend.

The soles of my penny loafers were worn and slick. The only way down was the way I came up. I would have to back down, one step at a time, until I reached the roof. The thought paralyzed me. What if my foot slipped off a rung as I was trying to get down? My knuckles were white with the effort to hang on to the ladder. Sweat threatened to loosen my grip. No one knew where I was, and the afternoon sun was headed for the horizon.

I clung to the top of the ladder, talking out loud to myself, afraid that screaming for help would make me fall. There was no way to see the rung below me. I had to feel for it with my left foot, knowing a misstep could send me plunging down the ladder.

I placed my left foot on the rung as carefully as I could. Then, I moved my left hand to the rung at my waist and held on as tight as I could. The moves stretched me out full length on the ladder. My left foot and left hand were on the next rungs down. My right foot was still on the rung right under me, my right hand was still gripping the rung above me. I took a deep breath and lowered my right hand to the rung at my waist. Then, I carefully lowered my right foot and placed it next to my left foot. One rung at a time, I slowly lowered myself down the ladder.

I paused each time I moved down a rung, working up the courage to go on. My muscles shook with fatigue. I don't remember praying.

I talked to myself, giving myself instructions and encouragement as I felt with a foot for the step below me, afraid each time that I would fall. The fear never left me until both my feet were planted firmly on the roof. Then I darted for the door, sneaked back down the stairs, ran outside, jumped on my bike, and pedaled home. I never sneaked into the coliseum again and I never told anyone about the water tower.

Terror burned in the lesson I learned that day. I was tough enough to save myself. I stopped crying when Daddy whipped me in one of his out-of-control rages, enduring it in silence. It was my own private badge of honor. One day, I overheard him tell my mother he couldn't reach me anymore.

I WAS THE OLDEST OF four girls. When I was born a month early, my father said I was too ugly to be his child. A thyroid deficiency, the doctor said, made my tongue too big for my mouth. It was taped to the side of my face to keep me from swallowing it. Tubes inserted through my nose into my throat helped me breathe. My arms flailed back and forth as though I were trying to pull them out of my throat. As my father watched me fight for my life, screaming like a red-faced monkey, something in my struggle to live struck a chord. He decided I might be his child after all. I had "fight," he would tell me again and again, recounting the story to me as I grew up.

My sisters and I quickly learned to tiptoe through life, never knowing what we would face next. One minute, my father was hugging us, and the next minute, he was a raving maniac with a belt. His mood swings were terrifying. He made rules that were confusing and hard for children to follow. They could change depending on how he felt. Punishments for even the slightest infractions were harsh. Challenges to his authority were met with whippings when we were small. When we were teenagers, his punishments were meant to demoralize: no dates, three months under "house arrest," no personal phone calls for weeks at a time, and, for me, religious boarding schools that were like penitentiaries.

We were irretrievably caught up in the vagaries of our father's moods and whims, prisoners of his inconsistencies. Shouts of childish glee invited a violent reaction. Running through the house triggered a whipping.

My sisters had their own ways of dealing with my father's sudden fits of rage. Carol, a golden blonde fifteen months my junior, simply hid, running from him as he came home or sidling away, mouthing respectful phrases as she eased out the door. Another sister, Kathy, was his stunning image, a tiny, irresistible creature able to elicit his laugh as a protective shield. He saw her as himself and only vented his violent temper on her when he was especially peeved. My youngest sister, Melanie, eight years my junior, left home in her early teens to avoid the violence and my father's blatant sexuality that was, by then, a daily part of her life at home, as mental illness and alcohol destroyed his hold on sanity.

My father raped my mind when I reached puberty. He gave me a thick book to read about the history of sex worship in cultures around the world. *Sex and Sex Worship* claimed the cross was a sexual symbol for the penis and testicles. Every time I saw the cross above the altar at Mass, profane images flashed in my mind. I loathed myself and spent time trying hard to atone.

When we lived on Watonga Street, our father forbade us to go to Mass for a time. He told us the Catholic Church brainwashed children. He wanted us to be free to choose a religion. We sat on the curb on Sunday mornings and watched playmates down the street leave for Mass with their mothers. We had been taught in Catholic schools that missing Mass on Sunday was a mortal sin. I stopped being afraid when I realized hell was probably a long way off because I was too young to die.

Our father had grand designs for us. We were Archer girls. We were meant to be debutantes and marry well in line with our last name. We were not allowed to call boys on the telephone, chew gum in public, wear mascara, or swear out loud. We wore matching hats and gloves to Mass. Our Sunday shoes were black patent leather Mary Janes. Our socks had no lace on the edges. Neither did our panties. We were ladies.

By the time we were five, we had been taught to say "how-do-you-do" when we were introduced to adults and "very-nice-to-have-met-you" as we parted company. We said "please" and "thank you" and waited with our hands in our laps for food to be passed to us at the dinner table after making a polite request.

Strategy governed our social lives. We were not to accept dates unless we were asked at least four days in advance. To further his plans for us to marry well, we were sent to the Kinkaid School, an exclusive private school for children of Houston's prominent families. US Secretary of State James Baker was a student there as he grew up. Kinkaid was in line with our "pedigree."

A cousin was a member of the Republican Magic Circle. Another was listed in Houston's social register. My grandfather was president of the Archer Development Company, a real estate firm he started in Houston in 1928. By the time he died in 1962, he had added more subdivisions to the city than any other developer.

My grandfather's brother was president of the Houston Fat Stock Show and Rodeo, and the Better Business Bureau, and chairman of the board of Uncle Johnny Mills. He was a national vice president and a regional vice president of the National Association of Manufacturers. His son, Bill, was a popular Republican congressman who represented Houston's Seventh Congressional District for thirty years, serving as chairman of the House committee on Ways and Means from 1995 to 2001. He would later be instrumental in helping Billy and me begin our investigation into the corruption at Angola.

My mother, Alice Elizabeth Mulligan, was a small, plain wren beside a peacock. I know she was afraid of my father. But she had grit. She could stand up under punishment. I relied on memories of her courage as I faced one crushing defeat after another in my fight to free Billy Sinclair.

I was born with her broad Irish cheeks. My father told her on their honeymoon that she wasn't pretty, but he had married her anyway. He made plans to change the contours of my face when I was a teenager, telling me he would have the molars in the back of my mouth—top and bottom—pulled out to make hollows in my cheeks, the way they did in Hollywood, to create an oval face, the standard of beauty in those days.

He prized beauty in women above all else. He looked like a movie star. He was so handsome that people quit talking to stare at him when he walked into a room. His devilish good looks, curly black hair, and flashy smile quickened the pulse. His charm was mainly reserved for others. But I believe he was often ashamed of the way he treated us.

One night on Watonga Street, he began slapping my mother's face every time she stepped backward up the stairs, first on one side of her face, then the other. Maybe she was drunk too. My sisters and I were in a bedroom on the second floor. The slaps woke us up. We cowered in our beds, not knowing what to expect. Suddenly my father walked into our bedroom and turned on the light. He sat on the side of my bed and began telling us why he had to slap my mother so many times. I listened in the dark, my heart pulsing in my throat. There had to be a way to confront his brutality. I turned my back on him, terrified he might hit me for disrespecting him. For a long moment, he sat there in silence. And then, inexplicably, he left.

I almost jumped over the second-floor balcony to get away from him one night in our palatial Westover Hills home when he flew into a rage. A winding plantation- style staircase swept grandly up to a hall with a balcony that overlooked the first-floor entrance. The first-floor ceiling was two stories high. A special demon must have possessed my father that night, taking away any semblance of self-control in the need to exhaust his anger.

It had stormed that evening. High winds had sheared leaves off trees and left small limbs lying on the ground. Lightning still occasionally ripped across the sky, illuminating pools of water on the lawn outside. I was nestled next to the window by my mother's dressing room vanity as she did her hair and applied her makeup. My parents were going to a ball that night at the Fort Worth Country Club. Without realizing it, I was leaning on a call button built into the windowsill that summoned the servants.

To me, my mother looked like a goddess. She wore a long black ball gown. It was cut low in the back, plunging dramatically from the nape of her neck to her waist. In front, the bodice was beaded up to the neckline at her throat. I stared at my mother as she wound her hair into thick coils that framed her face. The hairdo was the last word in fashion in the 1940s. The dress sparkled as she applied deep red lipstick to her mouth.

Suddenly my father was at the door of her dressing room, demanding to know why I had called our chauffeur in the rain. J. C. and his wife lived in the servants' quarters over the garage. She was our live-in maid. They had gone to bed early that night with my father's permission. When J. C. heard the call bell I was accidentally leaning on, he quickly dressed and arrived dripping wet in the kitchen, politely asking my father what we needed.

My father was incensed. Rage played over his face, distorting his features as he yelled at me from the dressing room door. How could I abuse a servant?

I was an eight-year-old begging him to talk to me instead of yelling, but my answer must have sounded like "sass."

"Daddy, yelling doesn't do any good."

"Oh, it doesn't? Then how about this?"

He whipped off his belt and began beating me. Beatings and spankings were usually over in a few minutes. But he had staying power when it mattered. And a direct challenge to his authority mattered. I ran down the second-floor hall close to the railing, screaming as I tried to escape him, headed for the bedroom so I could crawl under the bed, the only other refuge I could think of besides throwing myself over the balcony.

In the 1950s, my father suddenly moved us to Mexico. Maybe it was due to the shock treatments he voluntarily sought out to "cure" his melancholy—the worst disease that anyone could have, according to him. He fully intended to live out his life there. He declared that anyone who worked after the age of thirty-five was a fool. He rented a mansion in Mexico City for a year and then moved us to a penthouse apartment in Acapulco, where we lived for another year.

He gave away two-thirds of his successful dog food business to his two best friends to afford the move. In return for majority control of the business, they were to send him a check every month for the rest of his life. The bizarre arrangement lasted two years before they voted him out of the company.

Acapulco was a small town in the 1950s, although it already exhibited signs of the international resort it would become. We lived in a five-story building overlooking the bay. Every morning, according to an arrangement my father had made, we had waterskiing lessons before school. A boat from Acapulco's Ski Club would head out across the bay to pick me and my sisters up at the apartment's boat dock. One of us would get in the water, sleepy and shivering, and ski out to the middle of the bay behind the boat where we took turns skiing for an hour.

After my father's partners reneged on the dog food business deal, leaving us with no income, we returned to the United States. I sat in the back of my father's station wagon looking back, out the window, as we left for Texas, staring at the last beach I could see in Acapulco before we drove into the mountains on our way to Mexico City, telling myself I would never see its beauty again. I hated to leave Acapulco.

My father quickly moved us to California to try and recoup his fortune. He rented a big, furnished house in Beverly Hills while he brokered oil deals to Hollywood movie stars for tax shelters. He was successful for a time. Oil deals, particularly Texas oil deals, had a romantic appeal for Hollywood's inhabitants, whose lives often resembled the movies they starred in.

While we lived in Mexico, I attended the seventh grade and part of the eighth, but Mexican schools didn't follow the same curriculum as stateside schools. My father said it wasn't a problem. He said there was no excuse for me not to do well since I was an Archer.

He insisted that administrators at Beverly Hills High School put me in the ninth grade. I struggled in school, almost hopelessly behind my classmates, enduring humiliation after humiliation, the result of one scholarly fiasco after another. When grandfather Archer offered to build a house for us in an exclusive Houston neighborhood, we moved back to Houston.

When I was thirteen, my mother tried to commit suicide after my father declared he was leaving her. I found her late one afternoon, lying on the living room couch in a coma at our home in River Oaks, Houston's most exclusive neighborhood. I took her pulse every thirty minutes the way I'd been taught in Red Cross classes at school. When she wouldn't wake up, her brother, who was staying with us, called an ambulance.

The next day, after we got home from school, my father ordered me and my sisters to take seats at the dining room table so he could talk to us about our mother. He said she was dying and that it was our fault. We were taken to the hospital to say a last goodbye. The doctors later said they had never seen anyone that far gone survive.

I rebelled in high school. I had read voraciously before I was thirteen, devouring the pages even by flashlight under the covers on school nights after I was ordered to bed, often enjoying books no one my age was expected to read. Adolescence interrupted my literary escape and hurled me in other directions. Defiance of all authority dropped my grades and kept me in constant trouble both at home and in school.

By then I saw myself as the perennial outsider. Nose pressed against the glass, I was always the observer, never the welcome participant in high school social circles. The only two friends I made at Kinkaid, Houston's most elite private school, were other misfits—girls like me with "easy" reputations.

I ran away from home and stayed with high school friends who lived down the block from our house in River Oaks for two days and nights until their parents became suspicious and called my parents. A Houston police officer picked me up and gave me a lecture before letting me out of the car in front of my house.

When I was a sophomore, I stayed out all night with a date. It was a daring, socially unacceptable act in the 1950s. We fell asleep in the car after an evening of what was called "heavy petting." When we realized it was after midnight, we were too terrified to go home. We had violated both our curfews.

I crawled into the back seat and went to sleep. He fell asleep behind the steering wheel. That night, my parents called the parents of all my sisters' friends at Kinkaid looking for me. By morning, word had spread that I had stayed out all night with a boy.

It ruined my reputation. There was no "comeback" for an "easy girl" in the 1950s in those circles in Houston. I wasn't invited to make my debut, a must for high society girls in Houston. My bad reputation followed me everywhere.

For my senior year, my father sent me to Our Lady of the Lake High School, a strict private Catholic boarding school in San Antonio. He had rejected Catholicism in his twenties, claiming it brainwashed its adherents. But it was better than teenage pregnancy—the next form of social suicide he feared I would try at Kinkaid that would embarrass our family.

At Our Lady of The Lake, I met girls from prominent Hispanic families in South Texas, Mexico, and South America. Girls from

Venezuela gave me vinyl records of Mario Suárez, a top Venezuelan singer in the late 1950s. I still sing along with them in Spanish, listening to the harp and guitar that made the music so beautiful.

Our Lady of the Lake was strict. I counted off the days until graduation like a convict, cutting myself slack when and where I could. I smoked cigarettes on the sly. I shocked the nuns dancing the "bop" to Elvis Presley's sexy music, gyrating like a pole dancer during the nightly hour of recreation that boarding school students were allowed. I raided the kitchen pantry near midnight with other "inmates," teased a mouse out of a garbage can into the middle of a screaming gaggle of girls to disrupt study hall, and tried as hard as I could for the rest of the time to be "good."

I received my share of write-ups from nuns who had their hands full with me. "You are a ringleader," Mother Superior said, shaking a finger in my face.

"I am praying for you, my dear," was the usual conclusion to my many "conversations" with her. Spring came. I graduated from high school in May 1956 with my virginity intact.

I was sent to Europe to restore my social standing. Extraordinary views of the Swiss Alps as our train crossed the Simplon Pass into Switzerland from Milan are imprinted on my mind. So are Venice, the Coliseum in Rome, the Vatican, and the Italian countryside.

MY FATHER DIED A DEAD-BROKE alcoholic in a VA hospital in Houston in 1973. I collapsed in tears in the hall outside the ward where he lay, his tongue black and swollen, as he struggled to breathe. I hadn't seen him in years. Sudden grief slammed me to my knees; love for him surged in my heart.

When he patted my head, calling me his "little buddy," I was a child with no worries: The handsomest man on the planet loved me. I was in seventh heaven.

But the monster in him terrified me. I never knew when it would escape. I tried as hard as I could to make him love me. Like any child, I stumbled in my attempts to live up to his standards. Clashes with the monster grew more frequent as some form of mental illness that led him into the alcoholism eventually erased the father I loved.

When I hear Debussy's "Clair de lune," my father's favorite piece of music, he is at my side again, smiling down at me. I don't believe he ever meant to hurt us. But he could never break free of the mental illness that destroyed his life and threatened ours.

After my mother died in 1981, my sisters sent me a small, ragged cardboard box full of the things my mother treasured most. They were letters from my father. He left her destitute. She lived with me in New Orleans and then with my sister in Houston in the last few years before she died. The letters were written while my father was away in the army, or on trips later in life, as he tried desperately to market "Speed Speech," an ingenious method of learning languages easily that he had invented so he could make enough money to take care of them both. Across the top of the cardboard box, mother had written "Betty Archer's Memorabilia." I burst into tears when I saw her handwriting. I put the box away in a far corner of the closet for years. One day, in 2017, I opened it and met a father I never knew.

November 17, 1961
My Darling:

I wrote you a letter earlier today, but I did not get to say the things I wanted to. Mainly, I wanted to say how very much I love you and how lonesome it is without you, my Betty. Your letters made me cry, not because they were so sad. It's just that I want my booted foot going up the stairs to see the beauty in your eyes when you see me, the warmth of your arms about me and the feeling of home. Home is where you are. Wherever that is, makes it home. I am so sorry to be a disappointment to you, my darling, to have you endure the misfortune that I have inherited because of my stupidity. I have no right to make you suffer because of my inadequacies. But I am, my darling. I don't mean to. I hope you understand. You know I don't want it this way and that I am bending every effort to eliminate this intolerable situation, to end it forever, where we can live in a world never separated, always as one.

CONSEQUENCES

"Two roads diverged in a wood and I—
I took the one less traveled by,
And that . . . made all the difference."
—Robert Frost, American poet, 1874–1963

MY HEART BEAT EVERYDAY WITH concern for the man who changed my life forever when we met in Angola's death house. But how was I to see him again? The answer was not long in coming. We would be allowed a follow-up meeting on a Saturday, the ninth of May, in an inmate-lawyer conference room at Angola. It was granted, ostensibly, so Billy, Wilbert, and I could discuss a project—maybe a book about their experiences as inmates. Billy would later tell me that the warden who granted permission for the meeting felt I might be able to help the award-winning inmate journalists change public perception in Louisiana about their cases with an appealing project that would allay fears about the two rehabilitated men. Instead, I became one of Angola's prisoners.

My personal feelings for Billy Sinclair would ultimately take me down a tortured path not unlike Angola's twisted, two-lane country road. There were no highway markers to warn me of its terrible cost, no understanding that the years would blow away behind me like dead leaves in the wake of my car, my dreams withering and dying, one by one.

Angola had always worked its convicts hard. In 1869, Louisiana granted Samuel Lawrence (Major) James a lease to run a state prison on his plantation. He used the convicts like dumb animals on Angola's lands, working them from dawn to dusk—"kin see to cain't see." It was a byword for his brutal farm operation. He built a fortune on the convicts' backs. He died in 1894 and the state purchased the plantation in 1901. Conditions didn't improve. A 1917 census shows even children weren't exempt from Angola's horrors. It listed thirty-one inmates under the age of sixteen.

Angola's geography makes it a natural prison. It lies in the middle of the state, surrounded on three sides by the Mississippi River and the Tunica Hills on the fourth. Those hills are 150 miles long, ten to twenty miles wide, and nearly five hundred feet high in some places. Poisonous snakes, briars, thick undergrowth, and the dense canopy of trees covering the hills, their steep ravines, and cliffs made foot travel virtually impossible. The greatest danger, though, was inside the prison itself: death at the hands of warring inmate factions. Between 1972 and 1975—some of Angola's bloodiest years in the twentieth century—at least forty inmates were stabbed to death in inmate wars, and 350 prisoners were seriously injured with knife wounds during this period. Prisoners slept with telephone books and department store catalogs strapped to their chests to ward off frequent midnight knifings. Homemade armor and even swords filled prisoners' lockers as they sought to defend themselves or fought to resolve territorial disputes and questions of honor. In 1975, a federal court order finally forced Louisiana's governor to stop the carnage.

As if to compensate, nature burst into a glorious celebration of life that Saturday, May 9, 1981, as I drove to Angola for the special visit with Billy and Wilbert. Sprays of flowers filled redbud trees and Japanese magnolias. Azalea blossoms covered bushes with intoxicating color in neighborhoods rich and poor. Dogwood trees dappled the woods with small white flowers, tiny stars in a universe of fresh, bright green.

Anticipation filled me with pleasure at everything I saw and left me marveling at the prison's improbable beauty as it spread out before me like a manicured farm. Herds of cattle grazed behind white wooden fences lining the road as I drove down the hill toward the main prison from Angola's front gate. In the distance, green stalks pushed up in sturdy rows, the crops at healthy mid-stride in the early spring.

Inside the main prison's "A" building, a woman in a caged-in office pressed a button unlocking the first of two barred cell doors that led in and out of a small cage between the lobby and building's interior. I stepped inside and signed the visitors' register. A guard ushered me around a corner down a short hall to the open door of a visiting room reserved for lawyers and their incarcerated clients.

I entered and froze just inside the door. Billy Sinclair stood all the way across the room, arms folded across his chest, a deep frown on his face. He was as carefully groomed as he had been every time I had seen him. I was dressed for Saturday errands in heels and faded jeans. I felt another surge of embarrassment. It was obvious he had worn his best. A brooding look flickered across his face. He put his pad and pencil on the table and sat down in one of three chairs surrounding it without speaking to me.

Clearly, to Billy Sinclair, I was just another visiting reporter. I had either mistaken his intent or he had changed his mind. I forced myself to face him as I walked toward the table. My embarrassment was so acute, I wanted to turn and run.

A catalog of his letters flashed through my mind. Except for one that revealed a sexual attraction and another about his childhood, his letters were about the prison, his case, his crime, and those opposed to his release. I took a deep breath, forced a nonchalant tone into my voice, turned, and held out my hand to Wilbert Rideau. I would get through the meeting until it was time to leave, making it clear that I, too, expected nothing.

Rideau greeted me as though we had been friends for years. Our conversation ran the gamut. He talked about his love of Ayn Rand's books. I recommended *The Mind of the South,* the best account of what drove the South to secede and inspired country boys, who never owned slaves, to willingly die in withering Union crossfire at Gettysburg to preserve the rights of plantation barons to own slaves.

When the conversation circled around to food—the sort that prisoners never got at Angola—Billy finally joined in. He said he loved salads at self-serve buffets. At Angola, all vegetables were cooked. By the time they were dished onto inmates' plates, few vitamins were left. Salad dressing was a dream.

Our conversation drifted back to conditions at Angola and our talk of death row. The prison was at its bloodiest in 1972, when Billy was sentenced to life in prison after the US Supreme Court ruled in *Furman v. Georgia* the death sentence was inequitably applied and he was moved from death row into general population.

Then both men stopped talking as though a signal had passed between them. Rideau rose without a word and quickly headed for the door. I stared at my hands to avoid Billy's eyes. I didn't want to be left alone with him. The morning's awkward moments had been too painful. Suddenly he reached across the table and grabbed my hands.

"This is a brutal world," he said, his voice a guttural whisper. "Are you gonna stick with me?"

I looked up to see the naked passion in his eyes.

"I have loved you since the first moment I saw you," he declared.

He stood up and lifted me to my feet, cradling me in his arms. I relaxed against his body, locked in the embrace I had been dreaming of. Passion surged inside me like an incoming rip tide.

"I had no way to read you when you came in," he said, rocking me gently back and forth in his arms. "I was so afraid I had misread your letters and that you were just coming to write a magazine article." His kisses cut off my words as he stroked my face and hair, telling me how much he had longed to touch me. Suddenly, he jerked away and sat down, slamming both hands flat on the table at the sound of keys in the hall.

"That's rank," he said, the fear evident in his eyes and posture. Terrified, I sat down, placing my hands flat on the table like his. Heart thudding in my throat, I trembled with fear, unable to stop shaking. If we had been caught in an embrace, he would have been stripped of his position with the *Angolite* and returned to the fields.

The day was a brutal introduction to the life I would lead for the next twenty-five years. During our visits, I would freeze, almost too frightened to breathe at the sound of keys and the trappings of rank. Even the lowest-level corrections officer would prompt my suspicious gaze, no matter the circumstance or occasion. The fear would be a reflex, carrying over into my life like a displaced phobia. It would leave me with an automatic dread when I caught anyone staring at me, as though guilt for his crime were tattooed on my forehead.

The threat was gone as abruptly as it arrived. The hall was silent. Tenderly, he reached for me. Blind with tears and the need for comfort, I relaxed against his shoulder as he smoothed my hair. Somehow, he'd said, touching my cheek after we quickly stepped apart, he would find a way for me to visit again.

I turned at the door to signal a final goodbye through my tears. The longing to see him once more, the callous brutality of the prison, the fear and outrage I felt at his continued incarceration were now part and parcel of my life. The pain of missing him was now the pain of being me.

OUR VISIT UNLEASHED A TORRENT of letters about his need for me—feelings that had ambushed us when a stranger standing in the death house met a reporter he sometimes saw on TV. Nothing warned either of us that we would be caught in a whirlwind of emotion we could not control.

I went home to find a letter he had written on the fifth of May, four days before our special meeting. It was a passionate declaration of love. A week later, I received the letter he wrote after our special visit.

May 5, 1981
Dear Jodie:

I simply need you—you are my reason for living now, you, simply you. What I have to give you, what I have to share with you, has long been in my heart. Why am I involved with you . . . to use you . . . to take advantage of you? Why? Unlike most prisoners, I don't need money, a lawyer, or female attention. I'm not without support or backing. I don't need you for any of those things. My world was turning before you came into it . . .

You crumbled a steel wall around my heart. I've seen many situations where I've looked many women in the eye, undressed them mentally and about all I got out of it was a passing physical interest or emotional yawn.

But I look at you and I fall to pieces. You tell me why I can't take my eyes off you; why I mentally make love to you as my eyes run over your body, why I'm torn with an uncontrollable need to touch you, hold you and embrace you; why I want to build my every life's dream and goal around you; why I think of giving up every part of my heart, soul and mind to you? How you stay in my brain . . .

May 9, 1981
Dear Jodie:

I wanted to touch and hold you from the moment you first walked into the room. I kept trying to read you, read anything in a gesture or movement or word. Nothing. I sat stifled and checked. I had to eventually force the door open. I've never ached as much to touch someone as I did those first few hours we sat there. Now, I've touched your flesh, tasted your kiss, caressed the softness of your hair . . .

I felt my heart soar today hearing you say that you couldn't walk away from me, that something was holding you to me. It made me feel I could reach up and touch the sky.

May 11, 1981
Billy—

I don't want walls between us, any more than I want people between us, clothes between us, or anything else that gets in the way of being filled up with you. With you, I have embarked on the greatest adventure of my life—however long it lasts. Whatever comes, it will be the best time, the time I risked the most, suffered the most and loved the most.

Every night, I drink a toast to you. I am committed to whatever the future brings. I want to live every moment of it. Good night, Billy. Sleep with me in your dreams.

May 12, 1981
Dear Jodie:

I don't know where this is going where it will lead or what awaits us at the end—all I know is that I have never felt like this about anyone in my life.

Few men can be more in control and in command of life situations than I. I can walk among the most dangerous men in this prison with contempt and I can rise from the bottomless pit of failure to the height of success with a sheer force of will and determination. Yet, at times, I feel so helpless, so powerless simply because I can't touch or hold you; because I can't say "I love you"; because I am so flooded by the ten million emotions you arose in me.

May 17, 1981
Billy—

Today, before I left to cover a story, I had time to play the tape of the first interview we did. I watched your face, loving all the expressions I saw move across it. Before I began asking questions, you were looking at me with the most intent expression and a softness around your eyes I was unaware of that day.

May 16, 1981
Dear Jodie:

I want to make love to you so intensely, so completely . . . until we both collapse in exhaustion. I want to feel an ancient animal strength because you are my woman, and I want my heart to pulse a tender peace because I love you so much. And if it should be me who awakens during the night, as I sometimes do, I want to gently touch your hair or kiss you lightly on the forehead. I am in love with you—so deeply and irretrievably in love with you. Why? How? I really don't know. I simply know what's inside of me.

May 24, 1981
Billy—

I love you. I don't know why. I've seen you three times in my life and maybe I have a dozen letters. And yes, there are numbers of people who would call me a fool. But you are what I want, for now, for later, for as long as I can have you.

May 27, 1981
Billy—

Why didn't I meet you until now and why not under other circumstances? If not until now and under these circumstances, why at all? How is it you understand me so completely without knowing me? How is it you know the words that touch my heart, fire my desires. . . . How is it you know my secrets, my passions, my fears without being told . . .

you saw the child in me and the woman. You are the only man who has ever understood that paradox.

BY THEN, MY LIFE WAS divided into two rigidly separate compartments—the reporter I was and the secret desire burning in my heart for Billy. Being a capital correspondent in Baton Rouge distracted me from the fear tugging at me—that Billy and I would never be together. The capital had a giddy side that amounted to much more than breaking news stories and covering legislative committees. There were wild after-hours parties where elected officials cut loose on the dance floor and at the bar. It was "*Laissez les bon temps roulez*"—let the good times roll, as they say in Louisiana. And they rolled every year during the legislative session until it was over.

Every night, I drove to my apartment hoping to find a letter from Billy or get his call. On the eighteenth of June, he woke me up from a deep sleep near midnight to tell me we had been granted permission to see each other every two weeks for two hours on a weekday.

Warden Peggi Gresham, the *Angolite*'s adviser, had approved the visiting arrangement. She was one of the first women to hold an administrative position at Angola.

"Is this relationship personal?" she'd asked Billy crisply when he requested to meet with me on a weekly basis in the lawyer-client visiting room.

"Yes," was his short, straightforward answer.

Gresham was a small, dark-haired woman who took her administrative job seriously. She had risen from the secretarial pool to the position of deputy warden. Even in Angola's macho world, few questioned her ability. She demanded a high level of performance from the *Angolite*'s editors and got it. She gave them her trust and enjoyed their unflagging loyalty. She was a bulwark against the magazine's detractors and its first line of defense.

"Be careful, Billy," she'd warned. "Remember the *Angolite*'s reputation."

She also insisted our visits had to take place on a Friday instead of the weekend, when most prisoners had visitors. Her concern for the magazine's reputation was the reason we were only allowed to see each other in the lawyer-client visiting room where we were monitored. It protected Billy from prying eyes and gossips in the main prison's visiting center. Jealous inmates might cause problems for him. But the arrangement also protected me. A reporter seen holding hands with an inmate was a setup for disaster. Many other visitors were from Baton Rouge, where I was a regular on the evening news. Billy already harbored fears that I might lose my job.

It was the visiting arrangement we had longed for. Billy's lawyer, Richard Hand, lived on Long Island, fifteen hundred miles from Baton Rouge. Since he couldn't visit Billy regularly to monitor his condition, he selected me to take his place. Under the prison's policies, prisoners' attorneys could designate anyone they wanted to serve in that capacity. While Billy and I would be shielded from other inmates' eyes in a room reserved for legal visits, we would still be strictly monitored.

The promise of love between me and Billy had blossomed into full erotic flower. And I flew on, like Icarus at the sun, drunk on the dream that had sprung up between us. I came to know him intimately as we visited through the summer. He laid out all his thoughts and hopes, his mistakes and regrets, his dreams and ambitions, and his crushing remorse for his crime. It was there I vowed to become his wife, and dreams of him at home began to seem real.

I CHANGED MY SCHEDULE AT Channel 9. I became the station's weekend reporter, so I could see Billy on Fridays. I would work Saturday through Wednesday and visit Billy every Friday. I would plunge back into work on Saturday—with all its demands—and focus on covering the news, not on missing the man I had just left the day before in Louisiana's most notorious prison.

Reporting on the weekend at Channel 9 was always an adventure. It kept me from brooding over changes in my life that left me seriously adrift at times, mourning my first marriage, missing my children, terrified sometimes of the strange love that was rocketing me to such heights.

Early one Sunday morning, I stepped inside the deserted newsroom and turned on the lights. Saturday night's usual chaos just before the news went on the air at 10:00 p.m. was evident everywhere: scripts lay on the floor, empty Coke bottles littered two tables, and old news wire copy overflowed wastebaskets. A Styrofoam container with what was left of a takeout dinner lay on a nearby desk, cigarette butts in the refried beans.

The weekend assignment editor was already at her desk.

"Hey Dorothy," I called out. "Hard night?"

She shrugged. I had never seen Dorothy Williams excited. She had a controlled, laid-back languor that served her well when stories broke on deadline.

The two of us and Abe McGull, the weekend photographer, were on our own, flying by the seat of our pants, no weekday assignments editor telling us what to do, no news director looking over our shoulders. The freedom got me up higher than a kite. I ran on adrenaline and imagination, hunting for stories or angles that weekday crews had overlooked.

Suddenly, the police scanner came alive with a burst of static followed by a short message.

"Code ten," it blared. "Nine hundred block of Gus Young. All units . . ."

Static cut off the rest. Dorothy picked up the phone and called the police department.

"This is Channel 9 calling on your code ten over on Gus Young."

After a quick conversation with the dispatcher, she hung up the phone and turned to me.

"They're working a drowning over in the nine hundred block of Gus Young. It's a city park. They've been on scene maybe twenty minutes."

She radioed Abe.

"Base two to Abe. Base two to Abe."

"Dorothy, when you get him, just head him to the scene. I'll meet him there."

Running, I stiff-armed the door onto the side street, car keys in hand. The drive wouldn't take long on a Sunday. There would be little traffic, especially on the low-income side of Baton Rouge. Turning on Gus Young, I saw police cars parked near a large field about three blocks away. I wheeled into a parking lot next to the field and pulled up next to a police car.

"Channel 9," I said. "I'm looking for my photog."

"Sorry, babe, didn't recognize you. Back there." The officer behind the wheel jerked his thumb over his shoulder, indicating a swimming pool and bathhouse about fifty yards away.

I backed away, thanked the cops, and headed toward the bathhouse in a dead run. Rounding the corner, I saw a policewoman, radio to her mouth, blond hair hinging in thin wisps from under her cap. A pair of purple swim trunks lay on the ground beside her feet.

"Where's the body?" I asked.

"In the pool." She pointed at the fence. "Still on the bottom, up near the diving board. But you can't go inside."

Abe stood near the fence, camera on his right shoulder, ready to shoot the scene.

I could see the body in the water near the diving board. A knot of police officers stood near that end of the pool. One yelled at me.

"Watch out, darlin.' He ain't got clothes on. Don't want your virgin eyes corrupted, Channel 9."

I grinned and sidled up to the fence.

"Hey," I called out to him. "I need some help."

He walked over to the fence. I looked up at him through the wire.

"Listen," I said. "Can my photographer just come inside the fence to shoot?" I pointed at a spot just inside the gate. "Honest to God, I gotta have a shot from the inside. Look, my photog won't come near the body. Just let us get one long shot inside."

"You're not a bad-looking woman, you know," he said, leaning against the fence, an intimate tone in his voice.

I moved closer, my hand touching the wire near his.

"Please," I said. "I swear we won't mess up the crime scene." He gave me a hard look.

"I gotta talk to my lieutenant," he said.

I watched him walk back to a group of uniformed police and plainclothes detectives hear the bathhouse. After a long minute, they turned to look at me. Abe stood behind me, ready to move inside the gate.

"Come on," the lieutenant said, motioning.

Abe nodded and moved toward the gate, his camera on his shoulder. He was cool and steady. Abe McGull was a young African American photographer with big ambition and a lot of smarts. I could always depend on him to get the shots we needed.

I watched as Abe worked his way nearer the body as the police snared the corpse with a long-wired pole, lifted it off the bottom, and dragged it out of the water. The man's rigid body rocked back and forth on the edge of the pool, his flesh puckered on soles of his feet, his knees drawn up toward his chest, his arms lifted in a final, frozen gesture.

I heard a scream and watched a large, middle-aged African American woman run across the open field toward the pool. She threw herself against the cyclone fence behind the diving board, hands clutching at the wire.

"My baby, my Jesus, my baby, my Jesus," she screamed.

Her voice trailed off as relatives tried to pull her away. Clawing the air, she fought free and hurled herself against the fence again.

"Let me have him," she screamed. "My baby, let me have him. Let his mama hold him."

Two attendants from the coroner's office came up the walk toward the pool, pushing a stretcher with a body bag on top. Inside the gate, they rolled it toward the corpse. They put on rubber gloves and picked up the body, lifting it onto the stretcher and into the body bag almost in one motion. They buckled straps around it and rolled the stretcher toward the gate.

Abe ran to get in front of the macabre parade coming toward him, pivoting on his heels, camera rolling. I waited while he got video of the hearse.

The hearse pulled away. In the background, the woman continued her endless screaming, her body racked with sobs in a timeless rhythm before she collapsed on the park bench.

I saw the cop who'd let Abe inside the fence.

"What happened?" I asked him. "How'd the victim get in there in the first place?"

"Dunno," the cop came back at me. "The assistant coroner, though, he'll give you some information. He's getting the stuff from the guy's mother now."

He pointed out a carefully groomed African American man standing in the crowd, holding the grief-stricken woman under the elbows, his head inclined toward her mouth in spite of her screams. The coroner dropped the woman's arms and the crowd rushed in to catch her as she collapsed on the bench. I walked after him as he made his way toward his car.

"Hey," I called, "wait up."

He turned, surprised. I trotted up to his side.

"I gotta get a statement," I said.

He hesitated, unsure about talking to me.

"I'm Channel 9," I said. "We need it for the six o'clock news."

Abe was already behind me now, handing me the mic.

"How did it happen?" I asked the coroner. "Is this death drug-related?"

"I can't say until I do an autopsy. Offhand, I'd say maybe. But that's just a guess."

"Listen," I said, "if you get anything on this later, I'll need it for the show."

Wordlessly, he handed me his card, anxious to get out of the heat. I started for the news car with Abe, sick of the heat, the humidity, and the screaming.

"Hey, Abe, need me to help load anything?"

"No, babe, I got it."

He unlocked the trunk and lifted the video recorder into its cushioned box inside.

Equipment loaded, we got in the car. Abe flipped on the air-conditioning. I put the tape he shot on the seat beside me and lifted the hair off the back of my neck.

"Put it on emergency, Abe," I joked.

I would miss days like that for the rest of my life, living on adrenaline, doing a job I loved, telling stories the way they happened, recreating reality.

REPORTING ON SATURDAY AND SUNDAY ended my weekend trips to New Orleans to see my children. I was determined to stay in Baton Rouge until Billy was free. And it seemed, given the forty-five-year clemency recommendation by the Louisiana pardon and parole board in 1977, that he wouldn't be locked up much longer.

But I was letting my children slip through my fingers without realizing it. All I had ever read in magazines and other articles was how devastating divorce could be for small children. Little had been written in the 1980s about how it could devastate teenagers.

I was on my own emotionally so early in life, given my parents' alcoholism and my father's erratic and often violent behavior when I was a child, that I couldn't wait to get out of the house. I thought my children could handle it. But I was leaving them and their father for a man in prison. My mind closed off the possibility that I was betraying them.

I said a final goodbye to my beloved New Orleans home at 1478 Camp Street on a June day in 1981. Memories of it haunted me for years. I would hear my children's voices in the hall, see the shafts of light that pierced the windows at noon, scenes full of enduring pain. The grief I felt that day would wash over me again and again for years.

The notes of a steam calliope drifted up from the Mississippi River the morning I left forever and hung in the upstairs hall as a paddle wheeler made its way up the river from the French Quarter. The music reprised the heyday of riverboats for the tourists on board. I paused at the top of the stairs on the second floor of my historic house to listen for the last time, knowing I would never live there again.

My husband, Tom, sat in his study on the second floor by the stairs. I was sixteen when we met, and he was eighteen. We both knew it was the last morning we would awaken under the same roof. The pain was paralyzing.

Out loud I asked, "One last thing. How will I know when to buy new tires?"

He took off his glasses and looked at me. Fatigue was written all over his face.

"Push a penny into the tread. If you can see all of Lincoln's head, you need new tires."

He made no move toward me. Silently, I closed the door and stepped into the hall. My mind screamed at me as I stood outside the door, my hand on its elegant handle: What had we done to drive each other so far apart?

We had been married for twenty-three years. The pain I felt was too deep for tears. We had lived in that house for ten unhappy years.

New Orleans was my husband's choice, but the house was mine. I had it painted yellow like sunshine. It implied a future for us, like always living in the morning.

The house stood on high ground near the Mississippi River on the corner of Camp and Race. Heavy timbers shoring up granite curbs were still visible in the gutters around the house. There was an old patterned brick sidewalk on the Race Street side. Across the front, on Camp Street, four white Greek columns supported a wide balcony overlooking Coliseum Square, a three-acre park. On summer nights, I often stood in the second-floor hallway as music from a steam calliope on board a paddle wheeler drifted up from the Mississippi. That house was the only thing I loved about New Orleans.

But we drifted away from each other like continents moving apart on tectonic plates. He saw life one way. I saw it another. He was content with a professor's life in New Orleans. I was desperate to move. I begged him to apply to colleges near the mountains in Wyoming or Appalachia, where I felt such peace. But his teaching job at Loyola was guaranteed. He was a tenured professor. He couldn't take a chance at another college, jeopardizing the family's well-being if he wasn't awarded tenure when he was hired. Quarrels had ripped us to shreds for years.

I opened the door to my seventeen-year-old daughter's bedroom and gazed at her as she slept. She had a double cowlick, one perfect swirl of hair on each side of her crown. I saw it as soon as they laid her on my chest still wet from the birth canal. How I had loved the baby fuzz that stuck straight up from the top of her head as she grew that first year.

Quietly, I closed her door and moved up the stairs to the attic. Early sunlight from the attic's dormer windows fell across the beds of my two sons. I smiled, remembering the oldest at three, running through the house in a diaper trying to keep up with his older cousins. I remembered his younger brother when he was two, holding an Easter basket on one arm as I tried to show him how to hunt eggs.

They were already off to college, one in Baton Rouge and the other in New Mexico.

I moved down the stairs from the attic, taking mental snapshots as I went, imprinting images of the house on my brain—every timber, brick, cornice, and mantelpiece in the house, the echoes of children's voices in the hall, their grade school drawings, Christmas mornings, a tent stored away for family vacations in the mountains.

My car was loaded with the last of the things that I was moving permanently to Baton Rouge. I pulled away from the curb, drove across the intersection, parked the car, and spent long minutes looking back at the house. It would be years before I saw it again. When I did, I wouldn't be welcome there.

1478 Camp Street belongs to another family now. But it will always be mine. On the rare occasions that I was in New Orleans after that, I would drive to Coliseum Square and sit in the car across the street, staring at my house's elegant façade, wondering about the family inside, remembering the conflict that tore mine apart.

THAT FALL, BILLY AND I were writing each other every day. The letters stitched our lives together. They were filled with words, thoughts, and observations we had no time to share in person.

We had each found in each other what we had searched for all our lives. I wrote of the pain I felt at leaving my children's father, how our love died, where Billy and I could move when he was free, and how careful we had to be to protect the love we shared. I saved his letters for years, in special files, so I could relive the first year we met.

He wrote of the passion that animated his days and nights, bolstering his belief that he would be free. My arrival in his life, he believed, was a sign from heaven that his ordeal was coming to an end. We wrote what we would have said if we could have been alone, sometimes returning to subjects again and again as the bond between us grew.

5-19-81
Dear Jodie:

Let me get something off my chest. I was cautious and reserved at the beginning when we met. But it wasn't because I didn't feel anything for you. When I first saw you kneeling down poring through your bag in the Death House, I wanted to reach down and help you. When we sat together as you interviewed me, I felt a desperate need to touch you. When you stood in the little hallway before you left, I thought, my God, this is the most beautiful woman I've ever set eyes on. A piece of my heart trailed after me when you left. For the next several days, I thought of you constantly. . . . I don't know what life has in store for me, you, us, but if the stars over Sunlight Basin shine on me, I will be free of this prison. . . .

5-20-81
Dear Jodie:

I already think about the possibility of losing you—and it is like taking a pair of bolt cutters and turning them loose in my stomach—and while I have experienced pain before, I don't think any pain I have ever endured could match what that would make me feel. . . .

I feel for you unlike I have ever felt for anyone . . . you could tear my heart out. But even knowing that, I will risk it. I must love you. I must not hold anything back. . . . So I live with the possibility of losing you by keeping it out of my brain. . . . If destiny holds that wordless, ungraspable hurt in store for me, then I will simply cross that death-bridge when I get to it.

May 30, 81
Dear Jodie:

You told me what you do each morning when you awaken. I'll tell you about mine. I sleep between a lady homosexual who is fond of bikini panties and a motorcycle hippie who snores, sleeps with a towel around his head and is afraid of water. Depending on which side I first turn, I get a disheartening shock every morning. I get up, dress and make my bunk. I seldom, if ever speak to anyone in the dorm. I tap Wilbert on the foot on my way out. . . . If anyone speaks to me, I nod or grunt. I come directly to the office and put the coffee on. I sit behind my desk and instantly turn my thoughts to you. . . . I love you, baby—I want to spend my life with you making you know just how much.

May 31, 1981
Billy—

I will always care for the man I married when I was nineteen and he was twenty-one. We literally grew up together. We worked hard over the years. We mourned the deaths of two children together. I nursed him at times when he was sick, as he did me. He helped me through the births of our three living children and he was always there to take on my tasks when I was too tired to carry on. I will always care for him.

He is part of me. It is a tragedy that our marriage died. . . . I hope he finds someone who will love him as he deserves to be loved. He is a fine and decent man, this father of my children. I will always miss him.

I have known him for twenty-six years, the better part of my life. Not seeing him will be like not seeing a brother, or one of my children, or a deep close friend, the kind with whom communication is unspoken because you know each other so well. . . . I am not blameless in this breakup.

6-2-81
Dear Jodie:

It's been a long time since anger settled in my gut as it did last night, thinking of those who have hurt you. From your father on . . . I can't fathom that. Maybe I'm dense. Maybe I'm lacking a bolt in this circuit, but I can't see how Tom loved you, yet destroyed that love. . . . I have discovered in you a mine of untouched love, the most valuable and precious thing on this God's green earth. . . . my precious darling . . . how I ache for you.

6-4-81
Dear Jodie:

I am so sorry for the ill things I said about Tom. I didn't intend to disrespect him. . . . I must learn how to handle this love I have for you—it is so wild and untamed . . . the thought of us, the future, our being together is so powerful in my heart. I have never felt such an unbridled, uncontrollable and powerful feeling as I do for you. I love you.

July 3, 1981
Billy—

My husband and I happened to each other too young, half-formed. We could not withstand the pressures life put upon us. I held his youthful love as carefully as I could, but I was a child myself. We grew each in our own way over the years.

I became the person I was meant to be as I grew away from him. At the core of me there remained a need, insistent but unfulfilled. Over time, I came to accept it as not to be answered. Having been reared a Catholic, I was ready to accept that crown of thorns. I was ready to accept never being able to share the things that touched me, make my soul stand still and take note, the things that put me in touch with eternity.

And then I found you that day. The first time I ever saw you, a shock went through me. . . . You personified everything I had ever found attractive in a man as no one ever had before. Later when we talked . . . I imprinted your expression forever on my mind. . . . Had I never seen you again, I would never have forgotten you. I was prepared to believe, that day was out of time . . . a treasure that would never come again.

July 21, 1981
Billy—

When you were a little boy, you sat on the railroad tracks and watched cars go by on the highway. You wondered, you said, where they were going. And you wondered about the people in them. And you had a terrible desire, you said, to be free.

When I was a little girl, I had the same dream. I wanted to be free to go any and everywhere. In the attic on Watonga Street in Fort Worth, when I was twelve, I could hear the wind better than anywhere else. And in my imagination, I rode that wind. Often, all the way up to the Great Plains and the Canadian border. I wondered about places like Cheyenne. It took me a long time, but I finally got there.

August 26, 1981

Billy—

Last night I dreamed I was home. But the house wasn't really clean. It was just a visit. I finally cleaned out some cabinets. When it was time to leave, I couldn't find anything to pack. My children were leaving too. It was late . . . and it was cold. Fall had come. I said goodbye. We were all parting. The wool of my husband's coat brushed against my face. I pushed him away. I woke up crying.

9-7-81

Dear Jodie:

I have thought it out, sifted through every possibility, and weighed every option. There is nothing worthwhile in this world without you. I am not one of Sartre's wretches who clings to life with the illusive hope that tomorrow the dawn will break and justify yesterday's existence. I have realized my life's dream—I have touched the greatest and most magnificent thing in this world when I touched you. I don't need the lyrics of blind little poet, not even the gifted expressions of Wolfe to make me realize that.

September 12, 1981

Billy—

We were picked out for a special experience. . . . But it is not going to be simply given to us. . . . I have seen love die—strong love—love that was sanctioned by church, family, society, the times. . . . It dies in a terrible way. It doesn't thunder, there aren't any speeches, no death knells, not even a quiet rattle. It simply ebbs away, and one day you wake up to the quiet realization it isn't there anymore. The bedrock is gone. In its place is quicksand.

I harbor the seeds that kill love as well as you . . . we must not plant these seeds. They are the products of fear. Ironically, it is the same fear that has us both by the throat. I fear being abandoned. You fear I don't love you.

If you and I cannot overcome these fears, we will never have a lasting bond. We will fall on the sword ourselves.

September 16, 1981
Billy—

It's best we confront the terrible driving fear that is at the heart of each of us—your fear of losing me because you've seen too much come apart in your life, too many of your dreams have been shattered.

As I grew up, I was taught that love is conditional. It's conditioned upon being brilliant, scintillating, mercurial and beautiful. And I was taught very early that I was none of those things. My father often told my mother that she was ugly and stupid. And he said I looked "so much" like my mother.

I learned to hide away a little something, to keep a small reserve of some part of me I could use to comfort the rest of me when I failed to meet his standards . . . an inner core I could count on for solace all the times I went to bed smarting from his scathing remarks or the blows from his belt.

I never told you any of this. Beside what you suffered, it seemed so insignificant because my father never tried to kill me.

Billy wrote me about life at Angola and the uncertainty of surviving, how he carefully inched away from big yard inmates who lived by the convict code after he was released from death row. He spent ten months on the big yard in 1972 after leaving the row. Inmates on the big yard often reacted violently to "Judas Goats" who rejected the code. "One on the stretcher" was a common call, referring to an inmate on the way to the prison infirmary after being stabbed, a victim who had violated the code.

After a rule infraction on the big yard, Billy was sent to a maximum-security lockdown cell block where he spent two years, from 1973 to 1975. It was an even more dangerous environment than the big yard. Inmates on the lockdown tiers were the most violent at Angola. They murdered others locked up in the "block," setting them on fire with gasoline or burning them with hydrochloric acid smuggled into that part of the prison. It was the most violent era in Angola's twentieth-century history.

When he was released from maximum-security lockdown, he was housed in a sixty-man dormitory side by side with inmates who would attack at the slightest hint of "disrespect." But his reputation as a slick jailhouse lawyer protected him. He could get sentences reduced and cases called back to court. His legal skills shielded him from violence.

I was growing familiar with Angola's history and its policies as I came and went each week. I thought of the prison as a charnel house in spite of its bucolic setting. A thief of souls where men sweated out their lives in summer's blistering heat and shivered in winter's chill when frigid temperatures blew in on a norther's winds, whipping across farm lines working in the fields or sleeping under the prison's standard issue at night—thin blankets over short rigid cots in dormitories and concrete bunks in cell blocks.

I struggled in the prison's grip, my heart torn with fear that Billy and I would never be free of its mindless dangers and restrictions. Still, I thought of almost nothing but Angola as I covered stories during my workweek, living for the hours on Fridays that I spent with him in the small visiting room reserved for lawyers and their clients where we had our first visit in May. Every morning, I stood in front of the mirror, admiring my body's curves before stepping into the tub. Tears stung my eyes as I stared at my reflection. How many years would it be before an old woman stared back at me? Would he want me then?

I felt like an eighteen-year-old. But the secret clock my body stored was close to winding down. I was poised on the edge of panic, focused on the end of monthly function and the youth-sustaining cycle that held my flesh firmly to my bones. My body stared back, its internal rhythms as secret as the length of its seasons. But the firm, young self I saw in the mirror reflected little of my fear.

Worry sat on my head like a ton of bricks. I knew I was walking on the edge of a precipice—one false step and everything I was trying to hold together would fall apart. I missed my children. Details of my divorce had to be handled. I was responsible for airing stories that did the station justice, accurately quoting what the people I interviewed had to say.

I was assigned to cover Colin Clark as a new death date for him approached. I hadn't included him in my death penalty series in May because his execution date had been stayed. I wanted to be done with the death penalty and the racking job of balancing coverage of that polarizing issue. But there was no way I could duck the assignment.

Clark's case had continued to garner media attention. In July, he fired his attorney and again asked US District Court Judge John Parker to drop his habeas corpus petition, so he could be put to death. On August 26, Parker dismissed it. The state trial court set a new death date for November 5.

September 29, 1981
Billy—

I am not looking forward to Colin's date. There are people in the newsroom that let out whoops of glee at the thought he's going to the chair. They revolt me. I get sick at the pure animal blood lust I hear from those types. I can see the ravening animal in their eyes. They can't even talk intelligently on the subject. They talk in circles, their reasoning distorted. I could stand it if someone came straight out and said. . . . "I believe in revenge."

But no, they couch their desires in fancy language, clothe it in respectability. And each and every one is a coward using the state to do what they themselves could never do. I hate it when they draw themselves up as arbiters of the right, paragons of civilization. It's then I know how close the civilized world is to primitivism. It's then I know what a thin veneer covers the jackal. Today I have to write the two Colin Clark scripts. I have put off watching the tapes. I suppose I should have stayed several nights on my own time just watching the video, so I could get a real feel on how to build the story. So, this will be a real test of how well I work on deadline. It will be interesting to see if I can come up with something that really has impact, pacing and balance under those circumstances. Friday when I will see you . . . can't come too soon. It's the only day of the week I'm alive.

September 30, 1981
Billy—

I guess you saw my Colin Clark story tonight. I was pleased with it. I had real compliments on it, too. Everyone gathered around to watch it. And that's unusual. We are all so inured to news stories and each other's work that we kind of view the show with a jaundiced eye. So, it really meant something when all crowded around to see it. In that script, I let Colin talk for himself as much as possible. That was the best way. Less of him would have frustrated viewers.

I will fall asleep tonight with you on my mind, and I will wake up wishing you were with me. That's the way it always is. I wouldn't trade having you for anything in the world. I love you, baby.

Clark's execution was blocked again on the second of November—three days before he was scheduled to die—when the American Civil Liberties Union won a stay pending a sanity hearing for the twenty-eight-year-old former waiter. His death sentence would ultimately be vacated in 1983 by a federal appeals court on grounds that his partner could have committed the murder when they robbed the restaurant. Clark was resentenced to life in prison.

I was deeply concerned about being an objective reporter by November 1981. Would I careen off into bias in my stories? Would I fail to cover stories accurately, no matter the subject? Was I so distracted by the stress I felt over Billy's situation that I would get the facts wrong? Would I somehow shortchange the public?

I'd been assigned to cover a legislative committee hearing at the state capitol about funding more vocational classes at Angola when my ability to remain unbiased was tested.

"Gentlemen," the burly warden had addressed the lawmakers, "I don't care what you say, there ain't no way you're going to get twice as many prisoners in class for the same amount of money. And there ain't no way you gonna get 'em trained in eighteen months if you platoon 'em. It's gonna take twice as long if they can only go to class in the morning or afternoon and not all day. We need to expand the program."

"Well, at Angola, it don't make any difference," a legislator behind the dais in the hearing room volunteered. "Most of 'em won't get out any time soon. I think we ought to gut that program at Angola and take all those classes down to the medium-security facilities and train first offenders. Let's forget it at Angola. Why do we have those classes up there anyway?"

"Now you know, sir, we've trained plenty of those prisoners at Angola. They've done well, too."

The lawmaker persisted.

"Well, I still think we ought to get rid of that program at Angola. Not as many gettin' out as used to. We need more classes for the first offenders, the ones we can save. There's nuthin' you can do for that hard-core bunch up there. It's a waste of money."

"Better leave the classes they already got anyway," another lawmaker responded. "Those guys are liable to come out shootin' if you don't give 'em somethin' better to do when they hit the streets again."

I counted three wardens at the hearing. To a man, they were afraid for their jobs. It would be political suicide if they publicly pressed for better conditions at Angola. Louisiana's criminal justice system would go on turning out inmates with no job skills. The least equipped, facing the hardest fight, would quickly turn back to crime.

I recognized that I needed a rudder to steer me straight. Someone I could trust to watch my work and make sure I was getting it right.

I drifted toward Chris McDaniel's desk. Channel 9's investigative reporter sat with his back to the wall as far from the newsroom's side door as he could get, behind a rampart of books and files he'd erected across the front of his desk. He trusted no one. In a town like Baton Rouge, knowing certain facts, saying certain things, was dangerous.

Chris kept his files locked and his mouth shut. We had hit it off from my first day in the newsroom. Maybe my strange background appealed to his offbeat sense of humor. He gave me an appraising look.

"How's it going, Bell?"

I half-sat on a file cabinet next to his desk. I loved listening to his gripes. He was always up against the wall, to hear him tell it, but his complaints were legit. I came around whenever I craved an accurate assessment of city and state politics. I waited, delaying my answer, studying my toes, hands jammed in the pockets of my dark brown slacks.

"I'm hanging in, Chris . . ." I stopped, not trusting my voice. My story that day brought Angola too close.

"Steady down now. You got something wrong with you, Bell?" His hand slapped his desk for emphasis. "Why let the newsroom in on it? What's your story? What the hell has been wrong with you lately?"

"Chris, I gotta talk to you. I need help. I'm so afraid."

My story about vocational classes for inmates at Angola brought the prison too close. He saw the desperation in my eyes.

"Come on, let's get out of here. I don't know what's wrong with you, Bell, but you gotta be careful. Lots of shits in here, baby. They'll do you in, sweetheart."

Chris had been calling me at home to check on me occasionally after he learned about my separation and divorce. He would later tell me he sensed something more was wrong. He was like the older brother I never had. Behind us, the madness continued: shouts, phones, typewriters. He took my arm and walked me out of the side door.

Outside, the heat rushed up like a welcome embrace after the newsroom's cold. It was fall in Baton Rouge. The season would be called summer elsewhere. Weeks would go by before we got any relief from the heat. Late afternoon light flooded the pale sky.

He climbed onto the trunk of a Channel 9 news car parked at the station's side door. I climbed up beside him. I watched a flock of birds wheeling and diving across the sky, the telephone wires their target—a perfect nighttime roost.

"All right, Bell . . ." Chris's voice was rough, impatient. I turned toward him, eager to get it out.

"Chris, I'm in love with Billy Sinclair. I have been for months."

"Jesus fucking Christ," he exclaimed. His head snapped back. The tone in his voice was like a slap in the face.

"Bell, get rid of this, get rid of it."

"Chris, I can't," I said my throat almost too tight to talk. "I love him, Chris, I can't help it."

I turned to look at him, begging for anything to ease my pain. He gripped my arms.

"Jodie, listen to me. This is going to ruin you. You gotta get rid of this. Jodie. I'm telling you; this will cost you your career."

His voice was rough, his eyes narrowed into slits. "It will take you down, and it'll follow you all over the country. You are finished if you don't give this up."

"Chris . . ." It was still hard to string words together. "If it's a question of him, or the business, it'll be him. It'll always be him."

"Then there's nothing I can do." His flat statement lay between us.

"Chris, I need you. I've got to know if I'm OK on the job, if I'm doing it right. I can't tell if some of my stories are off. I try. I want to be fair. Chris, I gotta have somebody I trust watching."

"Dump this man, Jodie. Dump this thing."

"I can't, Chris. I'll never leave him."

The words unreeled in agony out of my throat. He gathered me awkwardly for a moment in his big arms.

"It's OK, baby, OK. I understand. I'll be there. I'll tell you if you are off. It's all right, baby. It's all right."

I leaned against him. He could help me for now, but not for long.

"Bell, are you sure, sweetheart?" He pushed me away, forcing me to look at him. "It'll kill you in this business."

"I know, Chris, I know. But I've got to keep on as long as I can. He's got to be able to see me, hear me, know I'm all right, see my face, know I'm on the job. I've got to stay here as long as I can."

Behind us, the newsroom door swung open. The station's photographers had finished editing their stories for the evening's news. We sat, trying to look casual. I stared at the sky. The moment was over. They'd be on us now, engineers leaving for home, photographers finished with the night's push, looking for a quiet cigarette in the evening air. The show was airing. Time to watch what we had done all day.

We slipped off the car's trunk and walked toward the newsroom door. The frantic activity inside was over. Several reporters gathered in front of the newsroom's TV monitor. The assignment editor pushed papers around his desk, previewing tomorrow's assignments. I could hear Channel 9's intro, the pulsating music, urgency in the beat, video cut on the rhythm, quickening the senses, exciting the viewers, pulling them in.

Chris walked back to his desk. I cleared away the few papers on my desk.

"Be careful, Bell," I heard his voice behind me.

I nodded in his direction and headed for the door. I walked across the street to my car, stuck the key in the ignition, and waited for the engine to kick over so I could ease into traffic on Government Street, hoping one of Billy's letters was waiting for me. But the mailbox would probably be empty. Angola's mailroom let his letters stack up before posting them. I wanted to be back in the newsroom with its noise, lights, and people. Loneliness and fear stalked me at my apartment until I fell asleep at night wondering how long it would be before the hammer fell, severing me from the career I loved.

If Billy and I had a future, it was riding on the pardon board's decision. I had called Jack Martzell, an old friend, hoping he would represent Billy before the board. He was one of the most successful and well-connected lawyers in Louisiana. He agreed to represent Billy pro bono, but he warned me in no uncertain terms that my relationship with Billy Sinclair would cost me my job.

Jack represented prominent politicians and celebrities during a stellar legal career. They included Muhammad Ali; Al Copeland, the founder of Popeye's Fried Chicken; and Charles Roemer, the commissioner of administration during Governor Edwards's first two terms in office from 1972 to 1980.

Roemer was charged with accepting bribes in exchange for using his influence. The case was known as the Brilab Scandal. It involved public corruption and labor racketeering. The *Washington Post* described Roemer as "once the second most powerful person in the state" during coverage of his trial for accepting bribes in exchange for using his influence. Ultimately, Jack got a federal appeals court to overturn Roemer's conviction in 1989. While he represented powerful and well-connected clients at his New Orleans law firm—Martzell and Bickford—many clients were "the hardworking poor," as one biographer put it. Jack was a Catholic, a graduate of Notre Dame's law school, and a staunch advocate of equal rights for African Americans when that was dangerous in Louisiana. He was still in his twenties when Louisiana governor John McKeithen appointed him to a new Human Relations Commission—a group of forty-two whites and forty-two African Americans in the 1960s with one goal: improving race relations. Jack's work reportedly put him on a KKK death list.

Even with Jack at the helm of Billy's plea for clemency and all his connections and belief in equal rights under the law, there was no way to predict the outcome of Billy's clemency hearing before a conservative Treen pardon board, given the nature of politics in Louisiana and Baton Rouge. He began working full-time on Billy's case with a young attorney, Tom Foutz, who had just graduated from the Tulane University Law School the year before.

Tom Foutz had been a member of Tulane's *Law Review* as a student. He received the Rittenberg-Weinstein Law Review Award before graduation, presaging a brilliant career for the young lawyer. The honor was reserved for a member of the *Law Review* with the "most published material of high quality." Billy would be represented by the best legal team in Louisiana.

June 15, 1981

Billy—

The offer from Jack to take your case for free is unbelievable. We have the best ally we could have. I'm overwhelmed with happiness. It will always stand out as the most beautiful gesture of friendship anyone ever made to me. What he is giving us is invaluable. He may well be handing us a life together. . . .

June 22, 1981

Dear Jodie:

I wrote Jack a letter last night thanking him for agreeing to argue my case before the Pardon Board. I suggested that he and I should meet. Once he officially enrolls as counsel before the board, the word will spread all the way through the power-vine. . . .

August 14, 1981
Billy—

Jack is beginning work this week on a brief in your case . . . the only thing Jack is worried about is the element of luck and the emotional pull the family of the deceased might be able to exert . . .but in terms of professionalism, logic and irrefutable argument, you will have it . . . in spades.

August 15, 1981
Billy—

Jack is very concerned about my part in this whole affair. I have written him assuring him that I'm not going to get in the way. I plan to do nothing but my work at Channel 9.

How foolish it would be of me to get you the best legal mind in Louisiana (if not the country) and then hamper his efforts on your behalf by mucking about behind the scenes politically. . . . I'm out of the picture. Jack said he would remind me every week anyway. I told him whatever makes him feel good.

Jack had agreed to represent Billy in June. But by September, the board still hadn't scheduled a hearing. Anxiety gnawed at me. Was there any benefit in the delay for us? The wait was agonizing. Fear invaded my heart every night as the sun set on another day with no answer about our future.

September 15, 1981
Billy—

We are running out of time for the hearing. If the Board is waiting for a propitious time, they are waiting too long. Unless you receive a notice soon, you will not be heard in October.

If they have it in their minds to give you a favorable response, to schedule it during the first three weeks of November—that's when the legislature will be in for a special session and you know what kind of forum that will provide for lambasting you.

Reapportionment caused a brawl in Texas. Don't remember how long it dragged out. If they don't hear you in November or December, they will be pushing into the time the governor begins preparing for the next legislative session which goes in March twentieth. The next budget round begins in earnest in mid-January. Then, the governor will have no time for a thorough review of your case if you get past the Pardon Board.

I have visions of it being next summer before the governor has time to personally review your case. All this could work another way, of course. The legislature could be so engrossed in reapportionment—which could mean reelection or defeat for many of them—that they will hardly give a damn about what happens in some crummy criminal's case.

September 29, 1981
Dear Jodie:

I will stop worrying about Jack and how he is handling things. He's right. The worry will only make matters worse. I am simply going to leave it with him. I really should know better than that. When I work on a case, as a jailhouse lawyer, I hate for the client to second-guess and haunt me with doubt. But usually when I worry, it is because the sun has gone behind the clouds and dark clouds signal a storm is ahead. That "tightrope" feeling sometimes rush up on me in a flood. . . .

I love you, baby. And some way, somehow, this thing is going to be behind us. I have a heart full of pride for how much you love me. It is my life gift.

The pardon board finally scheduled Billy's hearing for October 28. I had dinner with Jack and Tom Foutz after it was over. I made notes at the dinner and wrote Billy that night, so he would have a full account. The victim's family and friends—twenty-one of them—appeared in opposition before the board, accompanied by Ossie Brown, the district attorney of East Baton Rouge Parish.

Ossie's pendulous cheeks quivered when he talked about crime, aflame with fundamentalist fervor, like a preacher at a small-town revival. But he was a fraud. Baton Rouge's tough district attorney had represented as many accused felons when he was a criminal defense lawyer as he had prosecuted during his twelve years in office. He was Billy Sinclair's first court-appointed attorney, meeting with him in his cell, until he resigned, citing his special friendship with the victim's family and his plan to run for public office. Given the Southern practice of returning politicians to office for decades once they were elected, Ossie's power was entrenched. He also knew how to manipulate the press. If the Baton Rouge newspaper, the *Advocate,* carried a front-page story about crime, he was on the air that night, denouncing crime in Baton Rouge. His interviews amounted to campaign ads.

I was not his favorite reporter. He had called me a snit and "Miss High and Mighty" on my TV horse after I complained about having to wait in his office for minutes on end each time I was sent to interview him.

One day, after an interview, he kept ranting about his opposition to the insanity plea, waving his arms in the air, demonstrating how he taught a murder defendant to pretend to be psychotic. The ruse got the prisoner sent to a mental hospital for two years, before he was tried on a lesser charge.

"I taught him to act nuts. Told him to keep up the arm movements in the psychiatrist's waiting room . . . to be sure and do it the way I showed him."

When the judge objected to his client's unceasing movements in court, Ossie whispered to his client to keep it up.

"You see how easy it is? See how light these criminals can get off? I taught him to act nuts. He's out now."

I was amazed as the Baton Rouge DA openly admitted behavior that could get him disbarred. Suddenly, he saw the tape recorder in my hand.

"That thing isn't on, is it? Well, is it?" he demanded, a menacing tone in his voice.

I denied myself the pleasure of a lie, careful not to let him know I knew how unethical he was.

"No, it isn't on," I said casually, wishing I hadn't shut the tape recorder off as soon as our interview was over. I had heard many times that Ossie Brown was one of the most corrupt politicians in Baton Rouge. He had just proven it right in front of me.

"Just act crazy and it will get you sent to the mental hospital in Jackson," Billy said Ossie told him before he resigned as Billy's lawyer.

October 29, 1981

Billy—

I made these notes at dinner with Jack and Tom, thinking you would want to know in detail what happened at your pardon board hearing. This is what they told me. . . .

At the beginning, Herb Eddington, the chairman of the board, said the hearing was to remain cool and the number of witnesses for both sides would be limited . . . Tom said your witnesses appeared in the order they did, not only for what they had to say, but for who they were. The Earnests came first because they were so nice and sincere and because Mrs. Earnest had faith in you when no one else did. Gary Brashear, the vice chancellor of the LSU campus, was chosen because of his position and because he knew you both before and after your change and can vouch for it. Rupert Richardson, the former head of Louisiana's NAACP, was chosen because of her support for The Angolite *and its editors.*

Mrs. Earnest told her story. . . . how she read about you in the paper, thought about her own son and then wrote you because she would have wanted someone to do the same for her boy. She then told the Board about how you responded to her and that you had corresponded for sixteen years.

Dr. Brashear, being a chemist, had carefully and methodically prepared a statement with six logically reasoned premises stating why you should be released. Jack had him read it all because Brashear's demeanor was so "professional."

Rupert Richardson was extremely well spoken and was obviously a person of great character given her leadership in the NAACP.

David Madden, a creative writing professor at LSU, told the Board he had meticulously gone through your criminal record and your prison record before consenting to testify on your behalf. He said when you first sent him your writing while you were on death row it was not particularly good, and he so wrote you. He said it got better over the years, astonishingly so . . . he told the board you are an editor, not just a reporter and he could get you a job in an instant. He said you were no threat to society, and you ought to be on the outside with the rest of the exceptional journalists. Jack said he was your best witness.

Your mother said she'd seen her "boy" on death row for seven years and that both of you had suffered enough. Jack said she was extremely effective. . . .

Then the other side had their chance.

Jack and Tom said that Ossie was there because it was patently obvious he was using the hearing as a campaign platform. . . . They said he consistently addressed the assembled group and not the pardon board. . . . He began by raving about the fact that you had him up before the Ethics Commission . . . he dwelled on it quite a bit. He then harped on the one string he could play—revenge for the family—after that he had all the people stand up, all twenty-one of them. . . . Jack said after Ossie's pontificating, it looked like he was cuing the Mormon Tabernacle Choir as he had the entire opposition stand. . . . he didn't even have the sense to introduce them all and cite their positions in the community to show they were leaders. . . . During his harangue Ossie tried to pull the symphony strings by crooning how well he knew your victim . . . Jack said he kept putting your name in when he meant the victim. . . . "Why I knew Billy Sinclair for years and years . . . we were close" . . . all this while the Bodden family is trying discreetly but frantically to get Ossie's attention. . . . when they did, he had to start that part of his presentation over again. . . . But the point was lost.

. . . a Methodist minister testified against you. Jack said the guy played right into his hands. . . . Jack said the foundation of Methodism is that a man can change . . . that was the basic message John Wesley preached. . . .

J. C. Bodden's widow was the other side's most effective witness. . . . She made notes during your witnesses' testimony and tried to refute them. . . . The chairman of the pardon board stepped out of his role and told her he had lost a relative to violent crime and he had learned to forgive, and he hoped she would. . . . In his close, Jack said he had also lost a relative to violent crime. He then set about discrediting the notion of revenge. He began with a Germanic tribal custom. If a family member was murdered, the family had the right to kill a member of the offending family.

The killing went on and on until the families began bribing each other to stop the slaughter. The bribe, then, became transmuted into law. It became "damages." He then pointed out that the governor's clemency powers are contained in the Constitution . . . meaning the people wanted it protected . . . thus what was taking place at the hearing was not between the Boddens and Billy Sinclair, but rather, between the Board and Billy Sinclair. . . .

10-28-81
Dear Jodie:

Except for perhaps adding an additional ten thousand gray hairs, I made it through the day. I spoke with Jack and Tom Foutz a short time ago. . . . Apparently everything went as smoothly as possible . . .

I have this feeling that we will not see each other Friday. Tom Foutz mentioned it on the phone this afternoon. That's why I have this feeling that you will tell me tonight that I cannot see you on Friday. It is during these moments when the words in your letter today are so vital . . .

"Remember that I love you. Focus your mind on how much I need you and how intense my desire is. Remember . . . I will be your wife and remember I will be waiting the day you step out of that gate."

That does not make my pain go away. But it does ease it, it does make it bearable. I literally lock those words, and their promise, in my brain and I cling to them as a drowning man does to an extended tree limb . . . the words are my strength. I could not make it through this time without them. I love you so much.

October 30, 1981
Billy—

Today I received the letter you wrote the day of the hearing. It brought tears to my eyes. The nightmare of not winning this clemency effort has stalked me as well. I am literally eating away the lining of my stomach. The thought of losing tears me to shreds, too. Not seeing you compounds the agony. Tonight, I am sitting here wondering how I will go to work tomorrow. I am literally burning inside.

There has to come a time, Billy, when right takes over. We cannot be made to suffer for all the sins and transgressions being committed on the streets today. The injustice of that cries out for redress. Surely you and I cannot be singled out for treatment different from that handed out to others.

I have thought about the worst. I have thought about it for months. Being locked away from someone I love is new for me. But you are not just someone. You made me come alive. You are my other half. Your soul is the mirror image of mine. You make the world make sense. Without you, there is nothing to strive for. Without you, I would not survive.

So, I will fight for you. I will do whatever I have to do. I love you. My love will not end. I am bound to you and I will seal that bond. I will speak the words that make me your wife. I was meant to always be with you.

Life had begun coming apart in October. The summer visits with Billy in the attorney-client room and the hot blood that pulsed in my veins every time I saw him came to an abrupt end. Warden Ross Maggio ordered them stopped. They had lasted a scant three months. Maggio had been appointed by Governor Treen to run Angola. He had a tough law-and-order reputation that appealed to the governor. He believed our visits could provoke a jealous attack against Billy.

A strict by-the-book administrator, Maggio had cleaned up Angola in 1976 following the 1975 federal court decision that demanded sweeping changes at the violent prison. He had personally assigned Billy to the *Angolite* in 1977 over the objection of his top security officials. It was his way of saying, "this prison belongs to me." He didn't allow objections, much less challenges, to his authority. He wore cowboy boots and a white Stetson. "Boss Ross," the inmates called him—a moniker of respect tinged with fear. He had been moved out of Angola in 1978 to become the warden at the newly opened Elayn Hunt Correctional Center outside of Baton Rouge.

Maggio was reassigned to Angola seventeen months into the Treen administration because the governor's top corrections officials believed the prison was ripe for a riot, and Warden Blackburn, an Edwards appointee, would be unable to prevent it.

C. Paul Phelps, the legendary secretary of the Louisiana department of corrections who oversaw Maggio's cleanup of Angola, was fired by Treen in September 1981. He was replaced by a businessman named John King with no background in corrections. Prior to his departure, Phelps had warned Rideau and Sinclair that Treen thought the *Angolite* and its freedom to report events at Angola was creating problems for his office. The magazine had published articles and opinion pieces that were critical of the governor's law-and-order rhetoric and his stingy clemency policy that had enhanced inmate hopelessness at the prison.

Phelps had refused to muzzle the magazine as the governor's office had instructed. Maggio was tagged to do what Phelps had refused to do: shackle the magazine's inmate editors. One of his first official actions upon his return to Angola was to visit the *Angolite* office to announce that the Phelps/Blackburn era was over and to announce a new sheriff was in town.

"I told y'all not to count me out," Maggio said, surveying the room from the door as he sauntered in. He walked straight to an office cabinet, casually opened its door, and inspected its contents. It was his way of saying, "This office, like this prison, belongs to me." He then settled into a chair in front of Rideau's desk and propped his feet up on the desk.

"The office is a little bigger than I thought, but not as plush as I've heard," he said.

"Who said it was plush?' Rideau asked.

"It doesn't matter. I was told y'all had carpet on the floor, all new furniture, a refrigerator, color television, and wall movies. There's a perception among a lot of people that the prison is being run out of this office."

"Sounds like we have some enemies," Rideau said.

Maggio bit into his trademark cigar.

"Let me tell you how it's going to be," he said. "There are some powerful people in this administration who want me to put a padlock on this door. They want the magazine shut down. I'm going to do everything in my power to keep you in print, but there's gonna be some changes. You won't like 'em but at least you will still be in business."

Neither editor doubted what Maggio said. They had lived under the cowboy warden before. Maggio never pulled punches or minced words. At thirty-six, he was the youngest warden of a maximum-security prison in the country when he was first named Angola's warden in 1976. With true grit and unflinching style, he changed the prison from the bloodiest to the safest in the nation.

To accomplish this feat, Maggio triggered an avalanche of change. He turned Angola upside down, systematically destroying the criminal subculture's hold on the prison. He cracked down hard on the Dixie Mafia and other inmate gangs running the prison. He locked up gang leaders and the drug lords. He fired prison officials for smuggling contraband into the prison and curbed the activities of guards he suspected were on inmate payrolls. He hired free people to replace inmate clerks, ending a dangerous and lucrative trade in inmate records. Prisoners could no longer buy assignments to another part of the prison, get disciplinary records destroyed, or have inmate clerks deliver "snitch notes."

Maggio enlarged Angola's security force and equipped it with the latest electronic devices. He created a special tactical unit to curb violent disturbances. He assigned passive gay men to segregated cell blocks or out-camps and assigned aggressive gay men to lockdown. He put 1,500 idle inmates to work in the fields.

At the same time, he instituted a streamlined system of prison management and spearheaded a massive construction and cleanup program. He opened a correctional academy for officer trainees and hired minorities and promoted them. He built a new dining hall at Angola and three five-hundred-bed out-camps. He painted fences, renovated buildings, cut grass, and cultivated fields. He also improved inmate services, upgrading medical care and expanding educational and recreational programs. But he brooked no resistance and backed up threats with immediate action.

"Baby, Maggio cracked heads, kicked asses, and broke legs the last time he was here," Billy told me quietly as he held my hand during our latest visit. "But there's a good trade-off. I'll be safe under Maggio."

It did little to soothe my anger. The warden's abrupt cancellation of our visiting arrangement left me stunned. His order ending it was succinct. Our visits looked like a cover for illicit sex.

"You boys are hard enough to protect as it is," he had declared.

The special privileges granted to the *Angolite*'s editors to cover news and events at the prison were a source of resentment that invited violence. *Time* magazine cited the danger in an article about the *Angolite*'s win of the George Polk Award in 1980 for stories about rape behind bars and the death penalty. Calling the *Angolite* the "most probing and literate inmate publication in the U. S.," the article said the "editors cannot afford to play fast and loose with the facts. For one thing, they have to live close to their readers. For another, their readers include murderers, rapists, armed robbers and other criminals with a history of violent overreaction when provoked."

But the editors had never been attacked despite official fears of inmate violence against them. I suspected that ending our visits had a different motive. I was a reporter with a direct pipeline into the prison. Maggio's ham-handed changes to the Phelps/Blackburn era of liberal policies were being implemented without regard for civil liberties, much less inmate sensibilities. Boss Ross was bringing the prison under the fist of submission the way he had the first time he took over Angola in 1976. Curtailing my relationship with the *Angolite* editor reduced the possibility of damaging leaks from a credible source.

John King and his corrections administration didn't trust Maggio since the warden had made his disdain for the businessman-turned-corrections-secretary obvious. He went so far as to bar corrections headquarters inspectors from entering Angola and kicked a dozen or more social workers out of the prison.

King's office sent an emissary, Angola's security chief Richard Wall, to secretly meet with Billy, asking him to monitor Maggio's activities and report anything suspicious to the secretary's office. Wall stressed the benefits Sinclair would enjoy if he took the offer. Billy rebuffed the offer. He thought he was being set up. Finely honed survival instincts also warned him not to involve himself in that kind of official power struggle. He never told Maggio about the overture. But it put him on a King administration "don't trust" list and made him a possible target for political reprisal.

I WOULD NOT SEE BILLY again for months. Loneliness stretched me into a thin, taut wire. I could hear his voice in collect calls near midnight once a week. I opened his letters knowing they would be full of love. The authorities could slap punitive restraints on our relationship, but they would never have the power to kill it.

October 15, 1981
Billy—

By the time you get this letter, you will know that your phone arrangements have been changed. All calls to you from reporters have to be cleared through Maggio's office now. I tried to call you several times yesterday. Both times I was assured you would call the newsroom in ten or fifteen minutes. I never heard from you. . . . I called back. . . . I was told that the rules had been changed with the new warden.

I guess you and Wilbert better stop writing that you are "free from censorship" and that you have freedom of movement. Every time you write that it's a lie. Don't make the new administration look good when they are fucking you.

Maggio will restrict our visits because I am a member of the press. I wonder how long it will be before he is the cause of people's marriages and relationships breaking up. Rigid authoritarianism may make the place safer for a lot of inmates, but it is going to make it a hell of a lot lonelier for a whole lot of others.

"God, I hate that song," I told Boudreaux one day as we rolled down the street on an assignment. I could feel tears behind my sunglasses.

We always rode with the radio blaring hard rock. But the chords and mawkish tunes would sometimes shake my control.

"What's the matter with you?" he upbraided me with mock severity. "You ain't got no goddamn sense. That's the best thing that group's had out in months."

Pain, loneliness, and the desperation I felt welled up in my throat. A sudden storm of tears spilled down my face. I slammed my palm against the window in disgust. I never cried in front of anyone. It wasn't safe. Van grabbed my wrist.

"Hey," he said, his voice soft with concern. "Come on, babe, you can tell me."

I stared out the window, fighting down the tears wrestling for control.

"I'll be all right. I'll be all right." It was a litany I repeated over and over in private. "Just sometimes, stuff hits you in the gut, you know."

He still held my wrist.

"You can tell me, babe."

My laughter came out of nowhere.

"You fool Cajun."

I pinched his cheek and slid my arm around his shoulder. I loved shooting with Van. His easy laugh comforted me. I leaned against his humor on days that were dark with despair. Riding the streets together on assignments we shared confidences, always relaxed in each other's company.

Leaves flew up behind the car as we downshifted on the run to the state capitol. Sometimes, on assignments there, I had to leave photographers while I searched for the politicians I needed to interview that day. Van never complained no matter how long I was gone.

"Van, you know why I like to shoot with you?"

"Because I'm so goddamn good?"

"No, 'cause you stay where I put you. That's the great thing about Cajuns. You put 'em somewhere, you don't come back for a while. They go to sleep right where you left 'em."

He laughed. But thoughts of Billy still hammered at me. I locked my guard in place as hard as I could to prevent any sign of the fear and stress I felt. Desperation dogged me every day. I was clinging to the desperate hope the pardon board's decision would recommend freedom for Billy. But there had been no word from them for almost two months. Early one morning, a bomb suddenly exploded when I made a call to Tom Foutz. His voice cut me off like a knife.

"We got the decision, Jodie. They cut Billy to sixty years."

I turned blindly away from the newsroom to face the wall. I had begged Foutz and Martzell to give me the news straight, like a quick shot to the head, a coup de grâce, if the decision was bad.

"Sixty, my God! He had a forty-five-year recommendation from Governor Edwards's board. You're telling me Treen's board added fifteen years after Billy served more time and his record stayed spotless?"

I was breathing in shallow gasps, trembling, hunched over, my back to the newsroom, trying to absorb the shock.

"Jesus, Tom . . . how can this be right?"

"It stinks!"

I heard the raw disappointment in his voice. He could hardly believe the decision. The board had never increased a time cut recommendation before. There was no appeal.

I couldn't stop trembling. Tears slid down my face, the injustice of it a heavy weight in my throat. Billy and I had traveled down the path of hope, believing in a future for us, spinning out suspenseful days and nights of sour sleep, one strung out after the other, no solace in it for either of us in the hard minutes alone, all for nothing.

We were trapped. Our forced march would go on. The possibility of no relief loomed ahead. Unless Governor Treen signed the time cut recommendation to sixty years, his life sentence—no parole possible—would stand. I moved closer to the newsroom wall, staring at the buff-colored concrete, seeing the visiting room's cement walls. My fingers traced the grooves between the cement blocks. I would stare at them on prison walls twice a month for years.

"Jodie, if we can get the governor to sign the time cut, Billy will be parole eligible in four years."

It would be four years before we could hope again—four times the earth would pass through all its seasons, us spending each of them alone, waiting on relief that might never come. My heart constricted at the thought of Billy's pain. They had already told him.

Jack's voice interrupted my thoughts.

"I guess I didn't do much for you, Jodie."

I tried to comfort him.

"Jack, you did everything you could, everything! Nobody but you could have gotten any cut out of this board."

How could the board increase Billy's forty-five-year time cut recommendation to sixty years in spite of his national journalistic achievements, his record of rehabilitation, and the numerous letters of support? Where was the logic in what they did? Or did it all boil down to politics and revenge?

I stayed that day, working on my assignment, knowing Billy would be watching the newscast hoping to see me in a story. If he didn't, he would take it as a sign that I couldn't bear the news about the decision. I was determined to let him know the "sixty" changed nothing, that I loved him and that we had a future together no matter what they did to us. It was one of the worst days of my life—almost worse than being fired. That would come two weeks later.

ON DECEMBER 23, 1981, GOVERNOR Dave Treen summoned the capital press corps to his office to announce he was granting a pardon. TV cameras ringed his desk. Light cables and cords cluttered the small space between their tripods and his bulky, antique mahogany desk. I walked into his office with print reporters who had been asked to wait in another room while the cameras were being set up. The governor smiled at me.

"Why, Jodie," the governor joked, "I didn't know you joined the print brigade."

A wall of cream-colored curtains rose eighteen feet to the ceiling behind him. In place of the pleasant view I imagined, I saw old roofing tar and gravel spread between the windows and a stone parapet. The scene was a snapshot of Louisiana government: an ugly foundation covered up by a fancy veneer.

A forest of microphones stood on the governor's desk on top of a stack of papers. He joked with another reporter as an old African American man, stooped over from the burden of years, a relative at his elbow for support, carefully made his way across the room.

The mood in the room was unusually relaxed. For once, reporters' normally cynical comments weren't part of the regular whispers as they waited for final arrangements to be complete, so the press conference could begin.

After the governor announced he was granting a pardon for the man, he seated the elderly ex-inmate at his desk and stood behind him smiling. A reporter for the New Orleans *Times-Picayune* described the scene in the paper's December 24, 1981 edition:

> *John E. Norris looked out of place sitting in the governor's chair Wednesday. But the seventy-three-year old, who had spent eight years in the Louisiana State Penitentiary at Angola—from 1935 to 1943—for stealing two coonskins, was obviously happy following his pardon by Gov. Dave C. Treen.*

I stared at the scene, revolted by what I saw. Pardoning a man for stealing two coonskins was a political stunt that made a mockery of the clemency process. Using a frail, elderly victim of Louisiana's Jim Crow laws for publicity and potential political award was sickening. The old man should never have been sentenced to eight years of hard labor at Angola for a misdemeanor. I swallowed down the acid threatening to choke me and asked the obvious question.

"Governor Treen, there are a number of recommendations for time cuts and pardons on your desk. When do you plan to review those cases?"

The question ended my career. Some official—and I didn't know who—had told a reporter from Channel 2, Channel 9's main competition, about my relationship with Billy Sinclair. When the Channel 2 reporter left the governor's office, he immediately called a reporter he knew at Channel 9, who went to Carlton Cremeens, my news director, with the tip.

The Channel 2 reporter decided I was using my position to get relief for Billy, betraying every reporter's fundamental responsibility: balanced reporting with no hint of bias or plea for favoritism. It was his duty, he felt, to stop me. Unknowing, I went back to the station.

On Christmas Day, my children and I met at a friend's house in New Orleans. I brought presents for them, and we exchanged gifts in her front parlor. They were polite. The visit lasted little more than an hour.

My daughter accompanied me to my car. We stood in the street to say goodbye. Her long blonde hair hung down below her shoulders. Autumn leaves littered the uptown New Orleans lawns around us. She had been a smiling baby, holding on to the side of her baby bed like a big doll as she waited excitedly for me to pick her up. How had we come to this—a mother and daughter, like strangers, exchanging pleasantries instead of love on Christmas Day? Our worlds had rushed apart before she was ready for me to go. What barren legacy was I leaving the child/woman in front of me? I longed for her embrace. I needed her to comfort me.

"The pain," I screamed inside, "the pain. My child, I can't bear it. Missing you is killing me."

We smiled politely a final time. I closed the car door, waved goodbye, and drove back to Baton Rouge. I tried to take her with me to Texas when I moved to Houston after what happened at Channel 9 three days later. She stayed with her father in New Orleans and her friends in high school. I didn't blame her.

The night of December 27, I wrote Billy a letter.

December 27, 1981
Billy—

Symbols are powerful things . . . the soul understands them . . . so do the heart and the mind. They have tremendous impact: the Star of David, the cradle at Bethlehem, Christ on the cross, the Menorah, a single candle in the window, ashes on the forehead on Ash Wednesday, bell, book and candle, the winged horse, the staff of life, a loaf of bread. They go on and on. They speak a thousand words in one image.

You are a symbol. That makes you powerful. You engender fear . . . somehow you are inhuman. You will not stay down. You will not stay put. You rise above situations that should have killed you or broken your spirit or both.

That makes you incomprehensible to the average person. There is awe. There is fear. That is why you are stuck in the system. It doesn't know how to deal with you. Instead of rejoicing in your change, the system must show that it still controls you. . . .

And for the life of me, I don't know how you bear it. That you do is one of the ten thousand reasons I love you, Billy.

Wherever I am, you are. Whatever I think, you are part of it. I am you. You are me. I will work every day of my life to free you. And when you are free, I will always be with you. . . .

The newsroom was humming as usual the evening I lost my job. The six o'clock newscast was about to go on the air. My photographer was making the last few edits in my story when Carlton Cremeens touched my shoulder and said he had to speak with me. I left the editing bay to join my news director in his office. My story would air on time. The photographer I worked with that day knew exactly where to put the last edits. He didn't need me to finish it.

I smiled and sat down across from the desk from Carlton, waiting to hear about a new special assignment or a change in my work schedule.

"Jodie, some people are saying you have a relationship with Billy Sinclair. I'd sue them if I were you."

I could see deep concern in his eyes. I folded my hands in my lap, took a deep breath, and looked up at him.

"It's true," I said. And with that, my world blew apart.

"Goddamn it, Jodie, why couldn't you fall in love with a state senator? That's a conflict of interest we could handle." He beat his fist on the desk in frustration. "Jodie, you were one of the two most talented reporters I've had in the last twenty one years."

Carlton Cremeens was known for spotting and nurturing on-air talent. I would remember what he said for years. I could have had a stellar career in TV news. The words that burst out of him that day would always be balm for the rough times and disappointments ahead.

Carlton and I were caught in a professional dilemma. He was responsible for the newscasts' credibility. Publicity about my involvement with Billy Sinclair would hurt the station's credibility and damage its ratings.

Reporters walk a fine line. They must be above reproach to protect the public's trust. The best reporters never put bumper stickers on their cars or label themselves as Democrats or Republicans or show support for questionable causes. We had to travel the middle of the road. But I loved a convict. And the public would soon find out.

"I'm taking you off the air," Carlton said. "We'll find something for you to do in the business office upstairs." Carlton didn't want me to suddenly be on the street with no source of income and nowhere to go.

"No, Carlton," I said. "No, but thank you, I appreciate your concern." Instead, I resigned.

Billy's case was so political and so infamous in Baton Rouge, staying with the station in any job would damage its reputation. The right thing to do was leave.

I sat in the news meeting the next morning, on the edge of tears. It was the last time I would ever be part of the "newsroom family" I loved so much. After Paul had handed out all the assignments, the others looked at me, waiting to hear about my assignment that day.

I said I had a sister in Houston with four small children who was suffering from a serious health problem and needed my help, so I was resigning. She had urged me for some time to come home to help her. I knew I would be safe there and there would be no blowback on Channel 9.

I have no other memories of the twenty-eighth of December 1981, the day I lost my job. Perhaps the shock of leaving Channel 9 erased them. That evening, I lay for a long time in the gathering gloom as day faded into night. Huddled under the covers, my bathrobe on top for extra warmth, I stared at the bedroom curtains. Slowly, they became the only squares of light in the room. Their shadows warmed to a dark brown as the day ended behind their folds. My face was raw and puffy from crying. Out of the corner of my eye I could see Billy's picture on the dresser, his right hand on the electric chair, his left hand firmly on his hip, as he stared at the wall built to shield the executioner from the witnesses' view.

Suddenly, I heard a loud knock on the door. I never had visitors. In the apartment, I was alone with Billy—his letters, his picture, cartoons he'd sent me, small squibs from newspapers he wanted to share.

Now my job and my home were gone. There were no more anchors in my life. Time stretched out endlessly in front of me. I wiped the tears away and answered the door. Chris McDaniel was on the doorstep with John Voinche.

"Are you okay, Chris? Was Carlton hard on you, Chris?" I asked anxiously as I let them in. I was afraid Channel 9's news director had somehow learned that Chris had known for weeks about me and Billy Sinclair but had said nothing. I didn't want Carlton to be at odds with Chris.

"You were worried about me? Goddamn, Jodie, you were worried about me? We came because we were worried about you."

He stared at me in disbelief as he sat down on the small, cheap sofa in my furnished apartment. I listened, grateful for his concern. There had been so little company in my life for so long—no one to talk to, too many frozen days, too many forced smiles, too much empty chatter.

"We've been trying to find this place for hours," Chris said. "We even went back to the station and looked in the 'crisscross.' Some reporters we are."

He leaned forward and flicked ashes from his cigarette into the ashtray on the coffee table. I knew what he was thinking.

"I'm not the pill type, Chris," I said. I knelt in front of the table and fished a cigarette out of his pack. I needed something to do with my hands. I hadn't smoked since I was twenty-six. I held the cigarette and looked at him. Holding it was enough. "I endure, Chris."

I had said the same words to Billy when I'd told him I resigned, and I heard the near despair and concern in his voice.

"It's over, Chris. Thank God, it's over. I don't have to pretend anymore," I said, sobbing with relief.

Chris was across the room in two steps, his big arms cradling me as I sobbed. Months of tension exploded out of me. I could finally say the words out loud. John sat on the sofa, smoke curling up from his cigarette. His eyes were dark with pain for me. My downfall had a less-than-surprising architect. Aligned with his tough penal rule, Maggio had ordered his security forces to investigate my visits to the prison as soon as he returned to Angola. A copy of their investigative report was leaked to the Channel 2 reporter. Maggio had to put an end to my visits with Billy Sinclair. I was a threat to Angola's security. Billy was an accomplished inmate journalist with the means to root out scandals at Angola. I had the means to broadcast his findings.

Reality woke me up the next morning. I was forty-four years old with no income and no home. I had lost the career I had fought so hard to realize against the hard odds that an older woman with no experience could be hired in TV news at all. My marriage of twenty-three years was ending. My home in New Orleans, my status there and in Baton Rouge, were gone. My beloved mother had died of cancer that spring. I missed her deep inside my heart.

My two boys were virtually grown. My twenty-two-year-old son was at LSU. My nineteen-year-old son was at college in New Mexico on a scholarship. My seventeen-year-old daughter insisted on staying with her father in New Orleans. She had lived there since she was two years old. All her best friends were there. All my best friends were there, too, after living in Louisiana for fifteen years.

Relentless activity, day after day, seemed the only sure road to safe and solid mental ground. Like an automaton, I readied myself to leave Louisiana, praying for the peace of sleep that evaded me for hours every night as I tried to believe my life would one day return to normal.

I forced myself out of bed early each morning as though I were still expected in the newsroom. I rewrote my résumé and took it to a Baton Rouge printer. Several nights, near midnight so I would see almost no one I knew, I made audition tapes at the station, dubbing off my best stories, examples of my work that I would need to find a new reporting job. I scoured supermarkets for discarded boxes in which to pack the few things from my furnished apartment that I owned. I notified utilities of my departure and told myself I was embarking on another great adventure that I would love.

I paid the price I had been told I would pay. Not wanting to believe it, I had done my best to avoid thinking about it. It was not that I questioned the source. Jack Martzell, one of Louisiana's most brilliant lawyers, a man who in grand quixotic gesture had decided to represent Billy pro bono, had told me shortly after I went to thank him for helping with Billy's case that I would be fired.

It had taken ten months, longer than he anticipated, for the station's management to learn that I even knew Billy Sinclair. I had never mentioned Billy in any of my stories. Nor had I used my press position to try and secure his release in any other way. I had, I thought, kept my private life private.

But Martzell, in his astute understanding of politics and knowledge of life in the state's capital, never doubted my tragicomedy would have any other denouement. Innocence, he knew, would be sacrificed on the altar of expediency. Appearances, he knew so well, meant everything. He would spend the next five years pleading before various Louisiana governors for Billy's release in the ardent belief he should be free. In an era of growing victim outrage, none would comply. The tight-knit group of the victim's high school friends and his family was unrelenting in its opposition to Billy's release. And they had open political doors all over Baton Rouge. In Louisiana, rehabilitation was of far less concern than being reelected.

I would live with a sister in Houston until I found work—any work—to meet my monthly obligations while I searched for a job in TV news, there and elsewhere. I had made my bed. But I had searing fears. Where would I end up? What would I do? Who would take care of me? No amount of self-assurance could quiet the panic that threatened me in the middle of the night.

I grew up in the 1950s when middle-class women were never left alone to fend for themselves. A father or a husband would always be there in a crisis. In return, wives were to be busy with the home, filling up our lives with its duties and obligations, its network of errands, expectations, and responsibilities that affixed us in the family firmament. Suddenly, I was in a terrifying free fall with nothing but ingenuity and self-discipline to save me.

I could still see myself in the Channel 9 newsroom, still hear the police radios and the clatter of typewriters, still see the faces of the other reporters, suspended in time. I remembered moments, words, experiences, laughter, and feelings. I kept copies of my scripts for fifteen years, their yellowed pages wrinkling and curling with age. They were all I had left from the best time in my life, gone forever like chaff on the wind.

I left Baton Rouge for Houston on a bright, cold Friday morning in January 1982, two weeks after I resigned. What little I owned was packed in the back of my car. A blue norther had blustered in the day before. Gusts of wind buffeted the car, making the steering wheel hard to hold. The sky was so clear, it glittered.

I could see for miles as I drove over the Mississippi River Bridge, west, to Texas, a last letter from Billy carefully folded in my purse.

12-30-81

Dear Jodie,

When you told me last night you would be leaving Baton Rouge, I felt a psychological rip sear through my brain. . . . While we have been separated these past months, we were still so close, our worlds so tied and blended together, even during the two months when we couldn't see each other.

Now, I must think of you in Houston or in some other place even more distant. I feel alone. There's a gnawing dread creeping through my thoughts . . . and I pray—ever so silently I pray—that this is not the beginning of the end . . . and before that thought takes active shape, I reach back and grasp your words. "There is no beginning or end to this love I have for you, Billy."

Those words—more than any you have ever spoken to me—have sustained me this day; have helped me make it through the pain and agony and doubt.

I prayed and hoped we would leave together. Now . . . I can only hope to follow. . . . I've never felt such agony and pain as I do now . . . that you had to be called in and dismissed because of your relationship with me . . . tomorrow is so uncertain . . . all I want is to be with you. I need you so much in my life. You are my life.

In Houston, I moved in with my sister Carol and my brother-in-law Allen, in their house near Rice University. I started searching for a job almost as soon as I arrived. It didn't take long. That night my sister stood at her kitchen sink, her back to me, pulling silverware out of the drawer to set the table for dinner.

"You got a job?" she asked.

"Yeah."

"Where?" I could tell she was delighted.

"Oh," I replied, "some receptionist thing." It was hard to get the words out.

"Yeah, but where?"

"Oh, you know, that foreign bank."

"Hey, that's great! Is that the one with all those perks?"

"Yeah, it's the Royal Bank of Scotland."

"Wow. I mean, free parking and a month's paid vacation. Hey, they don't have those kinds of jobs hanging around just for the taking!"

The job was everything I had worked so hard to avoid—the years in college, the belief that I was smart enough to earn a degree and become a reporter. It was all gone; all my striving amounted to nothing.

I headed for the kitchen door. I didn't want her to see me crying.

"Hey." She grabbed my arm as I went by. "Is it bad tonight, Jodie?"

She held me in her arms as though I were the younger sister. We clung to each other, weeping for all the parental wounds that never healed, all the times our parents betrayed us—two sisters in their forties, children again in their grief.

It was the first time we had ever cried together to mark our pain and console each other as we had never been able to do when we were children, each struggling alone, walled off by the terror of Daddy's next choleric rage.

"It will be all right, Jodie," she said. "You can see Billy this weekend."

She blotted the sweat on my forehead. I was grieving for all of it: a career that had slipped away, my children, Billy Sinclair and the revenge paralyzing us. Maybe he would never be free.

"Tomorrow's Friday; you'll be leaving on your first trip to see Billy," she said. "It will be okay."

I didn't tell her I was afraid. I had never driven on the highway alone at night. Unlike the news cars I traveled in with Channel 9 photographers, my car had no two-way radio. If there were trouble, I would have no way to call for help on the long dark stretches of I-10 between small towns in Louisiana.

By the time I hit the highway on Friday at five o'clock after work, heading for my Saturday-morning visit with Billy, it was almost dark. By the time I reached Beaumont, just fifty miles away, my headlights were the only light on the road for the next 224 miles until I reached a cheap motel on the outskirts of Baton Rouge, where I would spend the night before driving to Angola the next morning. The trips eventually became routine. But the dark shadow of revenge and its extraordinary hold on Baton Rouge politics rode with me on every trip for the next quarter century.

A few months later, on June 9, 1982, I became Billy's wife. Angola's warden opposed marriage for lifers, but Billy had found a way around his objections, thanks to a proxy-marriage law that dated back to America's frontier.

It allowed a Russian dissident living in the United States to marry his sweetheart in Moscow. Billy stumbled on a story about it in a newspaper. The article described the ceremony in Missoula, Montana, one of only two states in the United States with proxy-marriage laws. Texas, as luck would have it, was the other one.

In the 1800s, ministers might not visit settlements or outposts on the American frontier for months, making marriage impossible for couples separated by miles of mountains and prairies. The Old West's proxy-marriage laws required only a sworn affidavit designating a stand-in and certifying the absent party's consent to the marriage.

On a Wednesday morning, at the Harris County Courthouse in

downtown Houston, my brother-in-law Allen and I stood before a justice of the peace. I gave him the notarized documents that Texas' sproxy-marriage law required from Billy. The justice checked our IDs, reviewed the papers, and signed the marriage certificate. In minutes, I became the wife of an inmate three hundred miles away, thanks to the American frontier.

June 9, 1982
Dear Billy—

I married you this morning at 9:45. Everything is right in my world. I can't wait until I can see you on Saturday. You are my mornings, my nights and all my days. You are my song of songs—the theme of my life.

We will make our future come true together. I told you shortly after I met you, in fact the first time I visited you and Wilbert alone last May 9th, that I would not give up until you are free. I love you, and I cannot imagine life without you.

How could I marry a man convicted of murder? The answer lies in scripture, liturgy, and all the great religions and the platitudes we learn in school. Redemption is a simple creed.

The man I loved was a new man, not the one who pulled the trigger in 1965. That man was molted like a dirty skin before I met the Billy Sinclair I married. But I knew, just as he did, that he was still responsible for the crime that put him behind bars.

I bought two beautiful matching gold rings to symbolize our union. I slipped his ring over mine the next time I visited him. I knew he would never be allowed to have it otherwise. Guards at the front gate didn't spot it when they patted me down before allowing me into the prison.

I slipped the ring on the third finger of his left hand as we sat in Angola's big visiting room. I could see the love and comfort in his eyes. I was his wife. He was secure. A smile lit up his face.

Our marriage was attacked as soon as the warden heard about it. Ross Maggio ran a tight prison. Nothing happened at Angola without his permission. But no one told him about the blood test Billy had to get at the prison hospital to comply with Texas proxy-marriage law or the statement he got notarized at the prison declaring his intent to marry me.

Angola's grapevine hummed with word that the warden and a member of Louisiana's pardon board had gone to see Billy Guste, the attorney general of Louisiana, claiming our marriage wasn't valid. Surely, they argued, a frontier-type Texas law couldn't possibly be legal in Louisiana. A Houston lawyer assured me that the "full faith and credit clause" in the US Constitution protected our marriage. It guarantees all states must recognize the valid laws of other states.

That Billy Sinclair and I met in 1981 was beyond improbable. What I faced for twenty-five years after our marriage erased the woman who walked into the death house at Angola to do a story about the death penalty. But I never regretted it.

WEEKS AFTER I ARRIVED IN Houston, I received a phone call that opened the door to an incredible future in TV news. I was invited to San Francisco for a job interview at KGO-TV, the city's ABC affiliate. I had sent its news director, Doug Ramsey, a copy of my audition tape, hoping for a recommendation that would help me find a job at a TV station near Louisiana. Ramsey had been the news director at WDSU-TV, the NBC affiliate in New Orleans, when I had an internship there one semester before I graduated from Loyola.

Chris McDaniel leaned on me hard to take the job.

"I don't care what you do, Jodie," he said. "You're never going to get another call like that, never."

Going from a small TV market like Baton Rouge to one of the nation's top ten stations was almost unheard of. KGO was an "O&O," a station that was owned and operated by ABC. The job might give

PICTURE OF THE WEEK

WILL'S PLAYMATES

In Fort Worth a photographer caught four girls and two boys in what seemed to be an act of lese majesty at the statue of Will Rogers, a man the Southwest has practically deified. But the picture he took also caught a tolerant look on the humorist's face that reaffirmed one of his wisest aphorisms: "A comedian can only last till he either takes himself serious or his audience takes him serious."

25

LIFE magazine, January 23, 1950. A twelve-year-old Jodie Sinclair helps a boy behind her as she sits astride a nine-foot, eleven-inch statue of Will Rogers, after having tried for months to climb on top of the monument. Two sisters are among the other children she helped climb onto the statue with her that day. © John Mazziotta. Mazziotta, a celebrated Texas news photographer, was one of the few in 1963 to get a picture of John F. Kennedy's assassin, Lee Harvey Oswald, after his arrest.

Jodie interviewing warden Frank Blackburn in the death house at the Louisiana State Penitentiary at Angola on March 17, 1981, where she met Billy Sinclair.

Billy Sinclair in the death house at Angola talking to reporters on March 17, 1981.

Billy Sinclair at the Louisiana State Penitentiary at Angola, 1981.

Jodie's prison visitor ID, 1982.

Jodie and Billy at Angola, 1982.

Jodie and Billy Sinclair at the Louisiana State Penitentiary at Angola, 1984.

Billy Sinclair on one of his numerous speaking trips around the state of Louisiana with an unarmed prison guard, warning school children not to break the law, 1980–1981.

Billy Wayne Sinclair

Jodie Sinclair

Tapped phone, hidden mike fed pardon-selling probe

By JAMES MINTON
and JOHN SEMIEN
Advocate staff writers

After almost giving up hope, Texas television executive Jodie Sinclair received the long-awaited telephone call from a Louisiana State Penitentiary official who claimed to have the key to her husband Billy Sinclair's freedom from prison.

It was 2 a.m. in Port Arthur, Texas, on Aug. 22, 1986, but Jodie Sinclair was alert and her telephone was wired to the tape recorder provided by the FBI in their budding investigation of a pardon-for-sale scheme at Angola.

The Morning Advocate acquired a copy of a tape recording of the telephone conversation and of other conversations between Jodie Sinclair and former Angola Food Services supervisor Berlin Hood.

The conversations indicate Hood was cautiously soliciting thousands of dollars in his professed role as a middleman in getting the Sinclairs a coveted "gold seal," a pardon approved by the state Pardon Board and signed by the governor.

The Aug. 22, 1986, conversation concerned an upcoming meeting between Hood and Jodie Sinclair, to which she was instructed to deliver $15,000.

Sinclair: "Tell me what to bring, now . . ."

Hood: "All you need to do is just bring the money in $100 bills."

Sinclair: "OK, it's 15?"

Hood: "Yeah."

Sinclair: "Is that ample?"

Hood: "Huh?"

Sinclair: "Is that enough?"

Hood: "Yes." (Both laugh).

Sinclair: "I mean I know that sounds funny, Mr. Hood, but I just, you know, I just, I knew Billy had mentioned to you that there was a little more than that, and I was just remembering that you said we ought to not 'nickel and dime it,' you know."

Hood: "Right. Okay, what time do you think you'll be in Port Allen, then . . . 'cause you always stay in Port Allen, don't you?"

Continuing the conversation, Jodie Sinclair and Hood agreed to meet at 9 a.m. on Aug. 24, 1986, in the coffee shop of a Port Allen motel. Jodie Sinclair also asked Hood when the money would be passed on to former state Pardon Board chairman Howard Marsellus.

Hood: "I'm gonna see him one day this week. I'm not sure which day, yet. As early in the week as I can get a chance to see him."

Sinclair: "At his office?"

Hood: "Oh, no. For lunch . . ."

Sinclair: "Is he still as greedy as you think he is?"

Hood: "Yep."

Sinclair: "So you don't think you'll have any trouble seeing Marsellus this coming week?"

Hood: "Oh, no. No. I see him often."

Sinclair: "And like you said, you're going to keep the money until he brings

SEE TAPE, 3B

Sunday Advocate, Baton Rouge, Louisiana, January 21, 1990.

Jodie in her twenties
in Houston, Texas,
mid-1950s.

Jodie in her International
House dorm room as
a graduate student in
journalism at Columbia
University (1984-1985).

Jodie Sinclair, assignment
editor and general
assignment reporter,
KBMT-TV Channel 12,
Beaumont, Texas,
1996-1998.

Jodie Sinclair with two of her grandchildren, New Orleans, 1988.

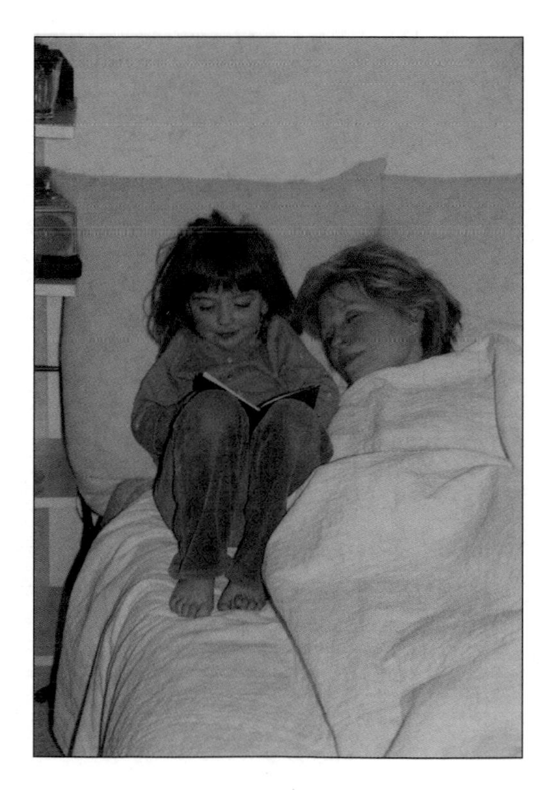

A granddaughter reads Jodie Sinclair a bedtime story, Los Angeles, 2005.

Jodie and Billy, 2019. © Waldenai Lafatiere Photography

me a chance at becoming a network correspondent. I flew to San Francisco, met with Ramsey and the station's manager, and accompanied a reporter on a story before flying back to Houston. The appeal of being a reporter in one of the most beautiful, liberal cities in the world pulled at me on the flight home. But the job had a critical requirement. I would have to be the weekend reporter for the first year.

I called Angola to find out if I could visit during the week. The switchboard connected me to Maggio's office. He was blunt. There would be no special privileges for inmates in his prison. Special privileges fostered violence by jealous inmates. Billy Sinclair would only be allowed to visit on the weekend like every other inmate. I began to explain what the offer meant to my career, how extraordinary and rare it was. He interrupted me.

"No exceptions. That's it."

There was no negotiating with Maggio. He exercised his power as he saw fit. He thought the special privilege of letting Billy Sinclair have visits during the week, instead of on the weekend like other prisoners, would make Billy a target of jealous inmates.

Conflict of interest also raised its ugly head. Was it fair to keep my relationship with Billy from Doug Ramsey? Billy was a nationally known prison journalist. Trouble the San Francisco station hadn't bargained for could follow me.

When I called Ramsey and turned the offer down, he was puzzled. Why on earth, he said would I reject such an incredible opportunity? I said it would be better for me to stay in Texas.

A news director in San Antonio called me, marveling at my work, astonished at how much I knew about reporting after just two years at Channel 9. I headed to San Antonio for an interview. It ended suddenly when he pushed his chair back from the table in the restaurant where he had taken me to lunch, looked me in the eye, and said:

"I called Channel 9 to find out why you left. I was told it was because you had a relationship with a murderer."

I was stunned. Why had he spent so much time praising my work and taking me to lunch before asking the question? But it confirmed what Chris McDaniel had said so many months ago. Billy Sinclair would ruin my career.

A few days later, a news director at a Houston TV station, who liked my audition tape, called to say that if I had worked even six months in San Francisco he might have hired me on the spot.

After I turned down the San Francisco offer, I walked out of my sister's house to the small backyard garage apartment where I was staying, crying so hard I couldn't sit in a chair. Night fell before I crawled into bed.

Billy called near midnight. He hadn't tried to talk me out of going to San Francisco. He'd said it wouldn't be fair, even though I knew he'd been worried that, if I did go, I would be thousands of miles away. When I told him I had turned it down, there was a long silence on his end of the phone. He would tell me later he was flooded with love that was so intense he couldn't speak.

As I adjusted to life in Houston, I prayed for a sign that that I was not sentenced to visits at Angola for the rest of my life. I imagined some unexpected opportunity rescuing me, restoring my career in TV news. It was a romantic dream I indulged as I hung on to hope. Would something suddenly occur to me that could open the door again to my career?

But the stark truth stalked me every day: My marriage to Billy was stillborn, a seed that was dead to every spring. I saw nothing but a bleak vista of secretarial jobs or positions as an administrative assistant if I was lucky. Reality hurt. But I had to earn a living.

For two months I stayed in the receptionist position with the Royal Bank of Scotland before I was hired as a public relations assistant at the Retina Research Foundation in Houston's famed medical center, a job I held for a year. Then I was hired as a medical reporter and producer at the University of Texas Health Science Center's TV production unit.

The answer I had yearned for came two years later, flooding in on the strongest of tides. In 1983, a new friend at the medical school's TV production unit urged me to apply to the Columbia University Graduate School of Journalism in New York where she had gotten her master's degree.

She had asked me one day how I had ended up working on medical documentaries. She said she could tell I had a background in TV news. I told her about meeting and marrying Billy, and what had happened to me as a result.

I scoffed politely at her idea. It was more than a long shot. I was forty-five years old, yearning after a career that rewarded youth, not middle age. The best journalism school in the country was not going to waste a master's degree on me. Columbia was an Ivy League school. Every year, one thousand applicants on average vied for the 180 slots at its journalism school.

"Do it," she urged me. "Do it. They'll take you," She smiled. "They like rebels. In my class, the FBI picked up a girl they said was running guns to South America."

I took her up on her dare. I filled out the application papers, writing the required essays in the required number of words—explaining who I was, why I wanted a master's degree from Columbia, and what I could contribute to the betterment of society. I took the pre-admission writing test on deadline at the local CBS affiliate in Houston under the supervision of a Columbia grad who was a reporter at the station. I packaged up all the papers and mailed them with a thirty-five-dollar check to Columbia.

And then I hedged my bet. I bought the most beautiful bed I had ever seen. It was a fairy princess bed, a Chinese Chippendale four-poster in cherry mahogany with a solid carved headboard and curving fretwork along the edge of the canopy that I saw at a Houston department store, a National Mount Airy reproduction of the real thing. I covered it with a dark green comforter embroidered with a crewelwork design.

It was my consolation prize, my sop against the disappointment I knew was coming. Every morning, I made it up perfectly so that it looked just like it did at the store. It was waiting every night when I opened the door and no one was there. I put it in a bedroom with a small balcony and planted vines in pots to shade my dream from reality.

And then, one afternoon, the phone rang in my office at UT-TV. It's probably a doctor's assistant, I thought, wanting changes in a script. I was doing medical documentaries for patients to watch in doctors' offices and ninety-second medical news stories that the school sold to TV stations nationwide. Doctors checked every word. Their assistants asked for conferences to discuss "and" or "the" and "but."

It wasn't a doctor's assistant. The call shifted my world 180 degrees. Energy crackled through me like a shot. I had been accepted at Columbia, the top journalism master's degree program in the United States. I was climbing back on the dream. I could have it and Billy Sinclair. It only took nine months to get a master's degree at Columbia and be back in Texas close to him.

I visited Billy the Saturday after I got the news. He said he was happy for me. One day in October, six weeks after the semester started at Columbia, a picture fell out of the envelope as I opened one of his letters. My heart stopped. Billy was sitting hunched over in a chair in the *Angolite* office, staring at the camera, a listless expression on his face. I could see what it had cost him to let me go. The fear that I would never come back was written all over his face.

A wave of guilt washed over me. He had never said a word before I left for New York, had never said, "Baby, don't go," had never talked about how he would suffer at Angola while I was gone. Instead he exulted with me over my miracle and said nothing about the knife in his heart.

I was off on a great adventure that frightened him. While the Department of Justice reported the serious crime rate in the city was down by 3.6 percent, New York was still tenth on a list of the nation's twenty-five most dangerous large cities. In the late seventies, the Son of Sam was stalking and killing victims in the city. In 1979, one of the most infamous kidnappings in US history occurred. Etan Patz, a six-year-old boy, disappeared one morning as he was walking to a bus stop to wait for a school bus in the Soho neighborhood in lower Manhattan. His body couldn't be found.

Much of the crime in New York City occurred on subways. Muggers jumped turnstiles with regularity, victimizing people waiting to catch the trains. On December 22, 1984, on a subway car in Manhattan, Bernard Goetz, a young white man, shot and seriously wounded four African American teens he feared were about to mug him.

But I was at home in New York once I got used to the city. My dorm room at International House in the historic Morningside Heights district of Manhattan overlooked Grant's Tomb, Riverside Park, and the Hudson River. I could see trees in the park and the river from my window. The national memorial to General Ulysses S. Grant, leader of the Union Army who won the Civil War for the North and later became president of the United States, dominated the neighborhood. It was one of the most imposing structures in the city.

I kept a picture of Billy on a table by my bed, taken when he was thirty-seven, a hardened-off man in his prime, squinting into the sun on the big yard at Angola. One day, a classmate from Jamaica picked up it up.

"He has a strong character," she said.

"Yes," I told her. "He does."

The seven hundred graduate students living at International House in 1984 were from one hundred countries. They were in New York to get graduate degrees from the city's top-flight universities. John D. Rockefeller founded I-House in 1924 to promote brotherhood among nations. My picture in the 1984–1985 I-House yearbook was surrounded by pictures of students from Japan, India, Italy, Lebanon, Norway, Iceland, South Africa, Pakistan, Greece, France, and a host of other countries studying a wide range of subjects from economics to design, cancer research, engineering, business, and other fields.

Three days after the fall semester started, as orientation ended, we were handed assignments with a deadline. I held my breath as I descended the stairs into the subway stop across the street from Columbia, pushing down my early fear of the city's crime rate. At Channel 9, I was always with a photographer. Now I was alone, and the stakes were higher than missing a deadline in a local newscast. Students who didn't get stories in on time didn't graduate with master's degrees. They got certificates of attendance instead.

But missing deadlines wasn't my greatest fear. If master's projects weren't approved, J-school students didn't graduate. I was fighting a negative attitude on the part of my adviser—a professor who thought I was too old to be at Columbia. I wouldn't live long enough, he felt, to make a difference in journalism, compared to someone in their twenties. He said he "despaired of ever teaching me to write." He delayed approving a subject for my master's project until late November. Most of my classmates' topics were already approved. They would have more time to finish them before the mid-February deadline.

My master's project was about women who were pregnant when they were arrested and ended up having babies behind bars. I flew to Houston for a few days over Christmas vacation, made a quick trip to see Billy, and then spent the rest of the month in New York doing everything I could to complete research on my thesis. I called every prison in the country with "maternity" programs for women and states that were considering it. My phone bill that month was five hundred dollars. The money came out of savings from my last job in Houston.

I found a former inmate living in New York who agreed to an interview. Her baby was born while she was locked up at the Bedford

Hills Correctional Facility in White Plains. It was only an hour away. But prison officials refused to let me interview women there doing time who had babies behind bars. They were afraid my real purpose was interviewing Jean Harris. Harris was doing time for killing her lover, Dr. Herman Tarnower, a famous cardiologist who wrote the bestselling book *The Complete Scarsdale Medical Diet* in 1978. Harris was convicted in 1980, four years before I arrived at Columbia. By then, she was running the in-prison nursery for babies born to inmates.

I wasn't interested in the lurid case that had made headlines all over the country. I wanted to know what it was like to give birth behind bars and what it did to inmates emotionally when they were ordered to send their babies home to relatives or put them in foster care after a year.

I turned in my master's project on time and held my breath. My master's project adviser said I had done enough research to pass, so he approved it. With that, I knew I had earned my master's degree. I was surprised when I later read his assessment of my work. He wrote that I was "an enthusiastic reporter with a strong desire to succeed," but my experience in TV news sometimes caused "too much voltage" in my work, although I seemed determined to learn the "more casual tone of print journalism."

The fear I felt as I worked on my master's project wasn't unusual. *In Cold Type,* a handbook of advice from the Class of '85 to the Class of '86, described the jolt that awaited incoming students. The book covered every course and aspect of the school year. But it assured the incoming class that the panic would ease, and the fear could be conquered.

Judith Serrin, a professor at Columbia, was my rock. She had been a reporter at the *Detroit Free Press,* United Press International, the Knight Ridder newspaper bureau in Washington, DC, and the *New York Times.* I was assigned to her required reporting and writing (RWI) I class that fall.

Serrin was demanding. But she constantly encouraged me. Her midterm critique of my writing helped me correct a flaw she attributed to TV news reporting. I was using labels or quick, sensational comments to start stories—a "broadcast teaser," she'd called them—that often didn't relate to the rest of the article. My "story organization" displayed some "jerkiness." But her critique also said I was an "extraordinarily hard worker" and researcher who tried to "pin down even the smallest question by deadline." She said I was improving, and she was confident I could polish my work.

I was forty-six years old that fall. Serrin knew I was nearly twenty years older than my classmates. But Columbia took the occasional older student, I was told, to make sure the applicants it accepted had a broad range of backgrounds. The school believed that the truth would emerge from the synthesis of their voices. Serrin called me "ma'am" and told me at the end of the semester that I had developed into a good writer.

"You could get a job at any newspaper in the country," she said, smiling at her triumph, and mine, at the end of my RWI class in late December. I kept copies of the stories I wrote on a variety of assignments. I remember the Dalai Lama, smiling at me and blessing me from the podium as I left a gathering for him, trying to get back to Columbia in time to get my story in on deadline. I covered stories at city hall and others that took me on the subway to dangerous neighborhoods in New York. I went on "rat patrol" in the Bronx on a story about the city's efforts to control rats in low-income housing projects.

I covered one of the most sensational trials in America that decade: *CBS v. Westmoreland*. General William Westmoreland was a commander of US forces in Vietnam from January 1964 to June 1968. He had sued CBS over a documentary that accused him of a "conspiracy" to show progress in the war by understating the size of the North Vietnamese and Communist Vietcong armies in order to boost morale and support, leaving the president, American troops in Vietnam, and the public totally unprepared for the Tet Offensive.

Columbia taught me that even though I was forty-seven years old, I could cover stories and meet its deadlines as easily as the most promising journalism students in the country. It confirmed my belief in myself. And it would open doors—even at my age—at TV stations near Louisiana so I could easily visit Billy.

LOUISIANA'S PARDON-SELLING SCAM

"Honesty is praised, then it's left to freeze."
—Juvenal, Roman poet, 47 AD

CASH AND CONNECTIONS WERE THE keys to freedom for Louisiana inmates at Angola in 1986. When Billy was told that for fifteen thousand dollars, he could be free, he never asked me for the money to buy him a pardon. The night he told me about the pardon-for-sale scam at Angola, he spoke in language so careful it was like a code. I could hear the excitement in his voice. I knew the odds of his ever being free legitimately were heavily stacked against us.

There was every sign in 1986, five years after we met, four years after we married, that his life sentence would never be commuted. The thought that he could be free left me breathless. I hung up the phone and pulled up the covers around me in bed, elated at the thought he could soon be there with me, his body pressed against mine as we fell asleep together. It was a short, but glorious, overnight ride.

For both of us, buying a pardon was unthinkable. It would have been the ultimate betrayal of his rehabilitation and my trust in him, and I could have been charged with a crime.

"Baby," he told me, "you are the best damn thing that had ever happened to me. I'd never smear you with dirt in return."

I was a reporter, in a profession with strict principles, bound to report wrongdoing. My conscience and Catholic grade-school mores prohibited paying a bribe. By the time they're seven years old, Catholic kids are taught to examine their consciences before they go to confession. If dancing on the head of a pin is a sin, they are duty bound to recognize it, calculate the degree—determine if it was a mortal or a venial sin—and confess it to a priest.

As we sat in Angola's main visiting room on that Saturday in late July 1986, Billy told me that inmates were buying pardons through F. Berlin Hood, a top prison administrator he knew well, and that he had the proof.

An inmate named Chris McAlister who worked for Hood told Billy about the scam one day in late July. He showed Billy his pardon. He said he had paid Louisiana's pardon board chairman Howard Marsellus Jr. five thousand dollars for a commutation of his sentence. He also said that Hood had brokered the deal.

Once Governor Edwards's signature was on the pardon, opening the door to freedom for McAlister, Marsellus demanded an additional payment. He wanted the jewelry he had seen McAlister wear on occasion, a necklace and bracelet that McAlister told Billy were worth $2,500. When McAlister balked, Marsellus threatened to have his commutation revoked.

Billy had suspected for more than a year that Marsellus was selling pardons. What he saw alarmed him. Marsellus had become a fixture at Angola. As soon as Edwards appointed him chairman of the pardon board in 1984, he began regularly attending inmate self-help functions, cultivating relationships with inmate leaders and key prison officials. He secretly set up a network of inmates and officials who could broker pardon deals for him. Hood and McAlister were the most important prison duo in the scam.

When Marsellus threatened to rescind McAlister's commutation, Hood and McAlister went to Billy for legal advice. As the most successful "jailhouse lawyer" in Angola, they figured he would know if Marsellus could legally revoke the commutation. Billy had been Hood's clerk in the food services office the two years before he joined the *Angolite* in 1977. They still had a close relationship.

Billy assured them there was no legal way a commutation could be rescinded once a governor had signed it. Then, Hood took Billy aside and told him he deserved to be out of prison and that fifteen thousand dollars would buy his freedom. Hood drove Billy to his house on "B-line," an area inside the eighteen-thousand-acre prison where guards and administrators lived, to lay out the plan.

That July day in the visiting room, Billy gripped my hand as he expressed his outrage.

"Fuck 'em," he said.

He had believed the mantra that prison officials preached—that rehabilitation was the key to freedom. Instead, he had just learned the bitter truth: He had to commit a crime to be free. It was the ultimate betrayal of a system that had held out hope to him for two decades.

I held his hand and smiled to deflect the guard's suspicion as I listened to the whispered rage in his voice. No one surveilling us in Angola's big visiting room could tell from our expressions that ours was any more than an ordinary visit that day. If anyone—guard or inmate—had overheard what he was telling me, his life would have been in immediate danger.

Some people later called us fools for not buying a pardon to get Billy out of prison. Everyone, they pointed out, knew that honesty had little, if any, reward in Louisiana. I had lived in Louisiana for fourteen years, and as a reporter at Channel 9 assigned to cover the state capital, I knew how casually corruption could be discussed in official circles.

I had at least twenty thousand dollars in a savings account, and Billy knew that. But he never asked me for the money. Buying a pardon meant turning his back on the man he had become. The thought infuriated him. His ethics were too hard won. If he betrayed them, he would become a common criminal again, guilty of public bribery. And so would I.

The vow we made to each other that day to expose the scam as we looked into each other's eyes added years to his sentence. Honesty has no coin in Louisiana. But there is a moment in every life when conscience demands stepping up to the plate. If there was any doubt about his rehabilitation, he proved that day his change was real. The lure of freedom could not seduce him.

EXPOSING THE SCAM PITTED US against corruption at the highest level of government. Louisiana's governor had to sign clemency recommendations to make them valid. Word could have easily come down to prison officials to have Billy shut up. Inmates waiting on pardons who had already paid thousands of dollars in bribes would gladly murder him to protect the scam. In the end, he barely escaped getting killed, and I became a target for reporting the corruption.

Initially, our only difficulty was finding a way to contact the right authorities without exposing Billy to immediate danger. We couldn't turn to anyone in the corrections system or state law enforcement. Billy's opposition was entrenched in both agencies. There was no one we could trust in the state government.

I called my cousin, Congressman Bill Archer, in Washington to ask for help. I told him about the request for a bribe and gave him all the information we had about the massive nature of the pardon-selling operation at Angola. He contacted the US Justice Department in Washington, DC. It began a federal investigation that ultimately involved FBI offices in New Orleans, Baton Rouge, and Beaumont, Texas. We asked for nothing in return.

I was in New Orleans visiting my son and his wife and my first grandchild when I received a call from an FBI agent in Washington early one morning. I told him that Hood wanted to meet me that afternoon in St. Francisville on my drive back to Texas, to tell me how much money he wanted to do the deal for Billy. The agent told me to put the meeting off. He said the FBI's New Orleans office didn't have the right kind of body wire to record an in-person meeting.

Agents came to my son's house in uptown New Orleans that afternoon and wired his phone before I called Hood and told him I couldn't make the meeting. I cried and said the distributor cap on my car had warped and it had to be replaced before I could drive back to Texas. He quickly agreed to reschedule it.

"You almost had me crying there," an FBI agent said, congratulating me on my performance. They warned me about entrapment every time they taped a call. They told me I could blow the federal government's case if Hood's defense attorney could convince a jury that I had led his client on.

The agents told me to meet them in a parking lot at a fast-food restaurant in Baton Rouge where I was to meet Hood. I pulled in the lot and spotted guys I thought were FBI agents. They came over to wire me up for the meeting with Hood at a "sit-down" restaurant down the road. When I saw the wire, I knew it wouldn't work on me.

"I only weigh 98 pounds. Hood will see it right away."

I suggested putting it in my purse. They agreed and assured me the mic was strong enough to pick up my conversation with Hood. They said an FBI agent would be having breakfast at the restaurant to keep an eye on the meeting. When I arrived at the restaurant, I spotted Hood and waved. He gestured me over to the table with a big smile. Hood was a likeable man who believed our opposition was so strong that the only way Billy could get out of prison was to buy a pardon. I hated betraying him. He was one of the few prison officials who had always been good to Billy.

During breakfast, we made small talk. I wondered when he might bring up a deal for Billy. When the waitress took our plates away, I put my purse on the table and took out my compact to powder my nose and touch up my lipstick, a typical gesture for any Southern woman after a meal. I wanted to make sure the wire inside my purse would pick up the conversation.

Hood told me how the scam worked and how much money I would need to get Billy out of prison. We finished our coffee and left the restaurant. On the way out, I spotted a man sitting alone at a nearby table. He looked like an FBI agent. I drove back to the fast-food restaurant where agents took the wire out of my purse. I asked if it had worked. They said it had.

Then they wanted me to have Hood arrange a meeting between me, Marsellus, and my "brother," who would be an undercover plant. Billy knew Hood would be suspicious. The prison official wasn't stupid. At first, I resisted. When I finally gave in and asked Hood to set up the meeting, he answered the way Billy knew he would.

"Jodie, when two people get together," Hood had said, "it's a meeting but when three people get together, it's a witness."

We had warned the FBI that Hood wouldn't go along with a three-way meet. He was too prison savvy. We told them to arrest Hood after he asked me in the restaurant for money to pay for the pardon. They had it on tape. We said Hood would "roll over" on Marsellus right away. Then, Marsellus would roll over on the contact helping him get the governor's signature on the pardons. The agents insisted they needed a three-way meeting for evidence. There was no way to set it up. The FBI investigation stalled in late August 1986, and Billy and I were left hanging.

We talked in whispers during our visits at Angola and never mentioned the FBI investigation or the pardons-for-sale scam over the phone. Billy would learn months later, through state police chief inspector Joe Whitmore, who was the detective handling the state pardons-for-sale investigation, that an FBI agent was drinking with a state police buddy in a local Baton Rouge bar one night and tipped the buddy off about the federal investigation.

"We have a man on the inside, and we're about to nail your governor," the FBI agent supposedly boasted.

The undercover agent went straight to his superiors, who reported the conversation to officials in the governor's office. They informed Governor Edwards immediately, and the state police launched its own undercover investigation into the scam.

An undercover state police operative made an offer on behalf of an inmate named Juan Serrato, who was serving a life sentence at the Louisiana state police barracks, a minimum-custody facility in Baton Rouge. Serrato had been convicted of strangling his wife with a pair of pantyhose. The undercover agent said he was willing to pay up to $130,000 to get the wife-killer out of prison. The sudden appearance of someone wanting to buy a pardon for that much money made Marsellus suspicious. But the pardon board chairman was greedy. It was too much money to resist.

To protect himself, Marsellus drew a powerful political benefactor into the Serrato deal. State representative Joe Delpit was one of Edwards's key legislative-floor leaders. On August 26, 1986, the undercover agent went to Marsellus's Baton Rouge home. Delpit stepped out on the porch when the agent showed up with a paper bag containing twenty-five thousand dollars in cash, the first payment in the deal. The state legislator took the bag and told the agent that the "deal" had already been "decided at the top."

State police officials in an undercover van across the street filming the exchange were stunned when they saw Delpit. He was the last person they thought might be in on the deal. But they now had one of the most powerful African American lawmakers in Louisiana on tape calling the governor's mansion to run a background check on the undercover agent's vehicle to make sure it wasn't assigned to the state police. Marsellus would later be convicted in the scam but Delpit was acquitted.

When Billy and I learned about the state police sting, we knew there was a chance he had been identified as the "snitch" on the inside. For the next two months, Billy was at Angola without protection. The door was open for prison officials to frame him and inmates with money in the scam's pipeline to kill him. He spent his days looking over his shoulder and his nights worrying if he would be knifed in the trusty dorm where he slept.

I was covering local news stories that did nothing to keep me from thinking about the danger facing Billy at Angola. If he needed me when I was out on a story, there was nothing I could do to help him. A call to US attorney Raymond Lamonica, who knew about our involvement in the FBI investigation, wouldn't prevent Billy's murder if it came after the fact.

What Billy was telling me in code on the phone and hinting at in letters was frightening. I could almost feel inmates bent on murder and prison officials with orders to shut him up closing in on him. Prison murders happen with lightning speed once all the elements are in place. The clues were there. Billy's instinct, honed from years on death row and the big yard, left no doubt.

Most inmates thought Marsellus had done nothing wrong. He was the only one helping them. Many had already paid Marsellus. When he was arrested, their pending deals were off. If they thought an informant was digging their hole deeper, there would be hell to pay. One inmate's dying father gave his last four thousand dollars to Marsellus. He knew it wasn't coming back.

Angola couldn't, and wouldn't, put inmates in lockdown who were likely to strike Billy. It didn't have the space or the moral incentive to do so. In more ways than one, Billy Sinclair was a problem the entire corrections system could live without.

I knew from all the stories Billy had told me over the years that it was dangerous to possess certain kinds of information in prison. I knew the pardons-for-sale information was dynamite. He had promised to call me if things started getting "hot." But I didn't know what he had to go through to get permission to call or how "dicey" it could be just before he got to the phone.

Afraid of the danger growing around Billy, I called Chris McDaniel, my old Channel 9 friend, and told him about our roles in exposing the pardons-for-sale scam.

"Holy crap," he yelled over the phone. "You were wired? It went that far? Fuck it, Jodie, we've got to do an interview. It's the only way to save his life. We've got to bring down so much heat, nobody would dare."

I could see his eyes, squinted into slits at what I had just told him. Chris had been the only one from Channel 9 who had kept his shoulder to the wheel for me through the years. Sometimes his loyalty brought tears to my eyes. There was no moment so low that he wasn't there.

"Chris, I can't do that. I promised the US attorney I'd keep it underground. A story could ruin his case."

"Jodie, what case? It's been fucked. They dropped the ball, sweetheart. You're stuck out there, and the fed isn't going to rescue you. They screwed up the investigation and you're paying the price. I'm telling you the only way you're going to save Billy Wayne Sinclair is by going public with this story. It'll blow the lid off this thing. You wanna be a fuckin' widow?"

I sat there mute, with the phone in my hand. He went on.

"You didn't take my advice and go with that job offer in San Francisco, and I was right. Not taking it helped ruin your career. Listen to me now. Don't be a goddamn widow."

"But what am I going to tell Lamonica?"

"Look, I like Lamonica. The US attorney's the only good guy in this fucking mess. Trust me on that. I'll call him. I'll embargo your interview until he says his investigation is finished. We'll hold it off that way."

"Suppose things go sour at the prison before he's finished? I don't like it, Chris."

"Baby, I'm telling you that you can save Billy's life this way. You've got to have an ace in the hole. If I've got the interview, we can run with it wild. Hell, we can do a crawl in the middle of the day. Look, I'm as concerned about ethics and that investigation as you are. You know me. I'm not just looking for a jump on this story to beat the competition. What I'm telling you is the God's honest truth, and you know it."

I met Chris in Baton Rouge and did the interview. He was right. While the white-hot heat of publicity might complicate the case, it would make Billy a priority for protection. Prison officials would have to step in and make sure nothing happened to him, even if they were among those who wanted him dead.

Meanwhile, corrections secretary C. Paul Phelps and the *Angolite*'s coeditor Wilbert Rideau were secretly planning to oust Billy from the national award-winning prison magazine. The ouster was something Rideau had wanted since 1985, when Billy began telling his coeditor that he suspected Marsellus was involved in corrupt activities that had something to do with the pardon board.

Rideau dismissed Billy's suspicions, saying they were based on "inmate gossip." Marsellus had promised to help Rideau get a clemency recommendation while Edwards was governor. But Billy's coeditor had another interest in the scheme. With Billy disgraced and removed from the *Angolite,* Rideau could take sole credit for the magazine's unique success and its long list of journalism awards, many for articles Billy had written.

In the weeks following Marsellus's and Delpit's arrests, Rideau began making secret "off the books" trips with an Angola security guard, ordered by Phelps, to corrections headquarters in Baton Rouge to meet with him to discuss Billy's removal from the *Angolite.*

When Angola's chief of security Eddie Boeker learned about Rideau's trips from his security staff, he became suspicious. They hadn't been cleared through him, the normal procedure when inmates traveled outside the prison. He assumed Billy would know. He called Billy to his office late one night to ask about the trips.

"What's Rideau up to?" Boeker asked. "Something big is going on for Phelps to keep me out of the loop. Should I be worried?"

Billy was stunned. He hadn't heard about Rideau's trips. He immediately knew that Phelps was aware of his undercover role for the FBI and that the corrections secretary had been ordered to destroy his credibility as a witness.

For years, Billy and Rideau had been close. Both had life sentences. Both had spent years on death row, and both were exceptional writers. Together, they edited and brought to national prominence the only prison magazine in the United States that was free to publish the truth about life behind bars. It had been a spectacular ride.

But their relationship ruptured when Rideau set up a deal with Marsellus to get Governor Edwards's signature on a recommendation for the magazine's graphic artist, Leonard Pourciau. Marsellus had commissioned Pourciau to paint his portrait for five thousand dollars. Rideau told Marsellus he could have the portrait for free if he could get the governor to sign Pourciau's clemency recommendation.

When Billy learned about Pourciau's deal, and Rideau's involvement in it, he moved out of the *Angolite*'s primary office into a smaller one in the prison's education department to put distance between himself and the pardon-buying corruption that had wormed its way into the magazine's operation.

When Boeker called Billy into his office to ask about Rideau's secret midnight trips, he thought he was Phelps's target. Billy made a calculated decision during their talk that night. He told Boeker about his undercover role with the FBI in the pardon-selling scheme and that he believed Phelps was aware of it.

"Shit!" Boeker exclaimed. "Here I thought they were after me, and it's your ass they are after." Boeker paused, letting the gravity of the situation sink in. "Man," he said. "This is some dangerous shit."

"Look, Colonel," Billy said. "All I ask is this: when whatever those two are plotting happens, let me get to a phone to call my attorney, Jack Martzell. He'll call the US attorney's office."

"I can do that," Boeker replied. "If I get wind of anything, I will do everything I can to get you to a phone." Boeker's promise saved Billy from the administration's plot to discredit him and lock him up in a maximum-security cell block, perhaps for years.

On November 13, 1986, Angola warden Hilton J. Butler and his warden for custody, Prentice Butler, went to the main prison control center where the *Angolite* office was located. They ordered Boeker to send all the inmates assigned to the area, except for the magazine's staff, back to their housing units. Then they locked down the entire main prison complex.

Boeker followed the two wardens into the office where Billy worked on *Angolite* assignments. They told Boeker they had things under control and he could leave. He refused. As the prison's top security officer, Boeker told the wardens he had the right to stay and observe any search made of the office. Boeker suspected they were there to plant contraband—probably drugs—in Billy's office to discredit him.

It was an old prison trick that prison officials used to frame inmates. If Boeker hadn't stood his ground, they would have pretended to find drugs in Billy's office with drastic consequences. They would have charged Billy with a serious disciplinary violation, one that would ruin his reputation as a prison journalist, remove him permanently from the magazine, destroy his claim of being rehabilitated, discredit him as a witness in the pardons-for-sale scam, and put him in lockdown for years.

Boeker stayed until the wardens went back to the security office to figure out what to do next. Boeker seized the opportunity and ordered the control center security officer to let Billy go "down the Walk" to call his attorney in spite of the lockdown. Jack Martzell immediately called Lamonica, who telephoned Phelps to inform him that Billy was a federal witness and warned him about taking any official action against a witness in the pardons-for-sale investigation.

When Billy came back to the control center, he and Rideau went back to the *Angolite*'s main office.

"What was that all about?" Rideau asked.

Billy suspected that Rideau had advance knowledge that the Butlers would search Billy's office that morning. He knew what it was "all about."

Billy decided to tell his coeditor that he had been working undercover for the FBI in the pardons-for-scam. That news left Rideau speechless. Phelps hadn't told him that Billy was the pardon-selling snitch.

The two editors were then joined by Tommy Mason, an inmate staff writer. He seemed surprised to find Billy in the office. Billy suspected Rideau had told Mason that Billy would be removed from the *Angolite* that day. Rideau quickly told Mason about Billy's undercover role with the FBI.

"You're a dead man," Mason angrily told Billy. "You won't make it through the night."

Late that afternoon, one of the prison's most notorious psychotic killers, Henry Patterson, was transferred to Billy's dorm straight out of a maximum-security cell block. Maximum-security inmates were never moved directly into trusty dorms— it was too dangerous. Billy knew Patterson was there to kill him. Patterson didn't strike that night. Billy wasn't surprised. It wasn't unusual for an inmate, ordered to hit another prisoner, to wait and see how security operated in the dorm before he attacked.

Billy watched Patterson all night long. When Billy went to the *Angolite* office early the next morning, he was greeted by a prison security lieutenant who was close to Hilton Butler.

"You know what happens to inmates when they say the wrong things to the wrong people about us here at Angola," he told Billy. "Something bad always happens."

"Is that a threat, Lieutenant?" Billy asked.

"Take it as some friendly advice," the lieutenant said as he left the office.

Billy immediately went down the Walk and called me from a telephone where inmates could make personal calls. I could hear the urgency in his voice when he said they had moved on him. I was terrified when he told me about the killer in his dorm and the lieutenant's threat, as well as the details about the shakedown at his office that Boeker had stopped.

Time to protect Billy was running out. I immediately called Lamonica and let him know that a leak at Angola had exposed Billy's role in exposing the pardons for sale scam. I told him about the psychotic killer put in Billy's dorm the night before and the threat made by the lieutenant that morning. The US attorney immediately dispatched two federal marshals to take Billy into federal protective custody and told me to do whatever I could to protect my husband until they arrived.

I knew the drive from Baton Rouge could take close to two hours, depending on early morning traffic. I called the prison and told the operator I was working with the FBI, that an inmate murder was in the works at Angola and federal marshals were on their way to stop it. She dialed the warden. When Hilton Butler answered, I dropped the federal government on him like a bomb.

"This is Jodie Sinclair. Billy and I have been working undercover with the FBI for months to expose pardon selling at Angola. He's getting death threats. The US attorney in Baton Rouge is sending federal marshals right now to take him into protective custody. If anything happens to him before they get there, Hilton, your ass is grass, and the federal government is the lawnmower."

For a long moment the phone was silent. Then the warden began stammering a reply. But I wasn't through.

"You better go down to the *Angolite* office yourself, Hilton, and make sure Billy stays alive until those marshals get there."

Then I called Chris and told him to run with the story. Chris phoned Lamonica and said the story was airing that night on the evening news. Lamonica told him that federal marshals were on their way to Angola to get Billy. I breathed a sigh of relief later in the day when Louisiana radio and TV stations reported that Billy was in protective custody in the East Baton Rouge Parish Prison.

The story that Chris aired on Channel 9 that night about Billy's role in exposing the pardons-for-sale scam prompted Nancy Harris, a Baton Rouge resident, to write a letter to the *Advocate* on Billy's behalf:

> *After seeing the television news about the bribe offers made to Billy Wayne Sinclair and his wife Jody [sic] Sinclair to gain his freedom from Angola Prison, I am appalled that such a fine person will be subjected to the additional rigors of being placed in the position of being an informant against some of our usual Louisiana politicians and bureaucrats.*
>
> *I have been a student of criminal justice at LSU and for other reasons have up until 1983 been involved in my own small way in combating the drugs and crime that proliferate our city. In my opinion Mr. Sinclair is a rehabilitated criminal and hopefully, after he testifies in this particular "pardons-for-sale" scheme, will be allowed to petition for his freedom again and will go free.*
>
> *I speak as a lifelong resident of this community and a Republican lady of middle-age who long ago gave up the pipe dreams of justice being fair. It quite often is only fair if you can afford an expensive lawyer or have a few well-placed influential friends. I, like many other Louisiana citizens, am tired of being embarrassed by our state politicians and I hope a committee to free Billy Wayne Sinclair can be formed.*

Harris was bombarded with death threats. The verbal abuse on her telephone answering machine frightened her so much that she turned the recordings over to the FBI in Baton Rouge. She changed her telephone number and ultimately moved to a new residence. Ten years later, Associated Press writer Alan Sayre wrote a favorable opinion piece in the *Advocate* about Billy's role in exposing the pardons-for-sale scam. He also received threats.

Five days after Harris's letter appeared in the *Advocate,* William "Judge" Roberts, Governor Edwin Edwards's executive counsel, informed the newspaper that he was recommending against clemency for the "convicted murderer-turned-federal-informant Billy Wayne Sinclair." Roberts handled all clemency recommendations that were sent to the governor.

"I am just not convinced and never have been convinced that Sinclair should be commuted," Roberts said.

The *Advocate* then published a letter from the Bodden family about Nancy Harris's proposal to create a "Free Sinclair" committee. Their account of Billy's crime repeated the false narrative at his trial that depicted him as a cold-blooded killer.

Billy's status was tentative. He was still in the East Baton Rouge Parish Prison, where he had been held since he was moved from Angola. His victim's family and friends were pushing hard to have him returned to Angola. I could hear inmates at the jail yelling at him when he called me, beating on the bars of their cells to drown out my voice. He was a snitch, and they were determined to make him pay. He had been placed on the tier with the three Colombian hit men who had gunned down DEA informant Barry Seal in Baton Rouge under contract from world's most dangerous cocaine kingpin, Medellín Cartel leader Pablo Escobar.

One night I sat bolt upright in bed at Billy's words on the phone.

"I got urine thrown at me when I came down the cell block hallway to call you."

"You what?"

I had to make him repeat it to believe it. His voice was low and husky. I could picture the cell block he was calling from. I had seen enough of the prison at Angola to know what the inside of the East Baton Rouge Parish Prison no doubt looked like.

"Yeah, they save it in plastic cups in their cells. They hit an inmate using the phone in front of me. They mistook him for me." Billy chuckled. "He's got a mustache, too."

Even in his dangerous situation, Billy found the mistake amusing. Among themselves, prisoners have a crude sense of humor. I knew he had used the word "urine" for my sake. Otherwise, he would have called it piss.

"Why, Billy? Why . . . ?"

"They yelled, 'That's what a rat deserves,'" he replied almost too casually. "A 'rat motherfucker'—that's what I am in the prison world now."

A loud din erupted in the background. The other prisoners were rattling their cell doors. They did it every night to interrupt our phone conversations. The urine signaled an escalation of their primal revulsion at the "rat motherfucker." The noise and the threats terrified me.

Prisoners who snitch are dealt with harshly by other inmates. The "FBI informant" label Billy had now was tantamount to a death sentence. I was frightened because he was being held in maximum-security lockdown on the same tier with three notorious informant killers. Attorneys for the Colombians had assured the jail's warden, Hayden J. Dees, that their clients posed no danger to Billy. Dees had known Billy when he was an assistant warden at Angola. The Colombians were the only inmates housed on the tier. Warden Dees believed Billy would be safer there than on a regular disciplinary lockdown tier.

I passed a hand over my forehead while I thought of him on the other end of the phone in a baggy white jumpsuit with "EBR" for East Baton Rouge stamped in big letters on the back. I knew he had on the orange thong sandals the inmates called "flip-flops."

Seeing him dressed that way was a shock. The look on his face shocked me too. He sat at the table during our first visit, listless and withdrawn, staring like a zombie as I tried to distract him from his situation. I held his hand, smoothed his face over and over with my palm, and kissed his cheeks with almost no response. Being a "rat motherfucker" was hard.

Each time we visited, he looked worse. I had the feeling I was trying to hold up a drowning man. I could tell he had lost another five or so pounds every time I saw him. It had been twelve years since he had spent time in a cell, and the lockdown confinement was taking its toll. He dreamed he would never be free. It had been years since he had thought about dying in prison. The circles under his eyes were visible evidence of the psychological torture he was enduring.

He had the "cell block look." I had seen it only once before in a photo taken of him at Angola in the 1970s for a prison ID He had spent two years in maximum-security lockdown between 1973 and 1975 in the most violent cell block at Angola. He was moved to lockdown after leading the peaceful integration of the big yard in the main prison complex because it infuriated the all-white prison guard staff. One of the prison's most racist security chieftains, Major W. J. Norwood, ordered an inmate to place three tabs of LSD in a law book before he gave the book to Billy. As soon as Billy took the book, Norwood and a "goon squad" surrounded Billy, threw him on the ground, handcuffed him behind the back, and escorted him to lockdown.

A local district attorney refused to bring criminal charges. He warned Angola's warden that Norwood's vendetta against Billy could have serious legal ramifications. Norwood settled for a two-year stay in lockdown to appease his rage against Billy for changing the prison's entire social structure. Now, he was once again in maximum-security lockdown for doing the right thing.

"Are you coming Sunday?" The strain in Billy's voice put tears in my eyes.

"You know I will be there, Billy."

"It's a long wait, baby, until Sunday."

I was counting the hours too until I could see him. In the meantime, my life went on as usual. During the week, I was a reporter for KJAC-TV, the NBC affiliate in Texas's Golden Triangle, near the Louisiana border, where refinery after refinery dotted the landscape around Beaumont, Orange, and Port Arthur. Every Sunday that Billy was in the EBR Parish Prison, I drove the two hundred miles from Beaumont to Baton Rouge to see him. Then I'd drive back the same day. Each of our visits required special permission from the US attorney in Baton Rouge.

I knew Billy had to steel himself the first time he walked through the door of the visiting room. Shame was etched on his face. The difference between the Billy Sinclair I was seeing and the man I had met five years before was dramatic. Then, he had the proud look of a free man, the sort of natural dignity you see in true cowboys. The man in front of me was struggling to keep his dignity.

"So, this is the thanks we get for helping the FBI."

I couldn't control the bitterness I felt at the federal government's betrayal. I had no idea about how our saga would end. Fear ate at me. I knew ranking Louisiana prison officials wanted revenge because we had helped the FBI. Corrections Secretary Phelps was incensed that Billy had exposed corruption in his prison system. He was working hard to have Billy returned to Angola, where he would almost certainly be killed. The Istrouma-based opposition was in a rage that our cooperation with law enforcement enhanced Billy's reputation as "one of the most rehabilitated inmates in America." They wanted Billy returned to Angola, too.

Billy's exposure of the pardon-selling scam had far-reaching implications. It led to a sweeping state police investigation of Angola that resulted in the indictment of F. Berlin Hood and several of his cohorts. It forced Warden Hilton Butler's resignation and Assistant Warden Prentice Butler's retirement. It also uncovered a massive, multimillion-dollar "homosexual mail scam" operated out of the prison by Dixie Mafia chieftain Kirksey McCord Nix.

The FBI joined that investigation. Federal authorities learned Nix had made nearly four million dollars from the scam. It targeted lonely gay men in the free world, ensnaring them in pen-pal relationships with fake young inmates created by Nix and his gang. They bilked the unsuspecting victims out of millions by making them think they were sending money to attorneys or to corrupt officials to help get the young men out of prison.

During their investigation of the homosexual mail scam, state and federal investigators uncovered Nix's involvement in the infamous 1987 "Sherry Murders" in Biloxi, Mississippi.

Nix had ordered the murder of Biloxi judge Vincent Sherry and his wife Margaret after the gang leader was convinced by his attorney, Peter Halat, who was Judge Sherry's law partner, that Sherry had ripped him off for hundreds of thousands of dollars. In reality, Halat had taken the money—which was supposed to buy Nix's way out of Angola—and used it to bankroll his successful campaign to become mayor of Biloxi.

If Billy hadn't exposed the pardon-selling scam, none of these wide-ranging investigations would have taken place. Yet he was locked in a cell near inmates who called him a "rat motherfucker" every time they saw him and tried to throw urine and feces on him.

Suddenly, there were no more calls from the jail. I swallowed hard. Maybe his opponents had sent him back to Angola. The US attorney had told me he was "stretching his power," hoping to get Billy transferred to the state police barracks where he would be safe. Perhaps his "deal" had fallen through.

I had no number for the state police and no way to get one without calling my reporter friends. But that would tip them to the story. I didn't want any publicity about his transfer to the state police barracks if that's where he was headed. The victim's family would up their crusade to get him sent back to Angola regardless of the risk to his life.

But I couldn't wait until morning to try and find him. Too much was at stake. Pushing down panic, I called information in Baton Rouge, got the only listing for the state police, and after several calls, reached the operator at headquarters. I took pains to sound as calm as I could.

"I'm Billy Sinclair's wife, Jodie. I'm calling to see if he's been transferred to the barracks from the East Baton Rouge Parish Prison."

"Sorry. I don't have any information about that."

Demons of fear started screaming in my head. I gripped the night table by the bed.

"Thank you. . . . Well . . . I thought that's where he was supposed to go. That's what the US attorney said."

I was finding it hard to catch my breath.

"I guess . . . I'll just have to call the US attorney at home. I don't know what else to do."

The woman on the phone was kind.

"Oh . . . I wouldn't make that call. If I were you, I'd just hang up the phone. Chances are it will ring before long with some information."

"Thank you," I whispered and hung up.

Within minutes the phone rang. I snatched the receiver off the hook midway through the first ring.

"Hello."

"This is Chief Inspector Joe Whitmore."

The voice I heard was a deep friendly baritone.

"Hello, sir. Would you know anything about my husband Billy Sinclair?" My voice broke off with a quaver.

"I've got Billy, Jodie. There is nothing to worry about."

He talked as if he had known me for years. Something in his voice made me trust him without a second thought.

"Mr. Whitmore, I was so scared when your operator said she didn't have any information."

"We have to do that for security reasons, Jodie. We never say anything about moving a prisoner until it's over."

Of course, I thought. What a dunce I'd been. I sat down on the side of the bed in relief.

Our conversation was short, although Whitmore gave me no indication he was in a hurry. I was cleared to come see Billy, he said, as soon as I chose. Visiting days at the Barracks were on Sundays and were nothing like visits at Angola. I would not be subjected to a pat-down search and had only to show my driver's license to be allowed in.

"You can bring him anything you want except booze and firearms," he said with a chuckle. "We don't allow those."

"You mean, I can bring him something to eat?"

"Sure, if you want."

I hung up the phone, full of amazement, shocked at the good news. Billy was safe in a humane place. I was free of the harassment that I had endured for years at Angola. I would be able to cook for him and buy him clothes. I turned out the light, snuggled down into the sheets, and breathed in their freshly laundered smell. For the first time in months, I slept without waking up in the middle of the night.

The change was hard to believe. Barracks inmates could visit almost all day long on Sundays. They could wear free-world clothes. Families could bring home-cooked meals. I bought Billy slacks and shirts right away from an upscale retail store for men. The pride on his face when he wore them the first time was unforgettable. For twenty-one years at Angola, he had only been allowed to wear standard prison garb. His voice was full of wonder when I told him about the surprise in our picnic basket.

"You brought a roast, baby, a roast?" he asked, wide-eyed during our first visit.

After we ate, we had time to talk about everything under the sun—Wall Street, medical breakthroughs, the weather, health spas, scientific discoveries, the price of gold and silver, anthropological theories and digs, dude ranches, pigs as pets, and freak events—instead of rushing through a two-hour visit.

MONTHS AFTER BILLY WAS SAFELY in protective custody at the state police barracks, he learned from Chris McAlister that the Dixie Mafia had ordered its henchman, Leoncio "Laredo" Castillo, to kill Billy.

Like Billy, McAlister was also in protective custody at the barracks as a witness in the pardons-for-sale scam. When news of the scam broke and Billy was removed from Angola, McAlister called Joe Whitmore and revealed his role in the scam. With his close ties to the gang and its leadership, McAlister had plenty of valuable information to give the state police on the corrupt inner workings at Angola. Whitmore had him transferred to the barracks.

McAlister's information proved Billy's suspicions had been right, that the Marsellus/Delpit arrests had led to his being identified as the "man on the inside" the FBI agent had bragged about in that Baton Rouge bar. Somehow, that information had leaked down to Nix, who was furious that the millions he had scammed from naive gay men couldn't be used to buy a pardon from Governor Edwards.

Castillo was more than willing to carry out the "contract." He had given Hood ten thousand dollars to get his fifty-year armed robbery sentence commuted. When Marsellus and Delpit were arrested, Castillo knew he would never get his money back. When he was told Billy was behind the bust, he wanted revenge. He lost his chance when Billy was taken into protective custody.

Rideau and Phelps weren't finished with Billy after the feds removed him from Angola. With Billy in protective custody and unable to speak to the media, Phelps gave Rideau unfettered access to his many media contacts to discredit Billy. The convict editor told them that Billy's informant role had destroyed the *Angolite*'s credibility and put the staff in danger. Prison inmates, he said, might think its staff members were snitches, too.

Their media campaign was so successful that Rideau convinced his longtime supporter David Anderson, a criminal justice editor at the *New York Times,* to write an editorial critical of Billy's role in exposing the scam. Other national media outlets including the *Columbia Journalism Review* questioned his whistle-blower role while he was a coeditor of the *Angolite*.

The 1987 May/June issue of the *Columbia Journalism Review* called Billy and Rideau the "Woodward and Bernstein" of prison journalism and said Billy's informant role left the magazine's staff "saddled with guilt by association." Rideau claimed his "best sources, built up over ten years, started clamming up." Phelps told the *CJR* that while he "was obliged to support undercover informants," he "had to put the integrity of the press first and disapprove of what Sinclair did," ignoring the fact that failing to report the pardons-for-sale scam was a federal crime, called "misprision of a felony."

But the *CJR* writer gave Billy the last word. Billy told Lee Kravitz that "convict journalists cannot function like free world journalists." He said Hood came to him to engage him "in a criminal capacity." He said he "did the right thing" when he worked undercover to expose the pardon-selling scam.

About a week after Billy was taken into protective custody, Rideau called me late one night. He said that he was "terribly concerned about me" and that he was calling me "as a friend." He talked to me for about forty-five minutes and then published a twisted version of my remarks in the *Angolite,* claiming he had "interviewed me."

Mary Sinderson, my friend and lawyer, had been terrified for months that I would be killed for exposing the pardon-selling scam. She was a former US attorney in Houston. She knew how things could go wrong even when witnesses were under federal protection. She told me that I would be a prime target for prison officials and inmates who wanted revenge for queering the scam. She said they would get back at Billy by killing me.

"You little fool," she scolded me one night over the telephone in a panic. "Don't you know how easy it would be to kill you? You're out there at all hours on that highway between Angola and Port Arthur on those trips to see him. On top of that, you live alone. You go to the TV station between five and five thirty in the morning to do the morning news cut-ins when it's pitch-black outside. Then you're there alone for at least two hours except for the overnight guy, and he's way up front in production."

A few weeks later, I stopped at a Popeye's in Lake Charles on my drive back to Texas after a visit with Billy. I paid for my box of chicken and turned to leave when two big men stepped in front of me.

"You're Sinclair," one of them said. The other one said, "Sit down, little lady. We want to talk to you."

The men appeared to be in their late fifties. They had on cowboy hats and boots. They said they had just attended a seminar on criminal justice in Texas and were on their way back to Baton Rouge. One of the men told me he was Jessel Ourso's brother. If they knew Ourso, they were connected to powerful people in Louisiana.

In 1963, Jessel Ourso was the youngest sheriff ever elected in Louisiana. In 1968, he was charged with thirty-three counts of violating state criminal laws "for failing to account for monies paid to him by construction and engineering firms for guard and security services he provided." He beat the charges and was reelected sheriff of Iberville Parish in 1971. He died in office in 1978 when he was just forty-six years old, still a revered, well-connected law enforcement officer.

It was lunchtime. There were a lot of people in the restaurant. Stories about the pardon-selling scam and the role a famous Angola inmate and his wife played in exposing it had been making headlines in Louisiana for weeks. The men wouldn't be able to hurt me without a lot of witnesses. I agreed to sit down and talk with them.

"Little lady," one of them said, "I hope you're not traveling our Louisiana highways without your buddies."

"My buddies?"

"Yeah, lady, Smith & Wesson."

I was incredulous. He was telling me I needed to carry a gun to protect myself. I remembered thinking what he said sounded like a line in a movie. How could it be happening to me? I don't remember feeling scared. In my car, before I left for Texas, I pulled out my tape recorder and made a recording of the incident, so I would have a record of every detail. When I listened to it later, my voice sounded like I was talking underwater.

The men told me they had stopped me to warn me. They said that "free people" at Angola would hurt me for busting up one of their "enterprises." One of the men said he had worked at Angola so he knew how its "free people"—guards and administrators—operated when they were getting "even."

One year after his September 5, 1986 arrest, Howard Marsellus was sentenced to five years in a federal prison for selling his vote in pardon decisions. In addition, he was sentenced to two years in state prison on "related charges."

During his trial on public bribery charges in the pardon selling case, Representative Delpit broke down in tears on the witness stand. His defense attorney argued in court that Delpit was "investigating" Marsellus when he accepted the bag with the bribe on Marsellus's front porch. The jury acquitted him.

In exchange for providing evidence against the officials running the scam, none of the inmates who bought pardons were ever prosecuted. Instead, they were released from prison. So was McAlister. Billy was the only inmate who was not released, even though he was the whistle-blower who exposed the pardons-for-sale scam.

Governor Edwards was never charged in the scam. Some suspected a signature machine was used to forge his signature on the clemency certificates of the inmates who were released after the scam. But why, I wondered, didn't Edwards react when he read news stories about inmates receiving clemency recommendations that he knew he hadn't signed?

Although the "Sinclair FBI tapes and recordings" were never used in state trials against those charged in the bribery scheme, in 1990 the *Los Angeles Times* reported that Billy had testified "before both state and federal grand juries in the investigation, putting his life in danger."

On January 21, 1990, after Berlin Hood and several other Angola officials were convicted of bribery in state court for their involvement in the pardon-selling scam, the *Advocate* published two stories about the roles that Billy and I played in exposing it.

The stories verified on the record that Billy Sinclair, the only inmate who reported the scam to the authorities, wasn't a criminal trying to con his way out of prison by exposing the fraud.

After Billy was transferred to the state police barracks, his opposition began making political and physical threats against anyone who spoke publicly on his behalf. They also started pressuring state police superintendent Wiley McCormick, who was in charge of the barracks, to transfer Billy back to Angola. Shortly after Billy testified before a state grand jury in January 1987 about the pardon-selling scam, Joe Whitmore escorted him to McCormick's office, where the superintendent had a frightening message.

"The state police and district attorney's office promised they would keep you housed at the state police barracks as a protected witness," McCormick told Billy, "but I'm getting pressure to move you. That pressure is coming from the highest power in this state—and I do mean the highest. If the governor gives me an order to transfer you, you're out of here. I suggest you and your wife contact the US attorney and the FBI to get me some help in dealing with this pressure. I cannot impress upon you enough just how intense the pressure is, Sinclair."

Whitmore, I believe, was somehow able to block the transfer. He was a highly respected member of the state police. He didn't like Billy Cannon, one of Billy's main opponents, or Governor Edwards. Despite Whitmore's help, the political pressure to have Billy sent back to Angola persisted through the rest of Edwards's 1984–1988 tenure in office. Even the federal government couldn't protect Billy.

"Mrs. Sinclair," US Attorney Lamonica told me, "I got your husband transferred to the barracks. I cannot force the state to keep him there."

In fall 1987, Wiley McCormick left the state police to begin a career in the private security industry. Edwards named a longtime political crony, J. C. Willie, to replace McCormick. Willie's first official act was to order Billy transferred out of the barracks. Whitmore blocked the move with a threat of his own. He told Willie that if the order were carried out, he would place a letter in Willie's personnel file, a copy in his own file, and a copy in Billy's prison file, stating that he believed the transfer had been ordered so Billy would be killed in the prison system. The transfer order was rescinded.

Edwards left office on March 10, 1988. A furious Joe Whitmore told Billy that outgoing Corrections Secretary Phelps had lobbied Edwards during his last hours as governor to order Billy transferred back to Angola. Edwards ignored the request. He knew he would run for governor again in 1992, and if Buddy Roemer, Louisiana's incoming "reform" governor, signed Billy's clemency recommendation, he would have to absorb the political flak for it. If Roemer denied Billy's clemency recommendation, Edwards would return to the governor's mansion in 1992 with the power to transfer Billy to Angola and curry favor with his opposition.

THE FIGHT FOR FREEDOM

"Freedom is what you do with what's been done to you."
—Jean-Paul Sartre, French philosopher and author, 1905–1980

WHEN GOVERNOR BUDDY ROEMER TOOK office in 1988, he found that Governor Edwards had left him with more than one billion dollars in debt and a legislature that was still controlled by Edwards's political machine.

But Governor Roemer had ignited a spirit of political reform in Louisiana. He appointed a new pardon board that would be independent and professional, free of politics and interference from the governor's office. Roemer chose Yvonne Foreman Campbell, an African American woman, to head the board. Campbell was a former reporter with the *Advocate*. Under Campbell, the board's decisions would be based upon facts and merit.

Billy's role in exposing the pardon-selling scam was having devastating, long-term consequences for his pleas for clemency. They were evident in 1988 after he was granted a hearing before Roemer's newly appointed pardon board.

We had strong support at that hearing. The conservative New Orleans Metropolitan Crime Commission was advocating clemency for Billy for his role in exposing the pardon-selling scam. During its decades-long fight against crime and corruption in Louisiana, the MCC had never supported the release of an inmate. My cousin, Congressman Bill Archer, supported Billy's plea for clemency. Henson Moore, a Republican congressman from Baton Rouge, also wrote the pardon board supporting clemency in Billy's case.

But assistant district attorney Mike Erwin told the *Advocate* that he opposed clemency for Billy. In response, I told the *Advocate* that Billy was the only inmate who reported the scam to the authorities instead of paying the bribe, and we were being singled out for harsher treatment.

Erwin dismissed my statement.

"What we had voluntarily on his part was information that might help him get out of prison," Erwin said. "There was not a whole lot we got from Mr. Sinclair we found useful."

Erwin's statement was refuted six years later by assistant Baton Rouge district attorney Charles Gray. Gray was in charge of the investigation into the pardon-selling scam in 1986. He would tell Cecil Goudeau, a probation/parole officer doing a pre-parole investigation in Billy's case in 1994, that Billy had been "very useful" to his grand jury investigation into pardon-selling.

I learned later Assistant DA Erwin's statements that Billy was no help in the pardon-selling investigation were the result of a threatening phone call to Erwin's boss, district attorney Bryan Bush, to stop any relief in Billy's case. After Billy was denied at the 1988 hearing, state police chief inspector Joe Whitmore and Charles Gray visited him at the barracks and told him about the call.

We knew why the caller targeted Bush. The year before, Bryan Bush had started advocating clemency for inmates in every pardon/parole case who cooperated with the authorities in the pardon-selling investigation. That included Billy. It was no secret. The *Advocate* covered the story.

Governor Roemer had already commuted the life sentence of Juan Serrato, the brutal murderer who cooperated with the state police in their pardons-for-sale sting. Serrato had served less than eight years for strangling his wife.

The *Advocate* reported that Serrato's commutation "was supported by the East Baton Rouge District Attorney's Office and the Louisiana State Police." Roemer cited Serrato's cooperation with the state police undercover operation and said that clemency was not something he took "lightly," but there would always be cases "worthy of consideration."

Charles Gray had promised he would recommend clemency for Billy just as he had for Serrato. But he was ordered not to.

"Bryan Bush told me I cannot recommend clemency for Billy Sinclair," Gray told Joe Whitmore. The lead investigator in the pardon-selling case was furious. He was keenly aware of the political pressure that the opposition had brought to bear in Billy's case from the beginning of the pardon-selling investigation. The veteran state police detective had taken a personal interest in Billy's case. He believed that Billy and I were "good people doing the right thing" and that corrupt politicians were trying to smear us. He also knew that prison officials trying to protect Governor Edwards would have Billy killed if he were sent back to Angola.

But there was little help from the federal authorities in Baton Rouge at Billy's 1988 hearing in late November. US Attorney Ray Lamonica told the *Advocate* that no one from his office would appear before the board on Billy's behalf. I never understood his reluctance.

"We have told them if there are any facts relevant to a decision," Lamonica said to the press, in an extremely guarded statement, "we will provide them with facts in writing, and that's the only thing we have ever agreed to do."

Thirty-five representatives of the victim's family and friends, including James Patin's father, appeared at Billy's hearing to oppose clemency in his case. I read all their names on the sign-in sheet. Despite their intense opposition, the board unanimously recommended that Billy's life sentence be commuted to seventy-five years. It was the fourth time a pardon board had unanimously recommended clemency in Billy's case.

Assistant D. A. Erwin immediately met with those opposing clemency for Billy. "Keep the community involved just like you are doing," he urged them.

Sadie Bodden DeLee, the victim's widow, who had since remarried, expressed bitter dissatisfaction over the recommendation.

"I don't think he (Sinclair) is rehabilitated enough to be out on the street," she told the *Advocate* following the hearing.

In my heart, I hoped clemency wasn't a popularity contest. Two governors had reduced it to that in Billy's case. I clung to hope this governor would be different.

December 16, 1988
Dear Billy:

The letter I got from you last night said you didn't know why you were being called on to serve so much more time, to pay so much more than others. After attending that hearing I know: Bodden's family. Pure and simple. They are the reason the system has singled you out. . . . They have poured hatred and vindictiveness into your case for all these years. And because they know people in power, they are able to influence it and direct it to hurt you.

They have made you pay more. And they are not satisfied yet. They never will be. At least now we have solved the mystery of selective enforcement in your case. For years, I have agonized over what was keeping you from me, what utterly irrational force could be blind to the merit in your case. But I have seen them now and it is absolutely clear. . . .

I love you, Billy. I will never give up trying to free you no matter how unfair they are or what they throw at us. I will always be your shield.

Less than two months after the pardon board issued its unanimous recommendation in 1988 for clemency in Billy's case, Governor Roemer denied it. A statement from his office said he had relied on Billy's falsified "cold blooded murderer, fourth offender" status.

I still believed Governor Roemer was an honest, decent man, that moral courage and political integrity would prevail with him. If we could get word to him through supporters who knew him and supply him with the truth about Billy's record, Billy's clemency effort might stand a chance.

At Billy's next pardon board hearing in 1990, we had even stronger support. Carol Costello was a prominent north Louisiana friend of the Roemer family. She had campaigned for Roemer when he ran for governor. She had also worked for North Louisiana senator Willie Crain. She was able to enlist Senator Crain's help in Billy's case.

She then turned to Gus Kinchen. She knew Kinchen had played football with Billy Cannon during their glory years at LSU. At her insistence, Kinchen and Senator Crain visited Billy at the barracks and decided to support him.

Billy's mother's family, a well-respected clan of farmers and planters in north Louisiana, also joined his freedom effort. They had never been involved in his case, but his uncle Charlie Patrick got the entire family together for a "reunion" to discuss it. They decided it was time to help. They were ready to fight "those people" in Baton Rouge. They enlisted the support of Representative Francis Thompson, a prominent north Louisiana legislator, to help in their effort.

The Metropolitan Crime Commission again supported clemency for Billy. Senator Tom Casey became another supporter. Casey was a political institution in Louisiana. He was also Roemer's executive counsel. While Roemer was governor, Billy clerked in the state police's fleet section at the barracks where government cars were serviced and repaired. His inmate job brought him into frequent contact with Senator Casey, who would personally deliver his state-issued vehicle to the state police compound for regular maintenance and servicing.

Billy didn't know Casey was a state senator. But he did his job and made sure Casey got an excellent motor pool vehicle while his car was in the shop and that his vehicle was spotlessly clean when he came to pick it up. Casey started bringing his vehicle directly to Billy when it needed to be serviced. When Casey was asked to support Billy, he reviewed the material in his case and became a supporter.

In October 1990, Roemer's pardon board again unanimously recommended that Billy's life sentence be commuted to seventy-five years with parole eligibility. When I spoke before the board, I said Billy had played a key role in successful cases against those who participated in the 1986 pardon-for-sale scandal, that the killing of J. C. Bodden was not a cold-blooded murder, that it was it was the irresponsible, stupid act of a twenty-year-old who did not intend to kill the clerk. I told the board that suppressed eyewitness evidence supported this account of the crime. I told the board that Billy would have been freed, along with the inmates who bought pardons, if we had paid the money like they did.

"But he did the right, the honest thing," I said. "It is a question of whether the right thing means anything in Louisiana."

When he was contacted by the media about the pardon board's second clemency recommendation in Billy's case, Governor Roemer had no comment. Billy's attorney, Jack Martzell, requested and secured a meeting with the governor. He led an entourage of Billy's supporters to the meeting. I went with him, along with Rafael Goyeneche, the executive director of the MCC, Senator Crain, and state Representative Thompson. While Roemer did not commit to a favorable decision, it was evident that he had a new view of the case—different from his negative perspective in 1988.

For the first time, the opposition had no insider access to the governor's mansion. When Representative Kennard led an entourage of Billy's opponents to Roemer's office "to speak about the Billy Wayne Sinclair case," Senator Casey graciously received them, listened to their concerns, and assured them he would convey their concerns to the governor. But he did not allow them beyond his office. He understood Kennard's political motivation for leading the delegation to the governor's office. The lawmaker had no choice.

Even though Kennard was one of the four suppressed witnesses at Billy's murder trial, he explained years later that he had to oppose Billy since members of Billy's opposition "lived down the street from his home."

Governor Roemer may have been the only governor who regularly reviewed clemency files until Kathleen Blanco, the first woman to be elected governor, took office. Every two months, Roemer would read through each file sent to him by his pardon board. Under the Louisiana Constitution, the governor could only act on clemency matters if the five-person board voted for a recommendation.

"I am cautious because I feel like I represent the victims and the general population," Governor Roemer said in a 1989 *Morning Advocate* interview. "I have got a fine line to walk. There's got to be a reason for hope on the part of prisoners, and I've got to honor the victims, too."

For a brief period during the Roemer years, Billy's opposition suffered from a vacuum of power. One of his chief opponents, Billy Cannon, had no political weight with Governor Roemer after the LSU football great was convicted of running a counterfeiting scheme and served time in a federal prison. Other well-placed people connected to the Istrouma High School opposition had little influence with Roemer. They included a high-ranking administrative assistant to the president of the Louisiana senate. But Governor Roemer wasn't controlled by the Baton Rouge political machine. He was from north Louisiana.

On January 9, 1992, Governor Roemer's last business day in office, he signed Billy's 1990 favorable pardon board clemency recommendation. While it made Billy parole eligible, the governor increased Billy's sentence from seventy-five years to ninety years. Senator Casey told Billy that Roemer had wrestled with the decision with his staff for weeks before finally making his decision to commute. It was the first time in Louisiana history that a governor had increased a clemency recommendation before signing it.

"The governor had a hard time getting past the fourth offender status," Senator Casey told Billy at the barracks when he turned in his state-issued vehicle. "I pushed hard for the seventy-five years, but I couldn't get around the fourth offender status. I cannot tell you how damaging that was in our discussions with the governor."

In the end, James Patin's false fourth-offender status would infect eleven pardon and parole board decisions during Billy's forty-year incarceration. It was nothing short of a criminal conspiracy by the Istrouma-based opposition to deny him due process. The department of corrections removed the false information in 1994, but it was too little, too late. Many opponents still clung to the false fourth-offender status regardless. Governor Buddy Roemer's signature on Billy's 1990 recommendation made him immediately parole eligible but it didn't guarantee a parole. It was only the first step in the long, arduous battle to bring him home. It would take a unanimous parole board vote to free him. We would lose again and again at parole hearings for the next twelve years.

Billy had served almost thirty years behind bars, and his rehabilitation was unquestioned. But the parole board refused to even grant him a hearing after the Roemer commutation. Led by its chairman, Ronald Bonvillian, the parole board ruled that Billy wasn't eligible for parole because he was a fourth offender.

The chairman of the parole board made the claim in defiance of a law the Louisiana legislature enacted in 1990 called the "old-timers' law." It made inmates who had served twenty or more years, on a sentence of forty-five or more years, and who were forty-five years or older, parole eligible. Billy met the criteria.

I hired Veronica Martzell Scheinuk, a longtime family friend and Jack Martzell's former wife, who was an attorney. She filed a lawsuit against the parole board asking for a hearing. Jack Martzell put a huge oar in the water behind the scenes for us. He asked Roemer to testify at a court hearing in February 1994 that it was his executive intent, when he signed the commutation order in Billy's case, that Billy would be immediately eligible for parole under the old-timers' law.

Based on Roemer's testimony, the court ordered the parole board to conduct a hearing in Billy's case. The opposition was furious that the rule of law had prevailed. They believed they had been denied justice when the United States Supreme Court vacated Billy's death sentence in 1972, when pardon board decisions recommended clemency for him, and finally, when Roemer commuted Billy's life sentence to ninety years.

Led by Carroll DiBenedetto and the Bodden family, Billy's opposition showed up en masse at the Hunt Correctional Center in July 1994 to oppose his parole at the court-ordered hearing. His opponents cited Patin's false claim of Billy's fourth-offender status, even though the department of corrections had since corrected it, listing him as a second offender. They called him a cold-blooded murderer, just as Ralph Roy had at Billy's original trial in 1966. It was the same false narrative they had used for nearly three decades to keep him in prison.

The board voted two to one that July against a parole for Billy. Ronald Bonvillian, who cast the deciding vote against parole, told the *Advocate* after the hearing that Billy "had done a fantastic job of rehabilitating himself during his twenty-nine years as an inmate," but he had to consider "other factors" in his vote against releasing Sinclair. He was obviously referring to the political power of Billy's opposition.

I told the *Advocate* that "the lesson in this is there is no virtue in doing the right thing." Inmates who paid the bribe had been free for nearly eight years by then. I deplored a board that granted paroles to convicted killers who served as little as twelve years and denied a whistle-blower who had served twenty-nine years.

On November 28, 1994, I drove to Baton Rouge the day before a hearing in another lawsuit Billy filed against the parole board. The suit charged the board with retaliating against him for the lawsuit that brought Governor Roemer into court. It also charged the board with using the false fourth-offender status that James Patin put in his record to deny him.

The next day, in a shocking move, Judge Kay Bates entered the courtroom and immediately dismissed the proceedings without hearing any evidence or taking any testimony, even though two important Louisiana officials were present to confirm Billy's allegations. Henry Goines, the DOC records custodian, was prepared to testify that Billy was a second, not a fourth offender. Ronald Bonvillian, the parole board chairman, had been subpoenaed to testify that the board had used the false fourth-offender status to deny Billy a parole.

I was furious at a judge who delayed the hearing to hold an in-chambers meeting with someone, according to our attorney, before abruptly shutting down our case. Ronald Bonvillian gloated over the dismissal. He sneered at me as I walked across the parking lot toward my car, making derogatory remarks about Billy and his lawsuit.

In 2014, Judge Bates retired after taped phone conversations with her son tipped off police that he was receiving special treatment in jail, according to the *Morning Advocate.* Her son had been charged with stealing large amounts of cocaine and several guns from an evidence vault in the downtown courthouse where the judge worked and he was an employee.

After Bates canceled the hearing, I drove to the barracks, where Billy had special permission to visit with me and his attorney. He was nervous and suspicious when we told him about the abrupt cancellation. He told me something was amiss; that it signaled impending danger. When it was time to leave, Billy escorted me to an approved area near the front entrance of the state police compound where we had said goodbye so many times before. I remembered seeing a state police official out of the corner of my eye as I turned from Billy's goodbye embrace for a moment. It was Colonel Paul Fontenot, the superintendent of the state police. He had been in charge of Edwards's security staff at the governor's mansion during Edwards's other terms in office.

I drove away from the barracks that day with a final wave at Billy, headed for Houston and my job at Channel 39. Less than an hour after I left, Billy was called before the top brass at the barracks. Even though he had permission to be in the parking lot with me that day and even though there were no DOC regulations against kissing a spouse, he was abruptly told he was being "shipped" for kissing me goodbye in public.

He greeted the news with characteristic aplomb. "Fine," he said, offering no resistance as he was weighted down with chains for a trip to lockdown at the Hunt Correctional Center. The transfer was no surprise. He had told me for months it was coming. It was a feeling, he said, that came from years of "reading cue" in prison and the consequences of challenging authority in court. When prisoners in Louisiana exercised their constitutional rights, they always paid a heavy price.

As soon as I got back to Houston, I stopped by my sister and brother-in-law's condo in Montrose to drop off Billy's Christmas present for them: two handmade folding chairs for the patio. The look on my brother-in-law's face when he opened the door should have warned me.

"Jodie," he said, "Billy called. He said to tell you they transferred him."

I remember screaming and slinging my purse across the kitchen, its contents skittering across the highly polished brick floor.

"No, no, no," I kept screaming as I fell to my knees, unable to get anything else out of my throat. When I could get up, I went home, a few doors down, to my own Lovett Boulevard condo. It was too late to drive back to Baton Rouge to try and confront Fontenot. I uncorked a bottle of wine and drank most of it. I paced the floor crying and calling out Billy's name over and over again until two o'clock in the morning, when I finally fell into bed.

The next day, no one at state police headquarters would take my calls except a state police colonel named Anthony Genusa. He told me he was sorry but there was nothing he could do. I would later learn that he and a number of other ranking state police officers had argued with Fontenot for more than an hour against the transfer to no avail. Fontenot would later tell a reporter who interviewed him about the transfer that what he witnessed "looked like a soap opera." In response to the reporter's question if Billy had broken any rules during eight years at the barracks, he said "no."

Two months after Billy's transfer from the barracks, the Louisiana State Troopers Association, in a rare move, announced it was mounting an "intense" effort to prevent Fontenot from being reappointed state police superintendent after Edwards left office in January 1996. Edwards had already announced he would not seek a fifth term.

Fontenot had made crucial enemies among the rank and file in the state police. He had been chosen for the superintendent's position over Colonel Genusa, even though Genusa had the backing of Jefferson Parish's powerful sheriff, Harry Lee.

In a January 22, 1995 interview in the *Morning Advocate,* the State Troopers Association's director, Bill Spencer, said he would "sandbag any attempt" by Fontenot to seek reappointment under a new governor. The paper reported that Fontenot had been "under continuous fire" during his three years as state police superintendent, "particularly" from the Troopers Association. The troopers could no longer stand Fontenot's arbitrary and abusive management style.

Billy filed a civil rights lawsuit against Paul Fontenot in January1995, charging the real reason for his transfer was his whistle-blower role in the pardon-selling scam and the lawsuits he had filed against the parole board. Almost simultaneously, state police lieutenant Ed Kuhnert filed a civil rights lawsuit against Fontenot charging the superintendent violated his due process rights when Fontenot summarily demoted him from captain to lieutenant. Kuhnert said Fontenot had a "vendetta" against him because of their differences in management styles.

Genusa, Spencer, and Kuhnert knew that Fontenot's decision to transfer Billy from the barracks had no basis in policy or regulation. Kuhnert's lawsuit worked its way quickly through the normal resolution process before US magistrate judge Christine Noland. Billy's did not. Once again, he was held to a different standard.

On July 15, 2003, in a rage that Billy's lawsuit against Fontenot had languished in federal court in Baton Rouge for nearly nine years, I wrote the judge and sent a copy of the letter to the Associated Press:

The Honorable Christine Noland, Magistrate Judge
RE: Civil Action No. 95-304-C-M2
Billy Sinclair vs Paul Fontenot Et Al

Madam:

"Justice delayed is justice denied." Are you not familiar with this phrase?

<u>You have had my husband's case for nearly nine years and you have yet to hold a hearing!</u> This, in spite of two remands from the Fifth Circuit Court of Appeals, the last a thirteen-page order that you received <u>three years ago</u>!

Under these circumstances, appealing to the court of public opinion via the Fourth Estate is a legitimate recourse. There should be <u>no</u>

consequences for my bringing this to the press. I am a wife crying out publicly on her husband's behalf about an unbearable injustice. My husband has been a hostage in your court for nearly a decade.

In March 1995, my husband sued former State Police Superintendent Paul Fontenot for transferring him from the State Police Barracks into the prison system without cause in late 1994.

The case was assigned to you. Last year, you finally ruled (when you denied Paul Fontenot summary judgement) that no evidence was presented that my husband had violated any disciplinary rule at the Barracks. Last December, you ruled there was an apparent agreement to house my husband at the Barracks in protective custody.

For nearly a decade I have watched my husband suffer while you have allowed delay after delay in response to frivolous briefs filed at taxpayer expense on behalf of the defendant(s). This is monstrously unfair to my husband and Louisiana taxpayers who are now paying two law firms hundreds of dollars an hour to defend Mr. Fontenot and the present Superintendent of the State Police, Terry Landry.

This summer, you named Mr. Landry a defendant in this case because Mr. Fontenot is no longer Superintendent of the State Police. Mr. Fontenot has not been Superintendent for nearly seven years (since January 1996). Why wasn't his successor named a defendant in the case seven years ago? I cannot imagine why this belatedly became so important. In any event, it now seems to be the cause of even more delays in this case.

I would remind you that this case becomes moot in April 2011—just seven years from now—when my husband discharges his sentence. It's been before you for nearly 10 years, so it's not inconceivable that it might still be pending in your court then.

Please make a final ruling. To do otherwise is exceedingly cruel. My husband does not deserve to twist slowly in the wind any longer while more time is frittered away on extraneous issues that do not reach the heart of this matter.

Noland never acknowledged my letter. A month later, on August 14, the *Advocate* published a story by Alan Sayre, an Associated Press reporter, that detailed Noland's delays, noting that the Fifth Circuit Court of Appeals had sent Billy's case back to her twice, rejecting Fontenot's "claim that Sinclair's suit was frivolous."

BY1997, THE PAROLE BOARD'S OFFICIAL bias against Billy was obvious. Aaron Brooks, an assistant DA in the East Baton Rouge Parish district attorney's office, called Billy "an opportunist who saw the offer of a pardon-for-sale as a means of getting out of prison," according to an account of the hearing in the *Beaumont Enterprise*.

I seethed with anger as I heard Brooks call my husband a fraud. He lied again when he said Billy was a fourth offender. He knew the corrections department had corrected Billy's record in 1994, listing him as a second offender, instead of a fourth offender. He lied a third time when he said Billy was a cold-blooded murderer. He knew there was mitigating evidence in the 1965 offense report proving that Billy did not shoot J. C. Bodden down in cold blood—evidence that was suppressed at Billy's trial.

Billy filed an ethics complaint against Brooks with the Louisiana State Bar Association. The state bar's Committee on Professional Responsibility conducted an extensive investigation. In 2000, the committee sanctioned Brooks, finding that he had knowingly and deliberately misrepresented Billy's criminal history to the parole board.

In 1994, after the parole board refused to recognize his second-offender status, Billy filed a second lawsuit against the board. The lawsuit worked its way up to the Louisiana First Circuit Court of Appeals. In September 1997, the court ruled that even though Billy was "fully rehabilitated," parole was a state-given privilege that did not enjoy constitutional protections. The parole board could deny a parole to an inmate for any reason or no reason at all.

This ruling, and others in different cases, allowed the department of corrections and the parole board to act with little regard for due process or fairness. It allowed Billy's opposition to use their political influence to repeatedly deny Billy a parole under Governors Edwin Edwards and Mike Foster. It also allowed the East Baton Rouge Parish district attorney's office and the department of corrections to continue hiding the real facts in his case.

It took Billy six years of legal battles in the 1990s to get the FBI and the Louisiana state police to agree that the single 1962 juvenile delinquency adjudication was not an adult felony conviction and that the juvenile adjudication never should have been put in his adult criminal record.

In 1998, he received a letter from Louisiana State Police Captain Randolph F. Johnson saying erroneous information on his state police rap sheet had been corrected as of October 13, 1998 and that the corrected information was forwarded to the FBI. It also corrected its record. Both listed Billy as a second offender.

Still, the parole board continued to ignore the state police and corrections department files, relying instead on false information in the 1979 Patin report.

Each time there was a parole hearing, the victim's family and the Istrouma-based opposition appeared to oppose Billy's release. Each time they damned him as a "cold-blooded killer" who was a fourth felony offender undeserving of parole consideration. At parole hearings from 1999 to 2003, all three board members voted against paroling him. The more time Billy served without a write-up, the harsher their votes became. There was more than enough merit in Billy's record. The parole board's treatment of Billy bore no resemblance to the rule of law.

By 2002, he had served thirty-seven years in prison, twenty-five of them without a disciplinary write-up. He was the only inmate who didn't try to buy a pardon. He was an accomplished prison writer with national journalism awards. A Louisiana appeals court ruled that he was "clearly rehabilitated." Corrections officials had publicly endorsed his rehabilitation. A parole board chairman had called his rehabilitation "outstanding." His release efforts were supported by a diverse spectrum of people, including the prestigious Metropolitan Crime Commission. His accomplishments and rehabilitation made no difference to the board.

A woman who loves a lifer must cross a sea of despair. I nearly drowned until I reached my own epiphany: Hope was the killer stalking me. It set me up before each pardon and parole hearing and smashed me to pieces each time we lost. I wrote a letter to each of Louisiana's governors in turn, stressing the merit and rehabilitation in Billy's case. I lived in a purgatory of suspense, swinging between elation and despair, as I waited for decisions from the pardon board, and then the parole board, in his case.

Hate exploded inside me like lava erupting from a volcano after each denial, triggering a battle with my conscience. There is no Christian rationale for hatred. But repentance and rehabilitation don't count in the barbaric world that revenge creates. Revenge doesn't concern itself with the suffering of another, no matter how intense, prolonged, or terrible.

On December 9, 1997, I watched a killer die as victims' families rejoiced. I was covering his execution for KBMT-TV, an ABC affiliate in Beaumont. That night, I was also chosen to be a pool reporter.

The state selected pool reporters to watch executions and describe them to other reporters who couldn't get in the witness room because it was so small. I was packed in shoulder to shoulder with another pool reporter, corrections officials, and members of the victims' families. A wall divided the witness room in half. A friend of the condemned man waited on the other side.

The inmate the state was about to kill, Michael Lee Lockhart, was stretched out on a gurney, crucifixion style, with needles in both arms. He was only a few feet away on the other side of a large glass window. We were told he would be dead in less than ten minutes.

A minister stood next to Lockhart, his hand on the inmate's ankle. It was the only place on Lockhart's body that his flesh was exposed, except for his arms where the intravenous needles were inserted.

The minister told me later that Lockhart was not afraid because his faith was real.

"I've assisted in thirty executions," he'd said. "I know when it's real and when it's not."

The minister left his hand on Lockhart's ankle throughout the execution so the condemned man would know he was not facing death alone.

"I'm ready, Warden." Lockhart's last statement was a quietly controlled flow of words. His voice was steady and easily audible. It included an apology to relatives of his victims. As his lungs collapsed with a rush of air that sounded like a cough, screams of grief erupted from Lockhart's friend on the other side of the wall. The victims' families appeared unmoved by her agonized cries. They had laughed and talked excitedly like they were on their way to a picnic as they walked into the death house before the execution. Now they were pressed silently against the window of the death chamber, watching him die. When he was pronounced dead, they turned away from the window smiling.

I mentioned little about the victims' reactions to prevent bias in my story. But I had no doubt that I had just witnessed a murder. I moved up to the window for a last look at Lockhart. His body was light blue. Prison officials said lethal injections starved the body of oxygen. They claimed it was a painless way to kill prisoners.

Outside the prison in Huntsville where Lockhart was executed, busloads of Beaumont, Texas, cops in uniform were squirting bourbon out of hypodermic needles into their mouths. "Joy juice," they called it. They erupted in cheers when Lockhart's death was announced.

I knew Lockhart well by the time he was executed. In early June 1997, six months before his execution, I interviewed him and edited a story about him. As I rolled the tapes of his interview back and forth, looking for edit points, I became familiar with his tone of voice, his gestures, and the variety of expressions on his face. He glanced away and then back at the camera, again and again, searching his mind for answers to my questions, wincing at queries about his crimes, refusing to answer them directly except for coded references to his victims, referring to conversations he had with them that perhaps only took place in his mind.

"Wendy and Jennifer know," he said. "I can't talk about it. But they know."

I was prepared for a con. Lockhart's legal appeals were exhausted. He knew a death date would be set for him soon. Perhaps he wanted to leave something on the record that would make sense of his life. I decided he was mentally ill. It was the only explanation for crimes like his. He said he was reading books to try and understand what was wrong with him.

Except for my interview with Lockhart in June and the second interview I did with him a few days before his execution, we had no other contact. The case was big news in southeast Texas. My June interview had been a big coup for KBMT. Until he talked to me on camera that summer, Lockhart had refused all interview requests for ten years.

His crimes were savage. He raped and disemboweled two teenage girls when he found them at home alone—one in Indiana, the other in Florida. On the run in Texas after the murders, he shot and killed a Beaumont cop to avoid arrest. Was there any sense to be made of his life?

My photographer, a twentysomething, wisecracking, tobacco-chewing good ole boy from southeast Texas was stunned as we left the death row visiting area after our June interview with Lockhart. His view through the camera lens—a tight close-up of Lockhart's face—left him shaken. There was a disconnect between the monster he had read about and the man he saw.

"Jesus," he said. "He's a human being."

I flashed back to a meeting with Louisiana's corrections secretary, C. Paul Phelps, in 1981 when I was asking for permission to interview inmates on Angola's death row for my Channel 9 series on the death penalty. The Wyoming native had a laconic way of expressing himself. He leaned back in a big leather chair in his office to size me up. He cocked his head and squinted at me before he replied.

"I never look at a man in a cell like an animal. I always remind myself that he's a human being no matter what he's done."

In our June interview, Lockhart told me he was afraid of the voices in his head that urged him to kill girls. He said he had checked himself into an Ohio mental hospital to control them. On the admittance form he was required to fill out, he wrote that he was "afraid of hurting someone." He said his family was ashamed of his commitment and persuaded him to check out of the hospital. He left a trail of blood across three states after his release.

I left Huntsville for Beaumont after Lockhart's execution, driving in the dark for two hours through dense fog in east Texas's Big Thicket. Sections of Texas 105, the two-lane blacktop that snakes through the heart of the Thicket, disappeared again and again behind the fog's thick white curtain as we crested low hills surrounded by a thick forest of pines. The headlights' glare reflected back into the car, blinding me and the news intern riding with me as we hurtled through the dark trying to reach the station in time to get my story on the air.

Tears came later in the station's garage, after I finished my 10:00 p.m. live shot from the newsroom at the start of the newscast. It was the only place I could be alone. I sat on a tire under the light of a single bulb, next to the live shot truck, with the Texas Department of Corrections press kit in my hands. It was the most complete press kit of any kind I had ever seen.

I stared at the names of the dead, their crimes, county of conviction, method of death, time of death, place of death, last statement, items ordered for the last meal—a statistical nightmare that buried the ugly fact of state-sanctioned murder in petty detail. I cried at the savagery I had seen that night—the smiles, the grins, the laughter, the cheers, the hypodermic needles full of "joy juice," the offhand conduct of the corrections officials who witnessed the execution. I thought of Billy. I knew that's how his victim's family and their friends would have reacted at his execution.

Years later, I read in the *New York Times* that revenge was rooted in altruism. It was programmed into our DNA millions of years ago as we rose from hominid to human in Africa. Any hominid jeopardizing the safety of the group had to be punished. That is why, the article proposed, revenge brings such deep feelings of pleasure and righteousness, and forgiveness pales beside the ancient god embedded in our genes. The man I met in 1981 in Louisiana's death house had brought me face-to-face with its brutality.

SURVIVING HIS SENTENCE

"Do what you can, with what you have, where you are."
—Theodore Roosevelt, twenty-sixth president of the United States, 1858–1919

AN EROTIC BOND BETWEEN ME and Billy Sinclair was evident in the fantasies that secretly haunted us both in the days after we met. The passion grew more intense as our marriage matured under the watchful eyes of guards in Angola's visiting room. It was a huge room with dozens of cafeteria-type tables for inmates and their families to visit. Prison officials ironically called them "full contact visits."

When they ended, I watched him walk away down a long corridor into the main prison, my body alive to every change in his gait, focused on his diminishing figure, until it was swallowed up by bars and cyclone fencing. Until I saw him again, I would only have his voice near midnight when he was allowed to call me. When he called, I could almost feel his caress.

I could feel the heat in his gaze when he looked at me across the table in the visiting shed. Our expressions never changed as we spoke our desires instead of living them. Our words glowed like hot ingots. His whispers were like small flames licking my ear. The noise and visitors around us would fade away. I sat with my body pressed against the table, yearning to feel his body against mine. I dreamed of the day we would have hours alone.

I almost always wore his favorite dress for our visits. He said he could see the shape of my body best in that dress, the curve of my waist, the length of my back as it rounded into my hips. He would hold his hands out together in front of me, thumb touching thumb, spanning the width of my ribs and then drawing his hands in the air down toward my waist the way he would if he could touch me. In letters, he called me "Baby Lion," a nickname he made up after my sign on the zodiac and my small size.

His hands were so big, they covered mine. He loved my blue eyes and the square shape of my jaw, a clue, he said, to my uncommon determination. He touched curls that fell across my forehead, his big hands awkwardly patting unruly waves into place. He sat as close to me as he could, breathing in my natural body odor and perfume. He called them a powerful aphrodisiac.

He marveled at my red polished nails, my high heels, and the shape of my ankles and calves. He watched me like a hawk. He was storing up memories, he said, visions he could replay in his mind until the next time I could visit. His prodigious memory for detail came from years of being locked alone in a cell. His eyes were starved for sights the average man had long since relegated to the mundane.

He told me I married half a man because he wasn't free. But I saw in him a phoenix with extraordinary achievements in the face of terrible odds. I was six and a half years older than he was, but he was in all important ways my senior. Billy Sinclair was a sophisticate, adept at deciphering body language and motivation, a skill honed to the fine precision necessary for survival behind bars. He had seen more of reality in his almost two decades behind bars than I had with all my education and travels. But he was always indulgent with me, sharing his brutal world without shame or patronizing explanations. He listened intently when I explained things that I deemed important, touching his face, tracing his mustache as I spoke. He would smile at me then, his eyes crinkling in amusement at the differences in our worlds.

He was six feet tall and heavily muscled when we met. At barely five feet tall, my head just reached the middle of his shirt pocket when I stood beside him. His body reflected his phenomenal will and the strength of his character. His dark eyes, hair, and mustache were part of what was so striking about him. When we met, his easy smile and self-confidence made me wonder about his roots. He had an air of command, a natural sort of authority. He never seemed to feel fear in a place where sporadic violence took lives without warning. One day, he laughingly told me he was part Native American.

"Billy Sinclair," I laughed. "You're all Scotch-Irish."

His first names, Billy Wayne, followed an old Southern tradition. The deep South was full of "Joe Bobs" and "Larry Dons." White boys with double first names were usually the sons of dirt-poor itinerant Southerners. And so was he. His last name was Scottish.

Billy stood up for himself in prison. He fought off a rape when he was eighteen years old after he was sent to Angola to do time on the carnal knowledge conviction. Prison rapes often prompted little more than a wink and a nod from guards. New inmates, especially if they were young, were frequent targets.

At Angola, inmates only had two ways to satisfy themselves sexually: sodomy or masturbation. Many prisoners didn't believe "studs"—inmates on the dominant side of the homosexual coupling—were gay. Louisiana's legislature all but openly endorsed homosexual sex when it refused to let husbands have real "full-contact visits" with their wives.

"It's masturbation or another man," Billy said when I asked him about sex in prison.

"Have you ever been with another man?"

"No. I'm not homosexual."

"Did anybody ever try to rape you?"

"Yeah."

"What happened?"

"I got a ball bat and broke his arm."

It sounded like the classic fuck-or-fight scene in a prison movie. He said he got forty days in the hole on bread and water for the assault—two pieces of bread with a tablespoon of oatmeal in the center for breakfast and two pieces of bread with a tablespoon of spinach in the center for dinner.

Nothing in my background had prepared me for the penal system's callous brutality and the guards' mindless adherence to rules. Over and over again, I complained about it to Billy. Over and over again he told me I would have to "suck it up" and adjust. He warned me that the guards could stop our visits if I didn't smile at them, if I asked questions, if I insisted on knowing why certain regulations and rules were imposed on visitors.

Billy warned me that I should always be afraid of some guards. They would taunt and tear at an inmate's sensibilities until blood ran in his mouth from biting his cheeks to stay silent. They roamed the prison like gunslingers, trying to shove an inmate off balance so they'd get a retort that they could classify as insolent or disrespectful. Then they could write him up and put him in lockdown.

A blowup was inevitable. That spring, a few months after our marriage in 1982, I sent Billy a pocket-size atlas with a map of Scotland so he could see how close Edinburgh is to the Arctic Circle and Sinclair Street, one of the oldest thoroughfares in the ancient Scottish city, named for his family. The Sinclairs were one of the twelve most important clans in Scottish history.

The atlas had a picture of the Sinclair family crest, its tartan and a brief history of the family, its origins in Normandy, and the original French version of their name—St. Clair. It was a treasure trove of information about his roots and medieval times in Scotland that were full of action.

The prison sent it back. Not allowed, the mailroom said. It breached security. I raged at the news. How could a small pocket-size atlas, with no roads except those in Edinburgh in a foreign country thousands of miles away, threaten security?

I sent Billy pictures showing him how we could furnish our home. I checked ads for furniture in the newspaper, searching for a coffee table, shelves to hold our books, and a large brown velvet sofa. I planned the rooms around a need that most men take for granted: a place to stretch out and relax at home. Never again would his feet hang off the end of a short, thin, rigid cot at Angola.

I took Polaroid pictures of the furniture I planned to buy in department stores. Billy had never had a real home. I smiled at the thought of his amazement when he saw the pictures and the love he knew would be waiting for him.

The prison sent the pictures back. I had mailed them in a small box stuffed with newspaper to keep them from tearing open an envelope. An officer I talked to after they were sent back said inmates were only allowed to have packages that came from a retail store. I sent the pictures to Billy again. I put a long piece of stiff cardboard in a big envelope, hoping it would protect them.

My outrage finally boiled over on a Saturday in July. I arrived at Angola that morning tired and irritated. The drive from Houston the night before had worn me out. I was staying in a truckers' motel, a cheap place for overnighters and my regular stopping place every two weeks. It was home to me more than once on Christmas.

When the slow seesaw of a mattress in the room above me began to accelerate, I got dressed and stepped into the muggy night, waiting until the rut upstairs was over before I went back to bed. Then I prayed the window unit would cool the room down enough for me to fall asleep. I left for Angola early the next morning, still tired from the trip the night before.

When I rounded the first bend in the Angola road, I slammed on the brakes. It was jackhammered to pieces. Gravel spurted under my wheels. The car lurched and potholes threatened the axles. Mud splattered the front and side of the car and the windshield. I drove through the rubble at fifteen miles an hour with the car bucking and shaking under me. There were no warning signs the road was under construction. Anger boiled up inside me at the lack of concern for those who regularly had to use the road—backwoods rednecks and inmates' visitors.

At the front gate, a guard searched my purse and found a stamp in my wallet. She lectured me in sarcastic tones about smuggling contraband into the prison. No one had ever told me a stamp was contraband. I tried to discuss the issue with her. I thought she would understand that I was merely commenting on the lack of information Angola gave visitors. I told her my husband was a trusty with no write-ups on his record. I wouldn't try to smuggle in contraband. But she made it personal. She said the man I married was trash.

"They all alike down there." She kept repeating the words in a singsong tone with a sly smile on her face.

"No," I told her evenly, "my husband is not the same as others." But she kept up the chant until I cut it off.

"Never speak to me in that tone again," I snapped at her. "Do you hear me? My husband isn't like the rest and don't you ever forget it."

She stepped back, surprised at the cold, hard tone in my voice. Then she laughed along with other guards in the room as I went outside to wait on the bus to take me down to the main prison's visiting room. I was seething with resentment at Angola's rigid policies and the sting of laughter deriding my helplessness.

I went back into the front gate processing center and demanded my stamp. Outside, I dropped it in the glove box, satisfied it was one thing Angola could not take from me. When I returned, the guard patted me down again. Her sly smile told me my outburst had been an unexpected bonus on her shift. But I wasn't through with her. Before getting on the bus that would take me to the visiting shed, I turned around and addressed her directly.

"Go out and search my car," I ordered her like a drill sergeant. "Look for the machine gun and all the dope I'm planning to smuggle in."

Then I took the bus down to the main prison to see Billy. The next day, he was notified that I had been suspended for three months. But Warden Maggio allowed me to visit Billy once to attend an event at the prison. He reassigned the guard to a watchtower at one of Angola's out-camps on the graveyard shift from six in the evening until six in the morning. She had charged me with smuggling. The warden suspended me for three months.

During spring 1983, I toyed with the idea of suicide. There was no sign Billy would ever come home. I had found the perfect place to end my pain. It was a rest stop on the westbound side of I-10 about twenty miles from the Texas border. It had a man-made lake four hundred yards from the parking lot. Pine trees towered over the water. I could lie down at dusk in the tall reeds near the water's edge, take a lethal dose of pills, throw the pill bottle in the water, watch it sink out of sight, put the gun in my mouth, and pull the trigger.

Anyone trying to save me from the gunshot wound wouldn't know that pills were slowly killing me. But my battle with the death penalty when I wrote my series for Channel 9 reverberated in my head:

"Thou shalt not kill. Ever. Even yourself."

Suicide is murder. It was a mortal sin in the eyes of the Catholic Church. And Billy's enemies would laugh and mock his grief, saying they knew I was crazy. Suicide would leave him to battle them alone and break my pledge to stay by his side. Alive, I could be a perpetual thorn in their sides. I smiled at the idea every time the rest stop receded in my rearview mirror on my drives back to Texas after a visit with Billy. And I never thought about suicide again.

I concentrated on learning to live alone, stringing out tasks one at a time to make the hours pass. Housekeeping made me feel normal. I had been a housewife for years, safe and secure at home while a husband earned a living and dealt with the outside world. Dusting, watering indoor plants, washing clothes, moving furniture, rearranging pictures, sweeping floors, and beating rugs burned off energy and revived feelings of security.

Housework became therapy at the end of a broom. It focused my attention on things I could do something about. Calm returned. Control reasserted itself. The fear of tomorrow, an impoverished old age, the highway, the pain of living without Billy, temporarily went out with the dust.

I tried to live as normal a life as possible. I went to weddings, funerals, and movies, ate out with friends, attended parties, visited museums, followed the stock market, planted flowers in terra-cotta pots on the patio in springtime, planned vacations I never took, browsed in bookstores, took aerobics classes, watched my diet, balanced the checkbook, paid income taxes, and never stopped missing Billy.

When I saw other inmate families on my trips to Angola to see Billy, my heart bled. We were all as suspect and reviled as the men we visited. I was struggling to accept my new role in my life, but I had far more resources to deal with the anguish and expense than they did. I will never forget a woman I met a few years after I became Billy's wife. Her pain and despair were typical of what I saw so often in other visitors.

We were sitting in the lobby outside Angola's main visiting room waiting for a prison bus to take us back to the prison's front gate. She was an older African American woman who looked like somebody's maid. White middle class stuck out all over me.

She was worried about her son. I was worried about my husband. We stared across the room at the bars now separating us from our loved ones. Age showed on her face in the deep wrinkles that ran from nose to chin.

"Lord, if I'd'a known they was gonna let me have such a short visit with him, I'd'a never come today," she said suddenly.

Politely, I glanced in her direction. A dime-store wig curled perfectly from under her knit cap, the flat waves shining dully in the sunshine.

"I hardly got in there 'fore they called out his name to go back. I ain't got but one day off, you know."

A guard leaving the building opened the door to the parking lot. A biting breeze blew across our legs. She reached down as if to brush it off. A tan-colored gabardine-looking coat was buttoned securely around her ample form. Slowly, she wrapped and unwrapped her wallet in a white handkerchief to keep her hands busy. Silence settled between us.

Suddenly, she was speaking again:

"It ain't right the way they do 'em. If it wasn't for us, they wouldn't have nuthin', if we didn't leave 'em a few dollars when we visit. They supposed to get that orange juice every day. But you know they don't. It just ain't right."

She sat impassively, her resentment a burning thing.

"What's your boy in for?" I asked.

For the first time, she looked directly at me. Her brown eyes accepted me without question. She shrugged her shoulders.

"I ain't sure. But he's got sixty-six years on him."

I stared at the flagstone floor. Carefully, I veered my thoughts away from my husband's life sentence.

"How long have you been coming up here?" I asked.

Thought furrowed her brow. She hesitated, rolling her eyes up toward the brim of her cap.

"Since 1976."

We went on waiting for the bus. I turned away and stared out across the parking lot. Angola's fields stretched into the distance; the winter grass was still green against the prison's white fences. Cattle grazed under the clear blue sky. Louisiana's Tunica Hills rose up brown against the skyline. In the distance, I saw the visitors' bus coming down the main prison road. We hurried across the parking lot when it arrived. Quickly, she settled in a seat in the sun and patted the seat beside her.

"Sun'll keep us warm till they get started."

I sat down beside her. We were the only two on the bus. A stretch of green lawn ran from the main prison to the road. A white lattice gazebo in the middle of the lawn looked strange without flowers. She stared out the window at the dirt in the empty beds.

"Fieldwork. No cause to have my boy doin' fieldwork. Looks like they'd wanna teach him a trade. Ain't no fields in New Orleans. What's a boy gonna do if he cain't earn no living where he's from?"

Other women filled a few of the seats behind us. The bus lurched forward in spurts, grinding its way through several gears as it accelerated. We passed herds of cattle. I wondered idly who cared for them. I had never seen inmates in those fields. Off to the right, more fields stretched a muddy brown to the horizon. Mid-afternoon sunshine lay across the land and high cirrus clouds streaked across the sky to the west. I knew it would be colder than the night before. A hard freeze, they said. I worried about Billy. Heaters in the trusty dormitories worked none too well, and the prison only issued two thin blankets. I knew he wouldn't be warm.

My visits to see Billy at Angola stopped in September 1984 while I pursued my master's degree in journalism at Columbia University. That fall, he had the flu for weeks. His deep cough interrupted our phone calls. It hung on for a month while I worried that he would develop pneumonia in Angola's dank environment.

In April 1985, he spent a week in Angola's hospital with a putrefying purple knot where a spider bit him mid-calf on his right leg. Until necrosis set in, hospital personnel accused him of cutting his leg and spitting in it to cause an infection, something prisoners did to avoid fieldwork or to be moved to the hospital's relative comfort from a cell. I was wild to fly home. I thought his leg might have to be amputated. But he refused to let me spend the money. A letter he wrote that fall still lives in my mind.

> *Angola, 1984*
> *Dear Jodie:*
> *The power to dream is the only true source of meaning in life.*
> *As a child, I dreamed of faraway places, fascinated with the white lines of an open highway zipping along beneath me. There had to be a place without abuse, torment and hate.*
> *As a teenager I dreamed of playing for the New York Yankees, of one day meeting Mickey Mantle, the greatest baseball player ever to play the game. As a petty thief, I dreamed of a "big score" only to end up marked for the electric chair.*
> *As an inmate, I dreamed of a woman who would bring balm to my failed life. The moment I saw Jodie Sinclair, I knew she had come.*
> *One day, the power to dream will set us free.*

I graduated from Columbia in May 1985 and took a job reporting for a small network affiliate in Texas close to the Louisiana border to be near Billy. It was just 183 miles from there to Baton Rouge. Angola was only fifty-five miles from Louisiana's state capitol. I drove to Baton Rouge on Friday night and up to Angola for a two-hour visit on Saturday. I drove back to Texas on Sunday.

I worried every time I made a trip that my car might break down or I'd have a flat on the interstate—emergencies I couldn't handle by myself. I didn't know how to change a tire. Personal cell phones didn't yet exist. I played a game to stave off fear for the first few years to make the trips easier. I pretended I was only driving to the next town—from Port Arthur to Lake Charles, from there to Lafayette, and from there to Baton Rouge.

The land was flat, uninteresting terrain. But I was alive with the thrill of seeing my husband. I imagined I was a cloud riding the wind, or a spiral of birds rising from a field or a lone pine on the edge of the road. I sighed with the wind at a Louisiana rest stop, thick and redolent with the scent of pine trees.

I spent money maintaining the car. I replaced every belt and bit of rubber in the engine. I changed the oil and air filter every three thousand miles. I bought new tires and kicked each one before I hit the road. I traveled with sealant in case I developed a flat. But a mechanical breakdown wasn't the only danger on the road.

I came close to being sideswiped near Beaumont one night. The driver had to have been drunk. A tire came bouncing down a freeway overpass in the dark directly at me. A late-model Mercedes-Benz almost ran me off the road near Orange, Texas. But one danger eclipsed them all.

In 1985, I drove through a hurricane off the Louisiana coast between Lafayette and Lake Charles. I was too terrified to cry. Tears would have blurred my vision. I crept along behind an eighteen-wheeler at thirty-five miles an hour, hugging the back of the truck, my eyes burning with the frantic attempt to keep his taillights in view. They were all I could see through the dark and the torrents of water pouring over the windshield as the wind howled and rocked the car. We were alone on the road.

There were no lights in the towns I passed in the dark. The power was knocked out all along the I-10. I could barely see the exit ramps. They were underwater, making me afraid the engine would stall if I tried to get off the freeway. Rain and wind kept battering the car as I crept along. After two hours, the truck reached Lake Charles. Hurricane Juan was behind us by then.

When I reached Baton Rouge after I left Angola that afternoon, I decided to head for Texas instead of spending the night in a motel. It was raining, but there was nothing to indicate that the leading edge of a hurricane were battering the freeway from Lafayette to Lake Charles, and I drove straight into it. When it hit the Louisiana coast two days later as a hurricane, some offshore oil rigs clocked winds as high as ninety-two miles an hour. Hurricane Juan killed twelve people and dropped eighteen inches of rain, flooding coastal towns.

Rain is a frequent companion on roads in east Texas and southwest Louisiana. A trucker once told me that I-10 flooded like no other major road in the United States, setting up the potential for hydroplaning—an irony, I thought, like walking on water at seventy miles an hour to see Billy.

BY THEN, WE WERE VISITING at Butler Park. It was a new privilege at Angola for Class A trustees who had no disciplinary write-ups for a year. Instead of two-hour visits in the main prison, Class A trustees could visit most of the day in Butler Park. The park was a first in Angola's history when it opened in 1985. It stretched across a full acre in the Tunica Hills overlooking the prison's fields about a mile from the front gate. Concrete picnic tables were placed far enough apart to allow inmate families some privacy. It was named for Angola's new warden, Hilton Butler.

Prison officials said it was a new kind of program designed to reinforce good behavior. Inmates secretly believed it was tacit approval for conjugal visits. Some Angola officials were partly responsible for that rumor. They were openly in favor of conjugal visits as a way to reduce homosexual activity and the tension it produced at the prison. If "good" inmates got to sleep with wives and girlfriends in mobile homes once a month, they reasoned, violence would decline.

The policy was working in Mississippi, a state with an equally harsh attitude toward crime. But "normal" sex was a penal policy the Louisiana legislature ignored. Still, some low-ranking prison officials and inmates saw Butler Park as a way around the legislature's refusal to implement the policy.

It resulted in at least one baby. He was born to a lifer's wife nine months after the park opened. He was named Butler in honor of the warden. But write-ups, long-term suspensions, and beefed-up patrols quickly ended inmates' ideas about the park's real purpose. After that, it took an extremely agile or very brazen couple to try having sex in the park. But some intimacy was possible. A furtive caress here, a touch there, a hand on a knee escaped the guards' eyes. The tables where prisoners sat with their wives and girlfriends were on the side of a hill in full view of the guards.

Down the hill, kids were hitting practice balls with inmates who were dads, uncles, or their mother's "friend." Children ran past playing tag. Other inmates and their families were busy setting out food on picnic tables. Smoke curled up from barbecue pits near each table. Visitors and inmates were supposed to barbecue at the park. When prison officials offered a privilege, it was best to accept. Billy said turndowns were an affront.

When I arrived for our first visit at Butler Park, he dumped half a bag of charcoal into the pit near our table, poured lighter fluid on it, and proudly whipped out a box of matches.

"My God, Billy," I said. "That's not the way you light a fire. It's dangerous. It won't stay lit anyway. First, you have to have twigs." I wasn't a Girl Scout. But at least I knew that much.

"Come on," I told him. "Off your duff. I could use some help."

He gathered pieces of small brush with me. We built them into a pyramid in the pit, putting the coals on top with crumpled paper underneath.

"Now the fire won't go out," I told him. "It's got to burn long enough for the coals to catch. You strike the match and it catches the paper. Then the twigs start burning. They burn long enough to ignite the coals. No need for charcoal lighter. It's liable to explode anyway and catch your clothes on fire. Or go out. And it makes the food taste terrible."

I remembered it from camping with my children on summer vacations in the Appalachian Mountains and out west in Wyoming and Montana. I put my arms around Billy and looked up into his eyes.

"Honey," I said gently then. "If your goal is a house in the suburbs with a two-car garage, then you've got to learn to barbecue. It's a religion out there."

I dreamed of sex with Billy. I was still a "virgin bride." We had imagined being together from the first caress to the moment of climax for four years in the main prison's visiting shed. But both of us were afraid of sex in the park. We were sitting side by side at the table, holding hands, thinking about it, when I told him I hated the park.

"I'm afraid we'll give in and get caught. It's getting harder and harder to resist. You know it and I know it. I don't want us to be here anymore."

The potential price for a few furtive moments of fulfillment was too much to pay. We decided to stop visiting at the park. Seeing each other for two hours twice a month was better than a onetime fling during a daylong visit and a permanent suspension.

When we stopped visiting at the park, some of Angola's officials thought Billy was trying to ruin the park's reputation to get revenge for a lecture we got one afternoon when a guard accused us of "suspicious activity" because we were sitting "too close together."

He had marched up the hill, confronted us, and ordered us to separate. Then he gave us a ten-minute dressing down about our flagrant behavior. Billy always kept his eyes on the guards. It was a prison survival habit. But the guard had caught us by surprise. His lecture was humiliating. I listened to the guard without looking at him or saying a word.

IN NOVEMBER 1986, WHEN BILLY was moved into protective custody at the state police barracks in Baton Rouge, we were allowed all-day visits every Sunday. It was just 183 miles from the carport at my Port Arthur, Texas, apartment, at most a three-hour drive one way if the weather was good. If I left at dawn, I could be at the barracks by nine in the morning and back in Port Arthur by seven that night.

I still wrote him every day and usually included one or two newspaper articles. His intense interest in the outside world was a double-edged sword. It gave him an acute sense of what he was missing, but it heightened his suffering. His interest in the "free world," as convicts called it, dated from his death-row days. It helped him escape thoughts of being executed, as each day edged him closer to the electric chair. When he became a lifer, he was determined not to become institutionalized.

Angola had shut out the twentieth century. For many inmates, visits with families inevitably became less frequent as lengthy sentences wore on, reducing their interest in the free world. After years of taking orders, some inmates lost the ability to order their own worlds. Once he was at the state police barracks, Billy was determined to be an even better husband. It led to the only lie he ever told me. I discovered it when I saw fresh needle marks on his arm.

"Tracks," he said, grinning feebly.

A state police bus made two trips a week to a blood bank in Baton Rouge where barracks inmates could sell their blood for ten dollars. Billy went twice a week to make twenty dollars in spite of veins that easily collapsed, making each trip a painful experience. He knew how much money I was spending on gas, maintaining the car and meeting daily expenses on a small TV market salary, coming and going each week to see him. He didn't want to ask me for money to buy "zuzu," the name prisoners gave items they could buy at the barracks' commissary.

He had promised me he would never sell his blood. He went against his word when I gave up a luxury that eased the physical shock of my weekly trips to see him. When he was transferred to the barracks, I gave up the overnight motel to save money, driving two hundred miles on Sunday morning to see him and then back to Texas in one day. He knew the trips left me exhausted, the arthritis in my left hip an inescapable pain after hours in the car with no overnight rest. But I was determined to see him every week.

I sat in his lap in a tent arguing with him. Inmates at the barracks visited in tents that were mesh on four sides to keep mosquitoes out and opaque on the top to protect prisoners and their visitors from the sun. He refused to admit he was wrong. Quietly, stubbornly, he insisted that lying was not the issue. At Angola, he was unable to help me financially. Contributing money to our marriage was a heady new freedom at the barracks.

"It was lying, Billy Sinclair, to hide it from me."

"No, it ain't," he said. "I swore to myself I would tell you if you ever asked."

"Lies, Billy, are lies, whether they're deliberate or lies of omission. What made you such a damn coward that you wouldn't tell me?"

"Don't be so hard, baby. I couldn't take money from you, not with you giving up the motel."

"Damn it, we are not so bad off you have to sell your blood."

He hadn't thought of it as lying. He was trying to care for me. The revulsion I felt at circumstances that would force a man to sell his blood to help his wife rose up to choke me.

In 1989, hope that he might soon be free began to fade when Governor Roemer denied Billy's clemency recommendation. I was shocked. Billy's case had so much merit compared to others. I had been making plans for our life together. We would live in a small place, nothing grand. It would be just big enough for two. Our days and nights would be filled with love and the fun of simple acts: brushing my teeth, smiling at him with a mouth full of foam, watching him laugh, shopping for groceries as we talked about fixing dinner.

We would have a stocked freezer. There would be no empty shelves and cabinets like the green house where he lived as a boy in Rayville, never knowing if he would have more for dinner than a few pieces of bread. The idea that he could open the refrigerator and choose not only the food but the amount was a dazzling proposition.

I saw myself in him: a small child crying in pain at night, nurturing the seeds of decency alone, sheltering unanswered prayers in a silent heart. I was beginning to fear that few if any in power would ever care that prison might compress his final years into protracted agony. But he would always know, no matter what fate held for us, that I saw through the web of lies they wound around him.

Sunday, May 7, 1989
Dear Billy—

We finally said the terrible words to each other on the phone Saturday morning we never thought we'd say—that you might never come home. My love has succeeded in the little it can do for you under our horrible circumstances. It has given you a measure of security, some feeling of normalcy in your otherwise abnormal world.

We have a good marriage in spite of it. We have genuine concern for each other. And deep love. And we are best friends. That was an element missing from our first crazy-in-love, drunk-with-emotion early days. In my heart, I knew it would grow into an abiding, many-faceted love because I knew how deeply we cared for each other.

Although the victim's family has never let us live together, we have a home. It's in our hearts. And we live there as though we had always been together, as though I'd nursed you through all your colds and viruses, as though you'd put up with my cold feet in bed on winter nights and I had put up with your scratchy mustache and you with my less than glamorous mornings and my irritable pre-coffee snits.

Together, we have worked diligently at our marriage. In spite of the constraints it has grown into a mature love that is dependable and comfortable, that lives with no truces or half-hearted commitments in the face of what may be a terrible future.

I will be at your side, with you, part of you and all that you are, and all that you suffer, for the rest of my life. You were what I believed you to be. A true and constant man, trying as hard as you can to right the wrongs you committed in the only way you know how. And you excelled. You were extraordinary. If I never fall asleep in your arms or see your dear face first thing every morning, I will love you nonetheless as though indeed, I had. Your home is in my heart. And my love will abide with you forever.

Still, I wondered how long it would be until we were only alive in someone else's memories and how long it would be before no one alive remembered us. In the middle of the night when the evening's wine wore off or a hot flash pulled me awake, I confronted memories and fears that tugged at me more often as I got older. Some were searing nightmares. Others were dreams that slipped in on bittersweet notes.

Tears slid down my face almost every morning as I drank coffee. I'd think of Sisyphus, condemned to push a rock to the top of a mountain where it slips from his grasp, rolls back to the bottom, and he is forced to start over, or Job, sitting on a filthy pile of rags outside a marketplace, still believing in a merciful God.

I had believed the system would reward a man who had worked so hard to right his wrongs. I had seen it work for others. My life lost its horizon each time the parole board proved me wrong. Hope pushed me to the edge of the cliff. I buried it for good as the parole board denials mounted up.

I lived in twenty-four-hour cycles. I made no long-term plans. Habit took me to work each day. I spent most weekends alone, reading or tending to chores, crying at the slightest frustration, before I went numb again, grateful to feel nothing at all.

Every day, I had to face the fear that I would lose Billy, that he would pay the ultimate price for doing the right thing and exposing the scam: a transfer back to Angola, where he would be killed. The treatment he received when he was abruptly taken from the barracks was horrific.

After Billy's transfer from the state police barracks to the Hunt Correctional Center, he was held in a maximum-security lockdown cell primarily used for disciplinary purposes. It had no heat from the thirtieth of November to the twelfth of December. It flooded during heavy rains that came in with cold fronts. Rain dripped out of the ceiling on his sheets and blanket. He had to shower in cold water. I was not allowed to see him. His attorney was granted a brief visit. She told me about his circumstances.

Curses threatened to explode out of my throat when I thought of his enemies. Hunt's warden, C. M. "Marty" Lensing, had been Maggio's deputy warden when Boss Ross returned to Angola during the Treen administration. Lensing had never been a fan of the *Angolite*. He welcomed the opportunity to cut Billy Sinclair down to the size of a regular inmate. I damned him and all the rest of the officials and Billy's enemies gloating over his transfer from the barracks to the hellhole at Hunt and swore I would do everything I could to expose their unwarranted malice and inhumanity. I would be the devil they couldn't lock up.

I wrote all of Billy's supporters, describing the conditions at Hunt and the abrupt, irrational reason for his transfer from the barracks. I asked them, in the name of decency, to write or call Governor Edwards and Corrections Secretary Stalder to protest the transfer. Billy was never given a disciplinary report for kissing me in public because there was no rule or regulation prohibiting it. Every prison in Louisiana allowed an inmate to kiss his wife or girlfriend at the beginning and end of each visit.

Although we had no proof, the only logical reason for the transfer was "catch-back" for his role in exposing the pardon-selling scam. Just as Joe Whitmore had warned us, there were people in the Edwards administration who wanted Billy back in Angola where he would be killed. It was our turn to pay the piper. Whitmore had already paid a severe price for his role in uncovering so much corruption at Angola in the wake of the pardons selling revelations. He lost his office in the Criminal Intelligence department and had to work from his car.

I wouldn't let them kill Billy without a fight. On Monday, December 19, 1994, I held a press conference on the steps of the federal courthouse in Baton Rouge about the punitive and inhumane conditions my husband was enduring at Hunt. I had letters from Billy describing his brutal confinement to deliver to US district judge Frank Polozola. Polozola had federal oversight over most of the Louisiana prison system.

In an article in the *Morning Advocate* the next day, Fontenot told the reporter he had observed "a convicted murderer . . . playing kissy face . . . that was grounds in my opinion to transfer him. I ordered it." He also denied knowing anything about the conditions at Hunt. The day after my press conference, Warden Lensing personally went to Billy's cell to inform him that he would be transferred to the David Wade Correctional Center in Homer, Louisiana, ten miles south of the Arkansas border.

A personal letter from Jack Martzell to Governor Edwards had blocked Billy's transfer back to Angola. Martzell told Edwards he would be held responsible if any harm came to Billy at Angola. It was Jack's way of telling Edwards that he knew what the governor was up to and that he should back off. Edwards did.

Rank greeted Billy at the Wade Correctional Center with a sneer.

"Hello, asshole," the sergeant said. "You ain't layin' out no more."

The officials at Wade were openly hostile. They scheduled Billy for a "mental adjustment." Orders from corrections headquarters said he should be stripped of all privileges, influence, or importance. He would spend a month in lockdown to "get his mind right," as one official put it. Other inmates on the tier told him that the officers had orders to "fuck with him." He was hungry most of the time that month. One day, an inmate orderly pulled a regular tray, loaded with food, off the food cart and started to hand it into Billy's cell. An officer stopped him and pointed to a tray with scant amounts of food. It was meant for Billy.

On December 28, Billy went before a disciplinary board at Wade to answer charges in a nondisciplinary "incident report" about his transfer from the barracks. The officer in charge of the proceedings found him "guilty of transfer." Months later, a handwritten administrative appeal that Billy filed about the transfer resulted in a ruling that the transfer was nondisciplinary and any and all references to guilt on Billy's part would be stricken from the record. His record of good behavior remained unblemished.

When I was finally allowed to see Billy, he had on an orange jumpsuit, prison flip-flops, and handcuffs like a dangerous maximum-security prisoner. The cuffs were attached to a chain around his waist. A "black box" between his wrists prevented him from moving his hands up or down more than two inches. There were chains and cuffs around his ankles, forcing him to hobble instead of walk. I watched his fingers swell up and deep red chafe marks appear on his wrists. Until late February, when he was deemed to have partially completed his "readjustment," he was shackled every time I was allowed to see him.

I was only allowed to talk to him once a month for ten minutes. I wondered if isolation was one of the methods meant to break him down. I protested bitterly to Wade's warden. Kelly Ward wrote me back on March 2, 1995, to inform me that inmates assigned to DWCC's working cell blocks could have one ten-minute phone call a week. When I received no calls, I protested again. After a month of "mental adjustment," Billy was transferred to general population in a unit called N-5, a special management unit at Wade for inmates in protective custody.

A former Angola warden, C. Murray Henderson, Luis Quintero-Cruz, Bernardo Vasquez, Ernest Comeaux, and Sam Teague were among N-5's most infamous prisoners. The former warden was convicted of trying to kill his wife. Quintero-Cruz and Vasquez, under orders from Pablo Escobar, assassinated Barry Seal, one of the most important drug informants in US history. Billy had spent nearly a month confined with them on a tier in the EBR jail after he was taken into protective custody in 1986. Comeaux was a former Lafayette Parish sheriff's detective convicted of serial rape. Teague was a former teacher and church youth leader convicted of molesting young boys with whom he came in contact.

Billy was assigned to N-5's Crew 20. While other general population "farm lines" sometimes "laid in," Crew 20 worked every day on the nastiest jobs at the prison. Inmates called it the "shit detail." Crew 20 worked in ankle-deep raw sewage in the "snake pit," Wade's sewer pond, chopping and cutting high grass. They waded through the pond with dull swing blades chopping down thick johnsongrass more than six feet high in record summer heat in 1995. They cleared piney woods from the driveway leading to Wade from its front gate.

Billy turned the work into a rebellious game that let inmates "beat the man" every day without breaking any rules. Drenched with sweat, the crew voluntarily worked harder and harder every day. It perplexed their "line pushers," corrections officers assigned to make them work. Billy set the pace, the mood, and the attitude on the crew. None of the inmates on Crew 20 complained. It was their *Bridge on the River Kwai*. They often whistled the movie's theme song as they worked, commemorating the heroic British soldiers forced into virtual slave labor in Japanese prison camps under inhumane conditions during World War II.

I swelled with pride when I read Billy's letter about the game. He had turned Crew 20 into a close-knit, hardworking group of inmates who robbed the prison system of the power to punish them by embracing the punishment. Crew 20 built a baseball field, planted grass on its field, and made it grow when prison officials swore it wouldn't work. They carved out a baseball diamond infield with shovels and rakes and reconstructed a jogging path around the ball field. They hauled dirt and grass on square pieces of wood to plant on the field when they didn't have wheelbarrows.

I pictured him picking blades of grass one at a time from the edges of the cyclone fence topped with razor wire that surrounded N-5 in July and August when temperatures normally hovered near the century mark and he slept on the concrete floor in his cell, the only cool place in the cell block, until midnight or so.

Inmates cooked in the summer's unrelenting heat. I followed stories all over the country about its deadly effects on prisoners. A *Los Angeles Times* report revealed that in 1991, three inmates died on the same day in a California prison during a heat wave. A prison official told reporters "the legislature might not stop laughing until Christmas" at a request for air-conditioning.

In the free world, the killer aspects of heat waves did concern the public. Temperatures of 105 degrees in the Dallas–Fort Worth area had hospitals preparing for heatstroke victims over the Fourth of July holiday in 1997. In 1999, summer heat killed a forty-five-year-old M. D. Anderson genetic scientist in Houston working in his yard.

After eighteen months on Crew 20, Billy was reassigned to the laundry. Working in the laundry was not as hot as fieldwork. It had big fans that helped to keep the temperature at tolerable levels. I quit worrying about heatstroke.

THE WADE CORRECTIONAL CENTER HOUSED a scandal so revolting it ended the career of an illustrious federal judge and raised questions about the ethics of Louisiana Corrections Secretary Stalder. It exploded in New Orleans in 1997 in a TV series on WWL-TV, and Billy was the source.

The story was about the friendship between Henry Politz, the chief judge of the Fifth Circuit Court of Appeals, and Gilbert Gauthe, a Catholic priest convicted in the worst pedophile scandal in Louisiana history. Gauthe was one of the first priests convicted of child sexual abuse crimes in the United States.

Between 1972 and 1982, Gauthe molested at least three hundred boys in four parishes in southwest Louisiana. In 1983, he was arrested on dozens of child molestation charges. But Judge Politz arranged a plea bargain that allowed the pedophilic priest to escape a life sentence for rape. In 1985, in return for a guilty plea, Gauthe was sentenced to twenty years in prison where he was to undergo psychiatric treatment. But after Judge Politz intervened, Gauthe was transferred to Wade, where he was assigned to N-5.

Judge Politz frequently visited the former priest in N-5 in a special attorney/client visiting room in Wade's administration building that was off-limits to security personnel. Secretary Stalder also allowed Gauthe to start a "special projects program" in the prison's laundry where N-5 inmates worked. He was given his own air-conditioned room where he painted portraits of young prisoners. Soon the paintings covered the room's windows, sealing it off from official view.

The priest and the federal judge were also allowed to set up a "prison ministry" that became a cover for Politz's visits with juvenile inmates in the attorney/client visiting rooms. It was rumored and widely believed, by both inmates and security personnel alike, that the so-called prison ministry visits were actually illegal sexual liaisons between the judge and the young inmates. Gauthe was rumored to be sexually abusing the inmates in his private room in the laundry. The pedophile priest had been at Wade for ten years, but he was moved shortly after Billy's arrival. The shocking stories about him remained.

In 1997, Bill Elder, a popular New Orleans anchor and investigative reporter at WWL-TV, told me that a high-level ring of pedophiles was operating in New Orleans. He suspected Judge Politz was part of it. He said he didn't think he could ever prove it, but he was convinced the ring existed.

Elder was a Peabody Award winner, an honor reserved for broadcast reporters who broke the "most powerful, enlightening and invigorating stories in TV, radio and online media." He was a two-time winner of the Edward R. Murrow Award, named for the pioneering CBS journalist. He was also a friend.

Elder had been suspicious of Politz and his strange relationship with Gilbert Gauthe for a long time. When he learned Billy was at

Wade, in the same unit where Gauthe had been held, he asked permission to talk to Billy. He had interviewed Billy on death row and again when Billy started winning national journalism awards. He knew Billy would have the inside scoop on Gauthe.

On the day of the interview, Elder's photographer set up the equipment in an office in the prison's administration building and rolled the camera, and Elder started questioning Billy. Billy began laying out details of what he knew and had heard about the Politz/Gauthe relationship and their visits at the prison. As the lurid story unfolded, the prison officer assigned to sit in on the interview was aghast at what Billy was telling Elder. She jumped up and bolted out of the room, heading straight for Warden Kelly Ward's office. Within minutes, Ward appeared. His face was beet red.

"You told me this interview was about Sinclair's rehabilitation," the warden spat out. "You never said it was about Gilbert Gauthe."

"I'm sorry you are upset, Warden," Elder responded. "I never said I was here to interview Billy about his rehabilitation. I just said I wanted to talk to him. You assumed it was about his rehabilitation."

"The interview is over," the warden told Elder. Then he motioned to a security guard standing nearby and pointed a finger at Billy.

"Get him back to N-5."

"Are you going to be all right?" Elder whispered to Billy as he removed the mic from Billy's shirt. Billy told me that he smiled at Elder and told him not to worry.

Elder's series on WWL-TV in New Orleans about the kind of special treatment the former Catholic priest was receiving at Wade because of his friendship with Judge Politz and Politz's special relationship with Secretary Stalder caused a political firestorm. A legislative committee and the Orleans Parish district attorney's office opened investigations. Billy was interviewed by investigators from the DA's office and a legislative committee investigator. Before Judge Politz could be called to testify, Governor Mike Foster shut down the legislative committee's investigation and removed

Lafayette Parish state representative Don Cravins, who led it from the committee.

Political charges and accusations were exchanged between Representative Cravins and the Foster administration. There was little doubt that Governor Foster had personally intervened to protect Judge Politz from the possible legal exposure and personal embarrassment that testifying before a legislative committee could bring.

As the political firestorm raged around Politz and Stalder, Louisiana's corrections department retaliated against Billy. It created "the Sinclair Rule"—a gag order directed only at Billy. He was never again allowed to talk to a reporter. For the next twelve years, I would be his only voice in the free world.

But the Sinclair Rule didn't stop coverage of the scandal. Elder's series prompted another major investigative story, this time by an award-winning *Houston Chronicle* reporter. In 1998, Evan Moore's front page, in-depth article broke in the *Houston Chronicle* under a banner headline in the Sunday edition. It revealed even more salacious details.

It began with a description of a cozy luncheon at Shreveport's Petroleum Club in 1997, featuring a "distinguished" group of guests that included Judge Politz, "one of the country's most respected jurists," Corrections Secretary Stalder, several attorneys, and a "quiet little man" named Gilbert Gauthe. The story covered all of Gauthe's offenses and Politz's interventions over the years on Gauthe's behalf that kept the former pedophilic priest from being convicted of aggravated rape and receiving a life sentence.

To explain his relationship with Gauthe, Politz told the *Chronicle* that the two grew up together in Napoleonville, Louisiana, the sons of sharecropping families that depended on each other over the years. That didn't deter the paper from detailing the extensive special treatment Gauthe received at Wade, thanks to Politz and Stalder. After examining Gauthe's record, the *Houston Chronicle* article called the former priest "a monster."

The story broke nationwide in 2002 with a blockbuster account in the *Washington Post.* The paper reported that after Politz intervened for Gauthe at the pedophile's sentencing, the former priest wasn't sent to the psychiatric facility where he was supposed to do time after his 1985 conviction. He was never given Depo-Provera to reduce his sex drive, a significant part of his plea bargain, while he was imprisoned. Instead, he was sent to Wade where he enjoyed "extraordinary freedom" in N-5 allowing him to indulge his pedophiliac inclinations while Stalder was warden there, before he was appointed by Edwards in 1992 to run the state's entire prison system.

With Stalder as the head of the corrections department, Gauthe's special privileges increased. He was given special furloughs so he could visit his mother for weeks at a time. The *Washington Post* reported that the *Houston Chronicle's* investigation and subsequent state hearings found that Gauthe took teenage prisoners, who had been placed in N-5 to protect them from older convict predators, and had them "shave their body hair and have sex with him" in his special air-conditioned office in the laundry under the guise of providing them with prison ministry.

Politz stepped down in 1999 after seven years as chief judge of the Fifth Circuit Court of Appeals, assuming "senior status" on the court until he died in May 2002. After Gauthe was released, he lived in a number of small towns in Texas over the years. There were other charges of sexual molestation of children filed against him in different parts of the state. He served two years in a county jail in Texas for failing to register as a sex offender. Once again information from Billy had triggered escalating investigations that destroyed the careers and reputations of powerful officials.

Billy's transfer to Wade had ended our bimonthly visits. Driving to see him at Angola and the barracks was hard. But driving six hundred miles over a weekend twice a month to get to Wade was too grueling. During the ten years Billy was at Wade, I only saw him once a month for four hours—two on Saturday and two on Sunday. But time and distance did not diminish what we felt for each other.

PRISON BROKE MY HEART. IT killed my dreams and shut off opportunities. For years, I saw bars in my nightmares, heard metal doors slam, endured pat-down searches, remembered the death house where Billy and I met and visits under the eyes of often unfriendly guards. I was a congressman's cousin with a private-school education in Europe and America, married to a "jailhouse" lawyer and writer who would have been a formidable foe in a courtroom.

In reality, I was speared by an awful truth: Billy's victims controlled the criminal justice system in Louisiana, and they hated us. When I thought of the people opposing Billy's release, I thought of the "Q," a collection of Jesus's sayings distilled from the gospels. No one, the "Q" says, has the right to ask for forgiveness if they cannot forgive. My soul, rooted in the faith of a Catholic childhood, gave me hope for a time. It didn't last.

In 1984, twenty years after Billy's crime, I begged an Istrouma classmate of Billy's victim to relent, but Carroll DiBenedetto rejected the word I brought of Billy's deep remorse and contrition and my fears.

"Please," I said, "my worst fear is not that my husband won't come home. It's that he won't come home until I'm old and sick and I don't have the money to take care of him."

A slow smile spread across his face.

"Mrs. Sinclair," DiBenedetto replied, his eyes burning holes in mine, "your nightmare has every potential for reality."

He had the absolute right, he believed, to make certain we spent our final years in pain. Ten years later, another of the victim's high school classmates rejected my plea for mercy.

"You knew what you were getting into. I don't feel sorry for you," football legend Billy Cannon sneered at me when I begged him to stop opposing Billy's release.

He was unmoved by my plea for mercy. He sat across from me in the waiting room in his Baton Rouge dental office, an aging mountain of a man, confident that his hatred of me and Billy was justified. Cannon and DiBenedetto, both close high school buddies of J. C. Bodden, assumed the right of blood kin to punish Billy. They waged their battle against him through their powerful political connections.

I clocked their hatred at hurricane strength as I stood with Billy before his 1999 parole board hearing. The victim's family and friends, led by DiBenedetto, had a private meeting with the board before the hearing to express their views, a privilege not extended to us. Then they were allowed to sit in on our presentation and interrupt our witnesses with their hostile, bitter comments. DiBenedetto called Billy "a dangerous career criminal," rudely interrupting Billy's attorney as he spoke to the board.

I had approached the hearing with skepticism. Billy had been denied a parole four times by then. His record was clean. He had served thirty-four years behind bars. We had proved the board could not lawfully use Patin's rigged criminal record to deny him as it had in the past. But I had no confidence they would make a favorable decision.

"We will vote our conscience," the board's chair announced as Billy and I took our places before the panel. I sat down with clenched teeth and braced for what I knew was coming—rank hypocrisy disguised as morality. Individual conscience was no substitute for due process of law. But it made no difference to the parole board's chair that day.

Peggy Landry wore a large cross on a chain around her neck. She was a grandmother, a crime victim, and a member of a crime victim organization in New Orleans. Local media nicknamed her "Pistol Packin' Peggy" after she said she stopped a robbery with a pistol she carried in her purse. She relished her role as a crusader against crime and she was a staunch advocate for crime victims. She was prone to tongue-lashing inmates who appeared before her if she didn't like the expression on their faces or their tone of voice.

The second member of the board was a hard-bitten north Louisiana political appointee with no criminal justice background who admired Landry. The third member of the panel was a former corrections department employee named Gretchen McCarstle. She lived in the same neighborhood as the victim's family and had always been a staunch supporter of Billy's opposition. We were facing a kangaroo court.

During a brief recess in the hearing, an old inmate beckoned to me from across the waiting room. He was sitting near a group of prisoners from a local jail. They wore shirts emblazoned with the sheriff's name. Most were young African American men in leg irons. They waited with bowed heads for a turn before the board.

The inmate's face was creased with wrinkles. Veins stood up on his hands. They were knotted and tangled with age. He was one of the few old prisoners in the room. He must have been close to seventy years old.

"How's Billy doing in there?" he asked me gently when I reached his side.

"Not good," I said.

"I knew Billy back at Angola," he said. He gestured toward the main body of the prison. "We been praying for him down there. We had a prayer going, you know, just hoping it would turn out okay this time."

Thoughts of his compassion and humanity stayed with me for months after the hearing.

"Thank you," I said, as I gently touched his shoulder. "What are you in for?"

"Drinking," he said with a smile. "I done a bunch of time for drinking."

"Good luck," I whispered before ducking across the room to join

Billy at a table near the door. He was staring at the wall. I knew he was bracing for another denial.

"Sinclair," a guard called abruptly. It was time to return to the hearing room for the board's decision.

The victim's family and supporters stared at us with open hatred as we took our places. They didn't care that Billy fired the fatal bullet in a blind panic in J. C. Bodden's general direction as the store clerk chased Billy across the parking lot in the dark. They didn't care that Bodden was disobeying direct orders from his employer not to confront the robber. While they had a legitimate right to their feelings, the parole board had no right to dismiss due process, fairness, and equal protection under the law to rule in their favor.

"You are denied, Mr. Sinclair," Peggy Landry said loudly from her seat on the dais above us. The pleasure in her voice was evident.

"You can have a hearing again in two years if"—she paused in the middle of her sentence for emphasis—"if you can get anyone to give you one."

I stood up, aghast at the open bias in her statement. Did she know she had just revealed the obvious prejudice in the board's decision? Or didn't she care?

"Mrs. Landry, are you telling us never to come back?"

"Mrs. Sinclair, don't argue with me."

"Please, Mrs. Landry; just tell us if you mean we should never come back. I could stop hoping then. It would be so much easier to bear."

"That's it," she said, slapping her hand down on the dais. "Get her out of here."

She jerked her thumb at a prison guard who immediately started moving toward me. I stepped out of the room in tears. Months later, I was still jolted awake in the middle of the night, remembering the guard heading toward me to forcibly remove me from the room.

I grieved like a madwoman after the 1999 hearing, until bit by bit, my body signaled that it could not take any more. I jogged at the gym with tears running down my face. I was nauseated. I drank Cokes and baking soda to settle my stomach. My gut went into spasms. I put anti-diarrhea pills in my purse and panicked if I forgot them. I downed two or three when I went to the prison. Resentment boiled up inside me like acid. I fantasized puking it up in front of the board and watching it burn smoking holes in the papers on their desks.

I went to the corrections department's headquarters to check Billy's file. I left Houston early on a weekday morning and drove to Baton Rouge. I met with the corrections department's executive counsel, who was also the legal adviser for the pardon and parole boards. He was polite. We sat at a large table in a first-floor conference room. Documents from Billy's file were stacked in neat piles on a highly polished table. They were separated into public and private stacks. Under Louisiana's open-records law, I could only see the public documents.

I was there to make a list of every error in Billy's file. When it was my turn to speak at Billy's next parole hearing, I wanted to name each deliberate error, so the public and the media would know about the lies in his record that the board was using to deny him parole.

Some of the files held letters opposing Billy's release. Even if they were full of lies, only board members could read them. The victims' movement had convinced the state that revealing their contents would expose the letter writers to danger. The state responded with a ban protecting them from public view.

I knew some of the records that I was allowed to see contained errors the parole board refused to correct, including the fourth-offender status the Board had used so many times to deny Billy. I was told that made no difference.

"Mrs. Sinclair," the legal counsel said politely from his end of the table, "the board has absolute discretion to do what it wants when it makes decisions."

"Sir, are you saying the board can vote against my husband if it doesn't like the color of his hair?"

"That's what I'm saying, Mrs. Sinclair."

"They don't have to consider his record of rehabilitation?"

"No, Mrs. Sinclair, they don't."

"I don't believe that," I replied.

I spiraled down into a deep depression after the hearing. A little voice inside said, "Not me. Not me. I wasn't meant to suffer like this." I knew then: Billy might never be paroled. I buried hope without a marker on its grave.

August 11, 1999

Dear Billy—

We are facing enormous prejudice on the Parole Board. Peggy Landry's sarcasm during the last hearing keeps reverberating in my brain.

"Mr. Sinclair, you may have another hearing in two years if you can get anybody to give you one." And Gretchen McCarstle the year before when we applied for a re-hearing: "Oh, that rap sheet."

I saw them in the ladies' room at Wade where I ran across them during a break in your hearing. I felt strange standing next to them washing my hands while they went through the polite nods and silent smiles women reserve for each other in that environment when they are strangers. They were going to chop my head off in the next moment and they both knew it, but they still trotted out the usual protocol.

"Would you like a cigarette before you die in front of the firing squad?" So concerned. So polite. I had seen it and read about it at executions in Sister Helen's book. Other places too.

Everyone becomes so concerned for those about to die. And they are oh, so compassionate. I would prefer a brutal assassin to that kind of vicious face-saving "politesse" as the French call it. Drawing room manners in those situations have nothing to do with good breeding or compassion.

People engage in it to make themselves feel better as they get ready to pull the trigger, drop the guillotine, or deny a parole. Some do it to be mean. They know it increases the victim's suffering when that victim realizes what appeared to be compassion was a farce.

The day after Landry denied you, I vowed that when I recovered, I would never let the Parole Board hurt me again, that I would never shed another tear, that I would find a way to live free of their hatred. I remember swearing something similar when I was nine years old just before another whipping. I never made a sound after that each time the belt hit me.

I CAME HOME ONE SUMMER afternoon after work to find the phone ringing in my downtown Houston condo. Billy never called then. He knew I didn't get home until eight since I usually went right to the gym after work. But that night, I had skipped my usual routine after a hard day at the office. Sensing trouble, I threw my purse on the floor and raced to the bedroom to get the phone before it stopped ringing.

It was a collect call from Wade. Billy came on the line in a ragged voice I had never heard before. He had just spent nine hours in a stun belt that could deliver up to 50,000 volts of electricity. A month earlier, on June 8, 1999, in response to a query from the Associated Press about stun belts, the department of corrections told the news agency that Louisiana prisons weren't using them. So why had they strapped one around Billy's waist for nine hours?

"I had a bad day," he said. "Two trip officers insisted I had a court date. I showed them the letter that said it was canceled. But they told me they had a court order and I had to go."

It was 254 miles from Wade to the courthouse in downtown Baton Rouge. The trip averaged four and a half hours one way. Before they left, the trip officers locked a stun belt around Billy's waist. If the guard activated it, the belt delivered a 50,000-volt charge of electricity into the inmate's body. Billy protested its use.

"Look, we don't like this either," one of the trip officers said. "This is some stupid shit. We don't know where it's coming from. We told the major we didn't want anything to do with whatever was being done to you. We were given direct orders to use this goddamn thing. This is not our doing, Sinclair."

The prison van had a blowout at seventy miles an hour near Alexandria. Billy was chained in the back. He said the van lurched and threatened to roll over before the driver could finally bring it to a stop on the side of the road where the two officers changed the tire. The button that activated the stun belt was on the driver's belt. If the van had rolled, the driver's body could have pressed the button on the stun belt. If he was knocked unconscious, how long would the belt's powerful current continue coursing through Billy's body? Who was responsible for this extraordinary security measure? Why?

Even if the driver were able to immediately deactivate the belt, it would have sent the 50,000 volts of electricity into a man with a heart condition, easily killing him. In a March 1997 booklet, condemning the spread of "stun technology" in tasers and remote-controlled electro-shock stun belts, Amnesty International said the belts "could be misused by officials to deliberately inflict pain, intimidate, humiliate, and degrade prisoners."

The organization's fifty-two-page report said the "literature distributed by one of the two American belt manufacturers clearly indicated the belt can result in cruel, inhuman, and degrading treatment." It also cited several deaths of American prisoners and a prison guard who died "after enduring two 45,000-volt shocks" while training with a riot shield.

In December 2000, more damning details of Billy's treatment were revealed in an Associated Press story in the *Dallas Morning News* about the lawsuit Billy filed against the department of corrections for transporting him in a stun belt that July.

The Associated Press reported that "a little over a month after the Louisiana prison system said it did not use stun belts when transporting convicts, a high-profile inmate spent nine hours in one of the devices while being taken to a court hearing . . ."

The AP reported the corrections department didn't deny locking a stun belt on Billy for the trip in spite of its publicly announced policy change a month earlier but said he didn't suffer "a true physical injury."

I pulled out letters about what he was enduring as I confronted cruelty so terrible it was hard to imagine.

11 July 1999
My darling:

There are times when the fatigue of legal combat saps me, leaving me drained of hope. But I always recover, always manage to set my sight on the next mile. There is an end of the line. You are my life, Baby Lion, and we must never, ever, give up on our efforts to be together.

22 July 1999
My darling:

Nothing has ever been easy for us. We are in a war of attrition. They want to kill me. That is why we must always fight—this day, every day. You are my life, Baby Lion.

10 October 1999
My darling:

Can you possibly imagine how difficult it was for me to breach the social chasm between us at the very beginning? Can you imagine the turmoil? The gnawing feelings of inferiority as I wrestled with a way to release the flood of emotions held in check by such a flimsy dam?

Of course, I pawed at the line. Stepping across was venturing into an abyss where I had never gone before. I was an inmate—not just any inmate but a convicted murderer. I was in love with a beautiful and extremely intelligent journalist. I understood prison. I knew how to play the big fish in the little pond, but I was completely lost and paralyzed trying to handle the feelings I had for you.

But the gates opened, and I was the happiest man in the world when the flood of emotions were allowed to rush free. I can still remember those moments so clearly, hurrying down the Walk at night at Angola anticipating the sound of your voice and desperately needing to hear your words of love. You've owned my heart since the moment we met. I miss you terribly. You are my life, Baby Lion. You were from the beginning. You are now. You will be forever.

August 6, 1999
Dear Billy—

This morning I am wondering if there is any way to satisfy the lust for revenge among those who oppose you. Maybe a net cam would work. I break into tears at least once every morning. They could tune in over coffee and enjoy watching me cry.

Better yet, what if they could tune in on you? They would see a national award-winning prison journalist and whistleblower reduced to weighing and loading thousands of pounds of dirty inmate laundry into prison washers and dryers every day.

No more national press clamoring to interview him, just brute work, day in and day out, in a monotonous routine.

Maybe they're entitled to the ultimate luxury—the right not to know how much pain they are inflicting or an obligation to care. Certainly, Louisiana has plenty of government servants to take care of that for them. Neat. Tidy. No bother.

Our visits changed after the 1999 parole board hearing. He had another twelve years to serve before he would be automatically released in 2011 after serving half of his ninety-year sentence. We were careful with each other's emotions then, respectful of the fragile core we each sheltered inside. Superstition played a part. Saying what we feared out loud might make it true. Our conversations were a careful minuet. We only inferred a tomorrow for us in what we said.

Home was a word we avoided. It wasn't likely to ever be a part of our daily lives. "I love you," we said to each other, concentrating on the moment, knowing it was all we had. We never worked at making it enough. It simply was, like breathing, ordained in the genetic packages that made him six feet tall and my eyes a dark blue.

April 18, 1999
Dear Billy—

Do you know what I am thinking when I sit with you in the cell-block lobby at Wade and look at your body stretched out in that chair? I am undressing you. I feel like I'm on fire, sitting with my hands in my lap, imagining your body stretched out against mine the way it was when we hugged this morning, me standing on my toes to fit against you, thigh to thigh, for the brief moment they let you put your arms around me—split second sex when I hug you hello.

It's hard to believe they haven't let us kiss for five years. That sanitary brush of the lips the guards allow us at the beginning and end of each visit doesn't count. Because I remember what it was like when we felt almost free at the Barracks. It rushes back every time I see you and so often in-between.

These days when we are together, sitting across from each other in the cell-block lobby, I watch your eyes and look for the child in the man I love. You smile, my mind comes alive with possibilities and I know I can get through one more day.

Hate kept me alive. I wanted to feel compassion, to imagine the shock the family and friends of Billy's victim endured, their grief at the random, cockeyed fate that took the life of their loved one when he was hit by an errant bullet fired by a would-be robber. But the massive weight of the prison system ate at my soul. It was too hard to look at the 1999 loss before the parole board and accept what it meant—another long march toward a receding horizon we might never reach.

I smiled every time hate jolted me alive. I slept with it every night. I felt it on walks under towering skyscrapers in downtown Houston. Nothing could banish the ancient beast that was living in my soul. I turned the cross in my bedroom around to face the wall. I was entitled, wasn't I, to hate Billy's lying prosecutor, the witnesses who committed perjury at his trial to get the death penalty, the judges who refused to grant him hearings or ruled against him, the governors who refused to grant him clemency, and the parole board members who denied him again and again? I wanted to scream at them, "Why are you killing me?"

But Catholic liturgy damns hatred. Thousands of years of Christian doctrine condemn it. Hatred is the root of evil, of love gone wrong, twisting in on itself, festering into a putrid mass. Still I had reveled in it, relishing each of Billy's legal assaults against his enemies, knowing they would be enraged.

At night I burst into tears under the covers alone in the dark trying to fall asleep. The state had total control of my life, my future, and all my aspirations. I wasn't really married. I was part of a trio—Billy, me, and the state.

As an abused child, Sunday Mass had been my refuge. So I decided to go back to church. I made an effort to believe again. I was determined to sit in Mass every Sunday hoping I would receive what the Catholic Church called the mystery of faith. I went to confession for the first time in almost forty years. But I confessed only one sin: the burning hatred for Billy's opposition that threatened to overwhelm me. It was exhausting me.

I told the priest I couldn't remember the Act of Contrition, the prayer that Catholics say as part of the penance they must perform to pay for their sins. He smiled and said that wasn't what he wanted me to do for my penance. Instead, he said my penance was to pray for the victims, their friends, and Billy's keepers every day.

"You cannot ask God for forgiveness with hate in your soul. Christ died to win forgiveness for us. You crucify Christ when you hate," the priest whispered to me in the confessional.

"Father, think of what they're doing to us."

"Try to think of their families, their children. You must forgive them. Christ wants you to forgive."

"Father, I cannot."

"Then think of your husband and what hatred does to him. You cannot ask for forgiveness with hate living in your soul."

I sat in Mass every Sunday and stared at a statue of Jesus on the cross. Ceramic blood congealed on its near-naked body hanging from nails driven into rough wood.

"Let me believe you died for something," I prayed.

I tried to cope by making plans, sending emails asking for letters of protest and support, calling for appointments with legislators, parole board members, and prison officials. But they were the reflexive moves of a decapitated body, like a chicken running across a yard after its head has been chopped off, flopping and jerking in agony.

There was more bad news after the 1999 hearing. A Baton Rouge judge ruled that Aaron Brooks, the assistant DA Billy had sued for purposely misrepresenting Billy's case to the parole board, had full immunity. In essence, he had the right to break the law when he brought up Billy's false criminal record. I listened in disbelief when Billy told me. I didn't think anyone in the United States, under any circumstances, was above the law.

Publishing Billy's story became my primary goal. If he never came home, part of him would be free. When I learned that Arcade Publishing, a prestigious independent publisher in New York City, had bought his autobiography, my prayers were answered. We had worked on it together for eleven years by then, me on the outside with a computer, Billy on the inside with a manual typewriter. He wrote all the searing chapters on life inside prison and mailed me the pages. I wrote sections about our meeting, our marriage, and our years together from his first-person perspective so there was no break in the narrative. It was his story, not mine. I knew how he felt when we met when I said I'd marry him. And I had the letters he had written me for years.

Arcade's founder, Richard Seaver, was celebrated in international literary circles for publishing works that "defied censorship, societal prudishness, and conventional literary standards," as the *New York Times* noted in 2009 in his obituary. Seaver released books by rabble-rousing authors such as the Marquis de Sade, Henry Miller, William Burroughs, and Samuel Beckett during his exceptional career, authors whose works violated "decency standards" in the United States.

Before he founded Arcade Publishing, a company he ran with his wife Jeannette, Seaver was an editor at Grove Press. Shortly after he joined the publishing company, Grove published *Lady Chatterley's Lover* by D. H. Lawrence, a book that "was quickly banned from the mail." In a breakthrough for US readers, a court ruled it was not obscene and it could be sold openly.

In 2000, Arcade published Billy's autobiography: *A Life in the Balance: The Billy Wayne Sinclair Story.* The cover had a picture of the electric chair and a subtitle—*A Journey to Redemption Inside America's Worst Prison System*—that deftly summarized Billy's battle behind bars to become a national award-winning prison journalist and "the whistleblower extraordinaire" who "blew wide open the pardons-for-sale scandal that rocked Louisiana government."

The *New York Times* called it "a numbing tale of crime, punishment, and redemption" with "graphic scenes of murder, mutilation, and turf wars over drugs and sexual slavery." *Publishers Weekly, Kirkus Reviews, Luce Press Clippings,* the Associated Press, the *Shreveport Times,* and the *New York Law Journal* also reviewed it. The review in *Luce Press Clippings* called it the "inside story" of thirty-five years in Louisiana's prison system for "a homicide that prosecutorial [mis] conduct turned into a capital crime." It ended with an observation that nailed the truth: "Billy Sinclair remains behind bars partly because his victim's family and friends are politically powerful, partly because he's blown the whistle on Department of Corrections corruption."

The *Dallas Morning News*, the *Houston Chronicle*, and a magazine published by Loyola University in New Orleans, my alma mater, interviewed me about the book, my marriage to Billy, and how it affected my life. After *Balance* was published, I made a ten-city tour to promote the book, but my appearance at the Barnes & Noble bookstore in Baton Rouge was canceled "because of possible protests at the store," according to the *Houston Chronicle* on January 6, 2001.

Billy was not allowed to be interviewed about the book. The "Sinclair Rule" was firmly in place. It just another example of the corrections department's ongoing retaliation against Billy for breaking the Gauthe/Politz scandal wide open

The Sinclair Rule also banned him from receiving newspaper clippings, so he never saw the book reviews. The corrections department tried to ban the book at Wade so Billy would never see it but relented after Billy threatened another lawsuit. The department then chose another retaliation tactic by banning manual typewriters in every Louisiana prison. They wanted to make sure another *Balance* would never be published. The letters I received from Billy after that were written with a dull pencil. They were almost illegible. But at least his story was free.

December 29, 2000
Dear Billy—

This holiday season is the saddest I remember since they took you from the Barracks six years ago. I forced myself to stop crying with this question:

"What is the one thing, above all others, Jodie, that is truly important when you scrape everything else away? It's that you are

alive. I have your voice and I get to see you from time to time and there's the book."

If you never come home, the book has freed you. Your story will live on after both of us are gone. And that is what I wanted. If I could not bring you home, I have at least helped to free you with the book. It is the stuff of myth and legend. It makes you bigger than life, and it will until the stars burn up the planet, the sun goes out or a black hole devours it.

You have achieved great things in your life. You rebuilt it against incredible odds. No one would ever have believed that you could literally come back from the dead to be the man that you are—patient and kind, with a piercing intellect and the strength of character to prevail against terrible fear and temptation. Yours is a triumph of the human spirit. You set an example for others. And that, in the final analysis, is what heroes do.

And that is what the book gives to the world, your portrait, and a look deep inside a forbidden world that routinely destroys its victims.

When Kevin Coleman died in a restraint chair at Wade in 2001, there were no detailed accounts of his last meal or his last words. Prisoners on the disciplinary tier where he was housed with other problem inmates said that when Coleman refused to come out of his cell, a "goon squad" charged in, shocked him with a stun shield multiple times, beat him, dragged him down the tier, threw him under a cold shower, and strapped him in a restraint chair, where he died seventy-two hours later. Some said Coleman was a "schizo" and his death was typical of the way Louisiana treated mentally ill inmates.

On August 10, 2001, the *Shreveport Times* reported Coleman's death but said the cause was "unclear." Wade's warden told the newspaper that Coleman was allowed out of the restraint chair every three hours under heavy supervision. But he was returned each time because he "remained uncooperative." Coleman had thrown a tray that hit a guard and kicked another one several times.

Assaulting guards was a felony. Coleman was supposed to face those charges at the courthouse the morning he refused to come out of his cell.

The newspaper also reported that ninety-three inmates died in Louisiana prisons in 2000. But the *Shreveport Times* didn't list the reasons. It couldn't. The corrections department told the paper that "causes of death weren't reported."

I thought about the corrections department's reaction to the national publication of Billy's autobiography. They saw him as a problem inmate like Coleman, not a protection case. Would I pick up the phone one day to hear he was dead from a cause they wouldn't disclose?

Fear engenders strange responses. I hung a picture of my mother on the kitchen wall. I stared at it every morning as I drank coffee, wondering how she endured the awful pain of living with the deaths of her husband and her brother. She was cremated after she died in 1981. There was no grave to visit, no way to kneel over the dirt above her bones, call her spirit out of the shadows, touch her cheek, and tell her how much I needed her.

Mother was generations removed from Ireland, but there was a Celtic sadness about her. At Mass, she sang the "Ave Maria" in a quavering voice ruined by a lifetime of cigarettes, worn out by time and tears, standing straight up in the pew, eyes raised toward a place high above the altar. I knew then I was more my mother's child than my father's, although his erratic and sometimes violent presence dominated our lives and caused the sorrow that racked us both for years as I grew up.

I tried to remember any advice she might have given me before she died, anything to help me hang on until Billy was free. But her secret died with her. And it made me question what I was leaving my children. They were teenagers when I left, growing up without me over that span of crucial years.

I took out a letter my daughter wrote to me after I left Louisiana for Houston in 1982. It was the story of an abandoned child, struggling to piece life together the way I had at her age.

Dear Mother,

I've been waiting three years for your letter. Sometimes I thought it would never come. But no matter how angry I was, I didn't ever quit hoping. I guess that's why I've hurt for so long. I wanted you to say those things so badly.

I always knew you cared. I denied it for a long time but that was just a defense. If I believed you didn't care about me, I didn't have to care about you. Sometimes it made sense you didn't give a damn. How else could I explain you weren't around? Even when I did see you, I still felt you weren't with me.

I desperately want to know you because I don't, and I feel I can't fully know me until I know you. . . . I feel like at times I am inventing the woman I'm meant to be. . . . I am constantly discovering things about me that are like you. . . . I scrutinize you when I see you to find what else about me is like you. . . . I have felt imprisoned by you because you denied me the one thing I needed to be happy: knowing that, yes, you do think of me.

I know you didn't want to alienate us, but that's all I ever felt from you. So, I decided to wait for you to contact me. I am very cautious, defensive, and cynical about those who say they care for me. I don't believe them until they show me beyond a shadow of a doubt. Now that I know for sure you care, maybe I won't be like that anymore.

We still have time. That's why God made tomorrow so we can do the things we couldn't do today, and we didn't do yesterday.

I love you, Mother. I always have. I am so happy to have you back.

I had asked her to write what she felt. She had the strength to do it, and I sobbed when I read it. Her stoicism and maturity were stunning. How could I have been so blind?

I should have known how hard life would be for her and her brothers when I left, like it was for me when I was their age. I should have reached out before I did. Her love and forgiveness filled a deep void in my heart and she became for me all I hadn't been for her—a rock I could lean on as I faced the powerful resolve of Billy's opposition to reach into the system and hurt him until he died.

IN EARLY 2002, I WROTE the parole board to protest its deliberately vicious conduct in Billy's case. I sent a copy to every member of the board. In spite of a state court order to correct Billy's criminal record, the parole board continued to base its denials on the false criminal report James Patin concocted.

MEMORANDUM
January 26, 2002

TO: Members, Louisiana Parole Board
FROM: Jodie Sinclair
RE: Victim Impact Statement

Everyone must face the consequences of his actions. You expect it of prisoners. I expect it of you. You have an obligation to read about the pain that you are causing.

On August 6, 2002, I will be sixty-four years old. The Board's vote against my husband (Billy Sinclair #64373) on 1-7-01 keeps me on the road alone, driving 630 miles over the weekend once a month for the next two years to see him.

You have deprived me of funds I will need in my old age. When Billy discharges in 2011, I will be seventy-two years old. He will be sixty-five.

Funds to sustain us will be extremely limited. He has job skills that make him employable now. Given your vote, he cannot contribute to our household or pay a share of federal personal income taxes.

I worry about my husband constantly. He needs surgery to correct an age-related eye condition. He has a congenital heart murmur and occasional high blood pressure that is worse in the heat. He sleeps on the concrete floor of his cell because the temperature does not usually fall below ninety-five degrees until well after nine p.m.

The average length of service on a maximum sentence in Louisiana is twenty-two years, according to a study last year in the Shreveport Times. My husband has completed thirty-six years of service, twenty-five of them without a write-up.

His incarceration costs Louisiana taxpayers twenty-five thousand dollars a year. Since 1992, when he became parole eligible, he has cost the state $250,000. Nine more years (at twenty-five thousand per annum until he discharges) adds another $225,000 to that total—a huge cost to taxpayers for a man whose prison record shows he is no threat to society.

Do I expect any of you to care? No. As a Board, you demonstrate little mercy.

But I believe appointed officials have an obligation to understand the ramifications of their actions, especially when they are cruel, unnecessary, and fiscally irresponsible.

No one on the board responded. I wasn't surprised. By then I knew the Foster parole board would deny Billy no matter how many years he served in prison, how many times I protested, or how many agencies like the New Orleans Metropolitan Crime Commission endorsed his release, or that a court ruled he was rehabilitated.

The times were too hard for hope. On the rare days that he felt discouraged, I did what I could to bolster Billy's spirits. I would be with him until hell froze over and angels fell out of heaven, dead. If he died in prison with only a prison chaplain by his side, reading loving parts of my letters to him, he would know my spirit was with him.

There was no doubt we were being targeted. Billy was one of the best jailhouse lawyers in the Louisiana prison system. He was married to a professional woman with credibility and easy access to local and national media. Inmates who exercised their legal rights infuriated corrections officials, who were determined to get even. So were members of Billy's opposition that Billy sued for interfering in his case. He lost some cases, but he raised significant hell with others.

Over the years, Billy sued the pardon board twice, the department of corrections at least a dozen times, and the parole board four times. As a result of one suit, three parole board members—Peggy Landry, Gretchen McCarstle, and C. A. Lowe—were subpoenaed for a court hearing. It was the first time a court had ever allowed members of the parole board to be subpoenaed. The suit was dismissed after Landry went to Governor Foster's office in a rage and a new judge was assigned to the case. But it rocked the board. He filed misconduct complaints with the Louisiana State Bar against two district attorneys. One of them, Aaron Brooks, was sanctioned by the bar.

Billy sued a hard-bitten opponent for using his government position to block his parole. He filed a complaint against another opponent for using her powerful position with the Louisiana senate to keep him behind bars. He sued a witness at his 1966 trial for committing perjury.

In another unprecedented move, he filed a judicial complaint against Judge Politz after the chief judge orchestrated a denial of a case he had before the Fifth Circuit Court of Appeals. After that, the court's judicial council forced Politz to recuse himself from any matter Billy had before the court. Another three-judge panel denied the appeal a few days after the Politz recusal.

Over the years, he sued two secretaries of the corrections department, five wardens, and a number of prison guards—including colonels, majors, lieutenants, and sergeants. He blew the whistle on the pardon-selling scam and the Politz/Gauthe affair, both of which sent seismic shock waves throughout the state's political system.

He reported corruption at the Louisiana state police barracks, leading to criminal and internal affairs investigations. He filed grievances about the corruption he witnessed in three of Louisiana's prisons, prompting investigations, employee firings, staff demotions, and forced retirements.

"You've done more to change this state's prison system with lawsuits you didn't win than with those you did win," former Corrections Secretary Phelps once told Billy before he left office. None of the suits were frivolous. But they engendered a powerful hatred against Billy for pursuing his legal rights, questioning officials' motives and their right to inflict pain, and revealing corruption wherever he saw it, no matter who was involved.

In March 2001, a long investigative article in *Gambit Weekly* took a hard look at Billy's case. The New Orleans–based alternative weekly newspaper quoted from a letter that Doug Moreau, a former Baton Rouge district attorney in charge of Aaron Brooks, wrote to the parole board in 1999, opposing "any clemency" for Billy.

"Sinclair executed J. C. Bodden," Moreau wrote. "When Sinclair made the conscious decision to enter the Pak-A-Sak store armed, he did so for the purpose of killing his victim. He succeeded by firing four shots, one fatally wounding his victim."

But the article also cited the sworn Kennard affidavits stating that Donald Ray and Ramona Kennard saw Billy running from the store with J. C. Bodden chasing him. They refuted the district attorney's claims to the parole board. But Moreau dismissed the affidavits and statements by other witnesses that undercut his claims to the parole board, saying he didn't believe any of the eyewitness statements that were suppressed at Billy's 1966 trial.

The *Gambit Weekly* article included numerous scathing comments from the victim's family and friends. Its report confirmed that Billy's opposition had no qualms about distorting his case to keep him in prison. The article was the second in *Gambit Weekly*'s three-part series, "The Keys to Freedom"—an in-depth look at criminal rehabilitation, redemption, and forgiveness. It cited Billy's accomplishments and released a long statement from Rafael Goyeneche, president of the New Orleans Metropolitan Crime Commission, in favor of Billy's release:

> *Billy Sinclair blew the whistle on the pardons scandals in the administrations of Edwin Edwards and (Pardon Board Chairman) Howard Marsellus. And he did it at great risk to his own personal safety.*
>
> *He did it because it was the right thing to do. And not only did he not receive any special consideration, he was actually penalized (by state authorities) as a result of his coming forward and doing the right thing. Yet people with more atrocious crimes who served less time and accomplished little or nothing in prison are at home right now with their feet up on the sofa enjoying the free life.*
>
> *The message that was sent by the way Sinclair has been treated is "Don't cooperate, don't blow the whistle in the system, because you will be treated the same way Sinclair has been. . . . That is you are going to sit in jail and rot."*

On March 1, 2003, a Discovery Channel TV crew taping a documentary about inmate relationships followed me to Wade to get video of the prison. By then, Billy and I had been married for twenty-one years. The producer wanted to end the documentary with our story to show that despite incredible hardships, inmate marriages could be stable and enduring. The crew had already taped segments in five states with inmates and their free-world wives. Each state gave permission for the interviews. The producer had called Wade's new warden, Venetia Michael, a number of times for permission to interview Billy. But she never returned their calls. When she didn't respond, the crew contacted the governor's office for help reaching her.

The crew flew to Houston on February 27 to interview me before following me to the prison the next day. Our story would have to be told only from my point of view because the crew never received permission to interview Billy. When we arrived that Saturday, Warden Michael sent a goon squad rushing out of the prison to roust the crew from the side of a public road as they shot video outside Wade—their right under the First Amendment. On March 5, the warden called me at my office in Houston to ask about the visit for an "incident report." While Warden Michael was polite, I taped our conversation since I had no confidence she would accurately report it.

Several days later, I received a certified letter notifying me that I had lost my visiting privileges and an internal affairs investigation of my behavior was underway. On March 15, I wrote Senator John Hainkel, the president of the Louisiana senate, that the department of corrections had canceled my visiting privileges, hoping he might have a way to help me.

That same day, I wrote Robert Barbour, the deputy general counsel of the department of corrections, to protest. I had telephoned him on February 27 to let him know that a TV crew would be with me when I came to visit Billy.

But Warden Michael charged me and the Discovery Channel TV crew with "subterfuge." The charge was ludicrous, since the deputy general counsel of the corrections department and the governor's office knew in advance the TV crew was coming with me. My letter to the deputy general counsel ended with three questions: Since there was no wrongdoing, what was the DOC investigating? Who was being investigated? What was being alleged to suspend my visiting privileges?

On April 10, five weeks after Wade's goon squad chased the TV crew down the road, I called the corrections department headquarters in Baton Rouge to talk to the prison official who had informed me by certified mail that my visiting privileges were revoked. He said they were restored but that it was the warden's duty to officially inform me. On April 13, I wrote Warden Michael asking her to expedite the "notification" so I could see Billy again.

That summer, I wrote Billy on a Friday night, two days after my birthday:

August 8, 2003
Dear Billy—

Sixty-five is such a milestone. It really rocked me. I remember my fiftieth birthday like it was yesterday. I can recall everything about that day, particularly the sadness I felt. There was no denying then that I was getting old. That wasn't what hurt the most. It was that I was growing old without you.

I look at my body in the mirror and I can see how age is affecting it. I'm probably a pretty hot looking chick to a man who is eighty (if a man that age still has the yen). In fact, that thought finally cheered me up. I started laughing at the prospect.

You know it's not so much getting older that disturbs me. It's what my image in the mirror symbolizes. It says we won't have much time together when they finally send you home. That's a pain so devastating, I can't describe it.

How have we survived this situation? People ask me that a lot now and I have no answer. I simply don't know. There's nothing I can point to that's hauled me through the last twenty-two years of suffering that your victims have insisted upon. I don't call them victims anymore—except for the immediate family. They've had nearly forty years of payment.

That is more than enough considering that other victims' families have received so much less from the state for crimes that were truly heinous. The inequity of it puts me in a rage if I let myself think about it.

I love you, Billy. From time to time, I still fantasize about being with you—what it would be like every day, in bed, at the grocery store, doing laundry, cooking, and all the things that people who were meant to be together, do together.

I don't let myself think about it too much because it hurts too much. I will turn my thoughts to the courts and hope we will find some relief there. I would so love to spend quiet Sundays with you.

THAT FALL, TWO OFFICERS AT Wade charged Billy with "aggravated disobedience." They grabbed him for a shakedown as he left the laundry, claiming they had found "extra items" in his laundry bag. It was a classic setup. The two officers, a sergeant and a captain, ran the laundry. They stopped him and another inmate at the end of a workday and went through all the items in their personal laundry bags. An hour and a half later, Billy was handed a disciplinary report.

On October 31, Captain Martha Henley had issued an order barring inmates working in the laundry from washing their own clothes during the workday. It was a common practice in the prison for decades. Three weeks later, Henley's superior, Colonel Michael Rhodes, ordered five inmates exempted from her order. Billy was one of them. He and four other inmates were handling hazardous waste every day—inmate garments smeared with blood, feces, and semen. As they stuffed the dirty clothes into washing machines their own clothing might be contaminated with the HIV and hepatitis C viruses. Rhodes ordered them to wash their clothes before leaving the laundry every day to prevent the viruses from spreading.

He also ordered Billy and the other four inmates to clean all the washing machines in the laundry with bleach before they left. A recent upsurge in infections at the prison prompted the colonial's orders. He had to submit regular reports about his efforts to contain the spread of hepatitis C, which was raging in prisons throughout the country.

Billy and another inmate, Earnest Comeaux, had been following Rhodes's orders for a month when they were suddenly stopped by Captain Henley and the laundry sergeant as they left work one day. Henley said she found two extra towels in Billy's bag.

Captain Henley was also in charge of the prison's mailroom. At the time, Billy had a federal lawsuit pending in a Shreveport court challenging the corrections department's new policy of forbidding inmates from receiving newspaper clippings in the mail. Stalder and Henley were ordered to testify about the "clipping rule" at a December 10 hearing before a federal magistrate.

Billy had already submitted credible evidence to the court that Henley made frequent exceptions to the policy for inmates she favored. The inmates told Billy that Henley was out to get him, and she had the blessing of Warden Michael.

Billy was ordered to appear before a prison disciplinary board. At the hearing, on the eve of his fifty-ninth birthday, he was reassigned to fieldwork—the hardest, dirtiest work at Wade. He would go through the winter working outside in the cold and rain, picking grass by hand all day, one blade at a time. I knew Billy wouldn't break. I also suspected the line boss was ordered to push him harder than other inmates, like the line boss running Crew 20 when Billy arrived at Wade nine years earlier.

In November 2003, right after the laundry write-up, Billy got word that Peggy Landry had scheduled a parole hearing for him. By then, he had served thirty-eight years with one minor disciplinary write-up. Just weeks before Landry scheduled the new hearing for Billy, she chaired a panel that paroled Thomas Laird, a man who served fourteen years for shooting and paralyzing a New Orleans police officer.

Laird shot the officer during a 1989 DWI stop, according to

the New Orleans *Times-Picayune.* He admitted to snatching the gun from the officer's holster, pistol-whipping him, and shooting him in the back. His parole outraged the New Orleans Police Department and the Orleans Parish district attorney's office. By then, the officer was back at the department on desk duty, paralyzed from the waist down.

An investigation was ordered after the board voted to parole Laird. Later, it would reveal that he was guilty of "misconduct" that occurred before and after his hearing. According to the newspaper, Laird had broken prison rules by trying to contact his victim before the hearing and "improperly" using a prison computer. On November 20, 2003, the *Times-Picayune* reported that Laird's parole was suspended.

Before the investigation concluded, the political pressure to have Laird's parole revoked increased, and the backlash against Peggy Landry grew. Billy was suddenly granted a parole hearing. It was scheduled for November 13. But circumstances surrounding it were suspicious. Billy wasn't eligible for another parole hearing until 2004. And he hadn't applied for one. Either a political deal had been struck in our favor behind the scenes or the Landry-led parole board had decided to give Billy a hearing, deny him, and use the inevitable publicity to deflect the political criticism bombarding Landry after the Laird parole. There was no way to know and little time to decide.

Billy's name wasn't on the official docket for the hearing. I was instructed not to attend. I was told the board wanted a low-key hearing, and I had a history of asking embarrassing questions. They knew I was a reporter and that I knew where the bodies were buried.

Billy's parole board hearings were like facing firing squads. Panel members were always rude. They allowed the opposition to stop our testimony with frequent "rebuttals." It was impossible to complete a presentation without being interrupted.

Billy's lawyer, a brilliant young New Orleans attorney named Thomas Corrington, had virtually been assured by a top-ranking attorney in the corrections department that Billy would be paroled at the hearing. Thomas was stunned when he first heard about it. He had been working with corrections attorneys to get Billy transferred back to the barracks. Based on the assurances that Thomas was receiving from one of these attorneys, Billy agreed to the hearing. Still, we were wary. We were being asked to trust a parole board and department of corrections lawyers that had done nothing but oppose us for years. The stakes were high.

In only six weeks, a new governor would take office in Louisiana, and Billy would be eligible to apply for parole. Was the Landry board holding the hearing to take a final shot at Billy? A denial would keep him behind bars for two more years.

On November 13, the Landry parole board unanimously denied Billy a parole. Peggy Landry's petty, vicious deceit was the parole board's final slap in our faces.

November 17, 2003
Dear Billy—

I suppose at some point we will come out of emergency mode and slump back into the prison system's routine. Once I'm finished at the office, I'm at a loss. I don't have a rudder anymore. The pain is so raw. Our future has just evaporated again. I am moving around aimlessly in the wreckage.

I cannot look at our loss before the Parole Board and accept what it means—two more years without hope, another long march toward a receding horizon that we may never reach. As long as I can stuff something between me and reality, I'll survive in the short term. But what happens when the few things that I can do, are done? What happens when there is nothing left to do?

It is hard not to believe that they are just killing us by degrees instead of in one fatal gesture. I look back on twenty-two years of our suffering and realize progress is an illusion. Moments like this rip the veil away so I see it clearly.

But I won't give up. I am your wife. Someday, God willing, our marriage vows will be said in person. But they will never be more heartfelt than they are today. I love you, Billy Wayne. Thoughts of you return a smile to my face.

November 20, 2003
Dear Billy—

Was it Chief Joseph of the Nez Perce who said, "I will fight no more, forever"? His lands were gone, his people dead, mothers and babies killed in their teepees, his corps of braves decimated.

I am writing this letter in a state of exhaustion at three in the morning. I am finally too tired to cry anymore. My life preserver is small. I can only survive if I accept the fact that 2011 is all we have that is real. I cannot bear the pain of hope anymore. It's a killer. Raised expectations, in this lawsuit or that, are, in reality, lethal doses of hope.

But not for you. Your way lies in fighting them no matter what—with requests for ethics investigations, lawsuits, any way you can stand up to them and their madness. A lawyer told me a long time ago—and I didn't believe it—inmates survive by filing lawsuits. Yours have been very good ones.

If you were less than a man, you would accept the way they lie and their betrayals and their corruption without protest. But you cannot. The proof of your rehabilitation lies in the efforts that you mount in court, not in violence. I am so proud of you for that.

Whatever you ask of me, I will do. If it's a trip to Baton Rouge to complain to the US attorney, I will go. If it's paying filing fees, I will write the checks. I will stand by you as you pursue relief from the vicious web of evil that holds you hostage.

If we survive to be together in 2011, we will have little time left. And I will be glad for every moment. But I cannot live for that anymore. For years, I have written you that we would always be together. And we will, if only in heart and soul.

December 24, 2003
Dear Billy—

I hope you can call tomorrow. I hate to think that Christmas would go by without being allowed to speak to you.

The fear that those officers at Wade caused as a result of framing you when you left the laundry will fade as the weeks go by. If nothing happens, I will create some repercussions. As soon as the new governor is inaugurated, I think I will go to Baton Rouge, hold a press conference, and ask why Wade is not being investigated, given our credibility and the kind of information I sent them. Nothing these people do would surprise me.

I was thrilled today; I got a letter from you I could actually read! I love you.

Billy was the only inmate in N-5 who wasn't allowed to call home on Christmas Day. His laundry write-up sentenced him to thirty days without a phone call as part of his punishment for having "unauthorized items" in his laundry bag. The phone ban began at noon on Sunday, December 21, 2003 and ended thirty days later at noon on Sunday, January 11, 2004.

On December 29, 2003, I wrote a final scathing letter to the warden at Wade, who, by then, I despised.

Warden Venetia Michael
David Wade Correctional Center
670 Bell Hill Road
Homer, LA 71040

Madam—

I will never forget your cruelty and the lying officers upon whom you depend to run your institution. The bogus charge against my husband for "aggravated disobedience" in the laundry, although he was following Col. Rhodes's orders, exhibits the corrupt and vindictive nature of those you trust. I wrote you in detail about what happened. You ignored my letter.

Your lying officers ruined my Christmas. I should be in Seattle with my children and grandchildren who are together for the first time in many years. But I will not leave this part of the country because I do not trust you. Normally when I visit the West Coast, my husband calls his brothers if there is an issue that needs to be addressed. They, in turn, call me at home in Houston.

Since Billy cannot call anyone because of the punishment being inflicted upon him due to your officers' lies, I am visiting him every weekend to make sure he is all right. Fortunately I can because it's Christmas and you allow visiting every weekend.

I am a 65-year-old woman making a 600+ mile round trip every weekend because of my fear that your officers will hurt my husband and that you will lie to protect them.

Have you taken a good look at my husband recently? That is, if you ever leave your office to visit his tier. Since no one has seen you there in months, I wonder about that. My husband is going blind. He has "ptosis." (It's in the dictionary). He is losing muscular control of his ability to open his eyes. In a few years, he will no longer be able to see.

You have a 59-year-old man, slowly going blind, who could not call home at Christmas after 38 years in prison. Your cruelty during the season of God's birth is beyond comprehension.

When I called the prison at noon on Sunday, January 11, an officer said the memo ordering the ban ended at midnight on Sunday, not noon. When I pointed out that was twelve hours longer than thirty days, I was told a "memo in the computer" couldn't be changed.

"Are you saying that if someone accidentally keys in an order to drop an atomic bomb on Paris, the computer wouldn't allow it to be rescinded? Do you mean that if a punishment is imposed and the inmate is later found innocent, it can't be changed because you can't override the original order?" Then I paused.

"Well, excuse me, I think I have it straight now," I said, in a sweetie-pie Southern lady voice. "I'm sorry. I don't know why I need to be reminded of this. I understand that anytime you can make a punishment worse, anytime you can hurt someone a little bit more, anytime you can be harsher, you will." Then I hung up in her ear.

December 26, 2003

Dear Billy—

I went to the office this morning. Finished up a few things and left at noon. Nobody else I had business with was around so there was no sense in staying. I pulled together the few odds and ends I needed to take care of and left.

Came home and read over your new laundry write-ups. They left me in a rage, especially the last one. Why am I so mad about it? Officer Hollinshead checked the "seriousness" of the offense. I notice there is no other box for something like assault with a deadly weapon. Is having a towel in the wrong place as serious as assault with a deadly weapon?

Can he find his backside with both hands? Does he know the difference between an organ grinder and a meat grinder?

Today is a very lonely day. I forget how much I depend on work to fill the terrible gaps in my life that exist because we are not together. My sister and her husband left this morning for their house in the Texas Hill Country. So, although I will be in their neighborhood to get a manicure and buy The Da Vinci Code *at a bookstore to send to you, they won't be home. Makes me sad.*

I really hate days off. Whatever I do, I mostly do it alone. My daughter and her husband flew to Seattle today to visit her brother and his wife and kids for several days. How great it would have been to go to visit them too. But I will NEVER leave this part of the country when you are trapped in this sort of situation—when you can't call my sister or your brothers to signal there is trouble. I don't trust anyone at Wade. Most of them are incompetent. They would hurt you if they could.

I love you. I always will. Whatever they do or say or however long it takes for you to come home, I will be at the front gate waiting even if they force us to do seven more years. I think of you every day, through the day. It always puts a smile on my face even if I am smiling through my tears.

The only light left in my world by then was my job. By 1998, I had left KBMT-TV, a network affiliate in Beaumont where I had been a general assignment editor and a reporter, to become director of public relations at the Houston Downtown Management District. My new position made me part of an historic turnaround in the city where I was born, and I was deeply grateful I could do something so worthwhile.

The district was a free-standing state agency created by the Texas legislature to turn downtown Houston into a twenty-four-hour center where people could "live, work, and play"—a challenging goal at a time when its suburbs had drained away businesses, homes, and shopping centers, weakening the city's heart. The district had a thirty-member advisory board of residents and business owners that included CEOs from major companies with offices downtown. Revitalizing downtown would also revitalize the old Houston neighborhoods surrounding it.

While I was with the district, downtown Houston added Enron Field—a $248 million downtown baseball stadium—built a park in front of the George R. Brown Convention Center, promoted a rail line between downtown and the city's world-renowned medical center, a first in urban transit for the city, and operated a downtown ice rink at Christmas that I also publicized and helped to manage.

In 2005, after I left the district, I was asked to join Houston's Joint Hurricane Housing Task Force in the mayor's office. Refugees fleeing Hurricane Katrina's devastation in New Orleans needed housing and advice on how to live in Houston's huge high-speed economy. By then, the difference in my life and Billy's was extreme.

Dear Billy,

I exist in a parallel universe with paychecks and dealmakers. I walk to work through blocks of skyscrapers that would look like the twenty-first century on another planet to you if you could see them. The people I'm around do million-dollar deals. They design light rail train stations and office towers. They plan huge construction projects.

Execute means get it going, see it through, give it life, prepare it for tomorrow.

You live in a place where revenge is God and people who call themselves Christians worship at its altar. It sears your insides. You spend your days silently screaming for a way out, focusing on litigation, the only thing that keeps you from going insane. We must compartmentalize our lives so we can keep putting one foot in front of the other down a road we know isn't going to end soon.

"I can live with today, if you give me tomorrow," goes a Fleetwood Mac song. But it's hard to believe. I wish you were with me tonight. You would see the sunset reflected in the glass skins of the skyscrapers. They shimmer and glow in the twilight as the sun goes down. Once it is gone, the sky turns a deep, luminescent, royal blue behind the buildings as the first lights inside begin to twinkle. Then, the sky turns black. And the buildings with all their lights look like pictures of New York City at night. It is gorgeous beyond belief.

The typewriter ban was still exacting its toll. Billy's letters were almost illegible given his handwriting and the dull pencil he had to use. So I read and reread a letter he wrote me eight months after we met. His words put him beside me, as though he were home with me at last.

11-10-81

Dear Jodie:

. . . when you are frightened, I want you to curl up beside me and let my warmth soothe and relax you—and if you need me, I want you to awaken me with a whisper and I will pull you to me, your head on my chest, and gently stroke away all the fears and uncertainties of the moment. I will hold you until you are safely and comfortably asleep again.

On New Year's Eve 2003 I wrote him about the love that began living in my heart from the beginning. Whatever the future might bring, I would be at his side fighting for his freedom and the life I prayed we would at last be allowed to live together if we could somehow manage to survive.

December 31, 2003
Dear Billy—

We begin the New Year with new things to think about. I may be no closer to bringing you home than I ever have been. But I will go against your enemies with my bare hands when I have nothing left to fight with if I have to. You are my reason for being. I live under your sun. And it knows no seasons. It is hot and tropical, always at zenith, shining on me with its full force from the top of the sky. I love you so, Billy.

Two songs that always make me think of you:

"There's an ocean between us. You know where to find me. You reach out to touch me. I feel you in my own heart. It helps to remember when it feels like forever, you're only an ocean away."

"I can hear you whisper in the silence of my room. My heart still surrenders like the sun to the moon. Love me now and forever were the last words you said to me."

THE FINAL MILE

"The strictest justice is sometimes the greatest injustice."
—Terence, Roman playwright, 195–159 BC

AS 2003 CAME TO AN end, I prayed the worst was over. But, as always, I was braced for trouble. Too many high-ranking Louisiana prison officials and others in powerful positions saw us as a threat. For ten years, Billy had forced them to attend embarrassing hearings, hire lawyers to represent them, and fend off news stories about their corruption.

The onslaught we would endure in 2004 eclipsed anything we lived through in 2003. It began in late 2003 when Billy overheard the Colombian Medellín Cartel assassin Luis Cruz make explicit death threats on several occasions against President George W. Bush. When Billy told me that he overheard Cruz talking to Roy Lee Casey, another inmate serving a life sentence for murder, about killing the president, I contacted the FBI in Shreveport. Gang members are notorious for getting members in the free world to carry out their orders. There was no way of knowing if the threats Billy was overhearing were real. I also talked to a Secret Service agent in New Orleans who told me that agents there knew Cruz's name "very well."

On March 24, 2004, two agents, one from the Secret Service and another from the FBI, finally came to interview Billy at Wade after the White House announced that President Bush was planning a trip to Louisiana. Billy told the agents everything he knew about the threats. Then they interviewed Cruz. After that, they talked to Casey. The FBI agent told Casey that Billy was the source of the complaint.

Word spread like wildfire at Wade that Billy had snitched on Cruz and Casey. That night, as Billy and I talked, guards signaled him to get off the phone. They told him to get ready for a transfer the next morning. When he called me back, I could hear the panic in his voice. After he was called away a second time, he called back to say he was only being taken to Baton Rouge for a hearing in his lawsuit against Paul Fontenot for transferring him from the barracks. We felt better after that. But our relief was short-lived.

I had sent a media alert to the Baton Rouge press corps about the hearing several days earlier. It said preliminary court rulings in the case found that Billy had broken no rule at the state police barracks to cause his transfer and that he had an apparent agreement to remain there. It also reminded them that he was the whistle-blower in the pardon-selling scam. And it listed the witnesses: a parade of top-flight state officials.

They included former US attorney Ray Lamonica, Corrections Secretary Richard Stalder, assistant East Baton Rouge district attorney Charles Gray, department of corrections deputy counsel Robert Barbor, Howard Elliot, a former lawyer for the state police, and Colonel Anthony Genusa. I was also ordered to appear and testify.

The next morning Billy was transferred to the Hunt Correctional Center. He was not allowed to call me before he left. He was told to take all his belongings. He was only allowed to keep his legal materials. The rest of his belongings would not be returned until he was transferred to a medium-security prison nearly three months later. He was headed for lockdown at Hunt.

At Hunt, he was put in a single cell on a lockdown tier with inmates too dangerous to be in general population, prisoners who had attacked guards or hurt other inmates. A week later, a deputy warden blew Billy's cover. He announced in a voice loud enough for all the other inmates on the tier to hear that Billy was a snitch. I was infuriated when I finally got to talk to Billy. When I challenged his lockdown status, I was told that Hunt was the only place in Louisiana with enough security to guarantee Billy's safety.

On Monday, March 29, the bench trial in the Fontenot lawsuit began. After nine years of waiting for a hearing in his case against the former state police official, Billy was finally to have his day in court. As I looked at all the high-profile officials in the courtroom who had been subpoenaed for the trial, I saw open hostility in their eyes. Only two, Charles Gray and Anthony Genusa, gazed at us with compassion.

I didn't trust the judge. For almost ten years, Ralph Tyson had been a state criminal court judge in East Baton Rouge. Before that, he was a prosecutor in the Baton Rouge district attorney's office under Ossie Brown. I knew the hearing would be rough. We were facing a prejudiced cadre of enemies.

I was shocked when I saw Billy. He was chained to a chair. A handcuff restrained his left arm. Only his right hand was free. His legs were shackled, and there was a restraint belt around his waist. Tyson had ordered him to be restrained for the entire trial. It was hard for him to leaf through his legal papers with one hand. His clothes had been confiscated along with all his belongings. He was dressed in pants that were two sizes too large, tattered shoes, and an ill-fitting, dirty-looking shirt.

As soon as Tyson walked into court, he overruled an order from the Fifth Circuit Court of Appeals to allow testimony about events leading up to Billy's transfer on November 30, 1994. His ruling excluded crucial pieces of evidence. The ruling came as close to defying the Fifth Circuit as it could, short of refusing to hold a trial. During the hearing, Tyson said several times if Billy didn't like his rulings, he could appeal again to the Fifth Circuit. Tyson knew Billy probably wouldn't get a third reversal of his rulings because of the appeals court's ill will about the Politz/Gauthe exposure.

Billy was not allowed to speak to his witnesses or consult with them in any way. Meanwhile, Fontenot's defense attorney talked to them during the recess, at lunch, and after the day's testimony. I wasn't allowed to talk to Billy during the entire trial except to answer his questions when I was on the stand. And then, Judge Tyson said I could only answer yes or no, nothing else, to any questions. Sometimes the judge turned toward me on the witness stand and parroted the questions I had been asked and my answers as though I were in kindergarten, almost daring me to add anything to the one-word replies he had ordered.

I sat in the courtroom for two days hearing my "inappropriate passionate conduct" discussed in front of me as though I were a whore, without being able to defend myself. I might as well have been a piece of furniture. I had never been accused of inappropriate physical conduct over twenty-three years as Billy's wife.

Billy asked me on the stand if the kiss we exchanged the day that Fontenot saw us was "prolonged and passionate." I said "no." In answer to another question, I was allowed to describe what happened in the barest of detail. The judge let me say the kiss was no different from any other kiss we had ever shared. That was all.

I watched Billy struggle under terrible conditions to question his witnesses. At the end of the second day, Tyson dismissed the case, telling Billy he could appeal. It was a sick joke. All Billy had was a dull pencil and no access to a law library. There was no way he could appeal the case in the allotted time, much less surmount the bias against him exposing Politz and Gauthe.

After the hearing was over on Tuesday, I saw them take Billy away in chains. I went crazy when I didn't hear from him after I got back to Houston on Wednesday. He should have been back at Wade by then. When the phone didn't ring, I called Wade. I was told Billy had been transferred. The officer there said he would try to locate Billy.

I started frantically calling anyone I thought might have information about Billy. I telephoned the Associated Press in New Orleans hoping the bureau would know. I found the home phone number of a former state police officer who was working for the department of corrections. I couldn't hold back the tears when I talked to him. He immediately asked for Billy's inmate number and said he would call back in five minutes.

He was as good as his word. That's when I learned Billy was being held in extended lockdown at Hunt. Then the officer at Wade called back and said he expected Billy would probably be returning to Wade on a prison bus over the weekend.

Late Friday afternoon, I called Wade to see if there was any word about his return. I had no idea why he was being held in lockdown. Had he been charged with some bogus offense? Was it revenge for daring to sue Fontenot? Was he sitting there like a dumb animal in a cage suffering in silence because no one told him why he was being kept in extended lockdown?

The extended-lockdown tier was a hellhole. The guards routinely used gas to subdue unruly inmates. When they were released, the suffocating fumes hit every cell. The first gas attack caught Billy by surprise. He didn't recognize the whirring sound of gas as it escaped from a canister near cell 4. He heard coughing and choking in the cells around him before it seeped into his cell. As soon as he smelled it, he instinctively took a deep breath. It was a horrific mistake. He rolled off his bunk, coughing and vomiting on the floor, afraid he was choking to death. His eyes burned and his heart was pounding. Desperate, he splashed water from his toilet on his face.

"Cell seven, you alright?" a young inmate called out to Billy. "You alright, old man?"

Then he passed out. When he came to, his nostrils and throat were on fire. Tears were stinging his eyes. He managed to get up and put his mouth directly against a small barred window in his cell and suck in fresh air.

"Turn on the blowers, motherfuckers," he heard other inmates screaming at the guards.

Sometimes, he said, it was an hour before the guards finally turned the fans on to suck all the gas out of the tier. After that, when there was a disturbance in the cell block, Billy instantly got ready. He had about forty-five seconds before the fumes crept into his cell. He grabbed his bedsheet and toilet paper. He folded the sheet lengthwise, made wet nose plugs from the toilet paper, and waited. As soon as he heard the sound of escaping gas, he stuck the wet toilet paper plugs into his nose, wrapped the sheet around his head covering his mouth and nose, pressed his face hard against the window in his cell, and rode out the attack trying to suck in fresh air.

Billy endured nearly a half dozen gas attacks in lockdown at Hunt. During his two and a half months there, he wrote me a letter I will never forget. I struggled to read it. When I finished, I transcribed it so I could read it every day.

4-15-04

My Darling:

The insane man down the tier from me in a distant isolation cell screams for long periods of time. Demons torment him, circling, hovering, and attacking. They tear at his thoughts, refusing to allow reason to plant seeds and grow. Their mission is to destroy any remnant of rational thought. When the guards have had enough, they put on masks and throw a gas bomb in his cell.

A picture steals into my mind. I see a kid about ten years old in denim overalls, too poor for a shirt to wear underneath them. The kid flashes a quick grin. A shock of dark hair falls into his eyes, He won't need a shirt until Fall. It's hot in Louisiana in July.

Why did God send that kid down a path that led to prison for thirty-eight years? But I have traveled it so long, I seldom question it anymore. Surviving is all that matters.

I drove to Baton Rouge on Sunday April 5, determined to get Billy released from lockdown. Early on Monday morning, I went to corrections headquarters hoping to see the corrections secretary, Richard Stalder, or the deputy secretary, Johnny Creed. I didn't have an appointment. I hoped one of the two would find a few minutes to speak with me.

Creed invited me into his office and spent a half hour talking to me. I was surprised. He was very kind. Johnny Creed said Billy was not charged with anything, but he would be at Hunt for another two to four weeks until Creed received all the reports he was waiting on. I wasn't told what they were. Perhaps the DOC was investigating some unknown threat against Billy. He also told me I would be allowed to see Billy at Hunt. I had been desperately worried about him after the first call that Billy was allowed to make the week before.

I told him that Billy was slowly going blind. The muscles in his eyelids were slowly being paralyzed, making it hard for him to hold his eyes open. There were signs his heart murmur was getting worse. He was almost sixty years old. He had no business being returned to Wade or Angola, where he might be attacked, given his age and his infirmities and his reputation as a snitch.

Had Billy gone to Hunt for the hearing with Tyson as a regular inmate from Wade, the guards wouldn't have taken away all his personal items and his clothes. Instead he was sent as a protection case, an inmate who belonged in administrative segregation, the classification for dangerous inmates.

I knew by then how easy it was for people to tell he was going blind. I left the meeting with Creed fearing Billy might be sent back to Wade or Angola. Wade might be as dangerous as Angola. Based on Billy's observations, N-5 was being run by Cruz and other inmates close to Henley. The first time Billy was allowed to call me from Hunt, what I heard staggered me.

"I am going to die in here," he said.

He was afraid the state might keep him in lockdown until 2011, when he would automatically be released on parole. His words resonated in my head like a tuning fork as I drove to Baton Rouge to visit him for the first time.

Seeing him made me feel better. But when I left, I knew we had reached a critical juncture in our long battle for his freedom. The scars of all the legal wars he had fought against the system were etched in his eyes. Nearly forty years of fighting had just ended with a crucial loss in the Fontenot case. I knew he would never give up fighting the threats, retaliation, and acts of naked revenge against him. But I knew then, I would have to lead the battle from the outside.

For twenty-three years, all I had longed for was to bring him home. I knew it might never happen. But I wrote him that I would carry his flag straight up the hill into his enemies' fire for the rest of my life.

April 17, 2004
Dear Billy—

I have just learned that the number of letters you can receive are limited. I don't see how that makes you "unsafe." Every time I think of you in lockdown under the same rules and policies for violent inmates, it infuriates me. I have never felt such outrage. It threatens to choke me.

But it may be by design. I think they want to cut us off as much as possible because they sense that we draw strength from each other. What they don't understand is that we draw strength from each other whether we have contact or not. Our minds are in sync somewhere in cyberspace.

People who believe in reincarnation have told me that you and I have to have been together in other lives. They say that because we instantly recognized each other when we met. There was a mystical quality about that meeting. Under their belief system, we have been partners for millenniums.

I agree they're out to humiliate you. They will do all they can to strip you of your sense of self and your humanity. That assistant warden who took you into a room at Hunt and told you to "quit running your fuckin' head" was one of them.

I believe they want you dead. They hope you will literally commit suicide by signing away your protection rights. They are trying to put so much pressure on you right now that you will give up those rights to get out of "the hole."

I have dealt with them for twenty-three years now and I know how they operate. If you get shanked in general population, they will be laughing themselves sick behind closed doors and crying crocodile tears in public.

That's their end game as far as I am concerned. You probably suspect it too. I am going to push for another appointment with Creed. He said it might take a month to evaluate your situation. I will give him that month. But after that, it's Katy bar the door, as we say in Texas.

Fear for his safety stole any peace I might have had. The system had mistreated Billy so long, I didn't trust anyone associated with it. I was on the verge of despair. I woke up every morning, knowing Billy was suffering. But there was nothing I could do. I needed power from another level, one they couldn't ignore.

I turned to Sheila Jackson Lee, a congresswoman representing the Eighteenth Congressional District in Houston, known for her power and bulldog tenacity. She had been a member of Congress for ten years. She was the first woman to be a ranking member on the Judiciary Subcommittee on Crime, Terrorism, Homeland Security and Investigations. She was a leader in efforts to reform the criminal justice system, dedicated to reducing prison overcrowding.

On April 20, I wrote to her, begging for help with Billy's situation. I included my résumé and hand-delivered the letter to her office in downtown Houston, a few blocks from my condominium at 2016 Main. My husband, I wrote her, should not be held in punitive lockdown for reporting threats made by a Colombian hit man in prison at Wade against the president of the United States. I described the conditions on Billy's tier, noting that Louisiana put protection cases on the same punitive lockdown tier as dangerous inmates. I suggested she might ask Louisiana senator Mary Landrieu, another powerful voice in Congress, to look into the matter.

My letter included the names and contact information of the top officials in the Louisiana's corrections department and Billy's role in exposing the pardon-selling scam, his record of rehabilitation, and his national journalism awards.

If powerful congresswomen from Texas and Louisiana began asking questions about Billy's situation, it might speed up his transfer from Hunt and ensure his safety in a humane environment.

In late April, I wrote Billy there was more evidence of the Foster parole board's bias in his case. I had learned Peggy Landry stopped to talk to Rafael Goyeneche, director of the Metropolitan Crime Commission, at a public event one evening in New Orleans. The commission was one of Billy's most powerful supporters. She ended the conversation with a casual comment:

"The board can't stand his wife."

I knew the parole board had "absolute discretion" when it came to making decisions. But denying a man out of dislike and contempt for his wife is unconscionable. And then I laughed. Would they parole him if I divorced him?

On May 4, in response to my letter to Sheila Jackson Lee, I was invited to meet with a lawyer at her office. By then, Billy had been at Hunt for seven weeks. The attorney, Carmen Mandujano, was horrified by what I told her. She said Billy's case was exactly what

Jackson Lee loved to fight for. I could breathe easier knowing she intended to help.

Marie Claire scheduled a photo shoot with me for mid-May. A Dutch photographer took my picture for the magazine's September 2004 edition. It was about true and lasting love in dangerous circumstances. Jennifer Lopez was on the cover. I was grateful to be part of a national feature. I wrote Billy when I could, assuring him we would get past their latest attack of "shock and awe."

Sister Helen Prejean also wrote Governor Blanco on Billy's behalf. I prayed the compassion and forgiveness embodied in her book *Dead Man Walking*, the story of two inmates executed at Angola, and the popular movie about it, would speak to the governor and her staff.

I also received word that another book, *The Impossible Will Take a Little While* by Paul Rogat Loeb, would be out in September. It was a book of essays about people who never gave up working against terrible odds for peace and justice. Billy's essay, "The Road to Redemption," appeared in the section with essays by Cornel West, Rosa Parks, and Dr. Martin Luther King Jr.'s "Letter from Birmingham Jail." Billy's essay was the only one in the book written by a convicted felon.

Billy's two brothers swore they would contact their congressmen if necessary. His younger brother, Dan, began negotiating with the corrections department to move Billy out of extended lockdown. His older brother, John, was afraid the DOC would pressure Billy to give up his protection rights to get off the discipline tier. He said signing them away would be signing his death warrant. Creed told me he had no intention of requesting a waiver of protection from Billy, but I had no guarantee.

On Monday, May 24, I got a warning call from Carmen Mandujano. She had just talked to Creed. She said he planned to visit Hunt and ask Billy to waive his protection rights so he could be transferred. She asked me to write a letter protesting his plan.

I immediately wrote the letter and sent it by FedEx after work. I also sent FedEx copies to William Klein, the top lawyer in the department of corrections, a Secret Service agent in New Orleans, and Bob Mann, Governor Blanco's communications director. I informed them all that I had written the letter at the request of Ms. Carmen Mandujano, an attorney on the staff of my congresswoman, Sheila Jackson Lee. I threatened to call every reporter I knew in Louisiana with a story. I was later told my letter hit the corrections department like a "nuclear bomb."

Mr. John Creed
Deputy Secretary
Department of Public Safety and Corrections
504 Mayflower Street
Baton Rouge, LA 70804
Re: Billy Wayne Sinclair, #64373

Dear Sir:

This is to put you on legal notice that if you ask my husband to sign away his protection rights to gain his freedom from administrative segregation at the Elayn Hunt Correctional Center in St. Gabriel, you are knowingly placing him in danger.

Today, I learned from Ms. Carmen Mandujano, a lawyer on the staff of my Congresswoman, Sheila Jackson Lee, that when you visit my husband on Thursday to discuss his future housing in Louisiana's prison system, you plan to ask him to sign papers relieving Louisiana of its obligation to protect him. Otherwise he cannot be moved out of administrative segregation, the most punitive status in Louisiana's prison system, although there are no charges against him.

That is blackmail. After nearly two and a half months in ad-seg, Billy's signature would not be worth the paper it is written on since it was clearly obtained under duress, i.e. the threat that he would have to serve the rest of his sentence there to guarantee his safety.

When you told me last Friday that Billy would be an "active participant" in the decision about his housing, I immediately asked you if that would shift liability from the state to my husband. You said it wouldn't. Yet, I learned today that your plan is to do exactly that—make Billy responsible instead of the state if he is injured or killed in your prison system.

My husband is in this situation because he tried to do the right thing. He was not in this fix until two members of the federal government visited him on March 24 and conducted an investigation in such an indiscreet, irresponsible, and sloppy manner that every inmate in the protection unit at Wade knew who had blown the whistle on Luis Quintero Cruz by the time they left.

My husband will not be blackmailed by the State of Louisiana or abandoned by the federal government as long as I draw breath. I promised you, Mr. Creed, that I would not contact the press about this situation. But if you ask my husband to sign away his protection rights that is the first phone call I will make.

You said on Friday that you "don't care about the press." I assure you the governor does. This is a nasty, damaging story that I won't hesitate to tell. Let me say it is what I expected that I would have to do all along.

I vehemently opposed Mr. Stalder's re-appointment as Secretary of the Corrections and he knows it. My husband's lawsuits resulted in two subpoenas being issued to Mr. Stalder in federal court in the last six months. This will certainly be construed in some quarters as an incredibly cheap shot at revenge.

Jodie (Mrs. Billy Wayne) Sinclair

I could picture corrections officials walking up to Billy's cell door looking so well-groomed, well-fed, and full of their sense of power, looking at Billy in a sweaty orange jumpsuit, with long dirty hair and long unkempt fingernails, offering him a quick way out of lockdown if he would just sign away his protection rights. That was no arm's-length contract, I raged. Were they offering him the Hilton or the Sheraton?

A few days later, two psychologists came to Hunt to conduct extensive psychological evaluations of Billy. Was it an attempt to make him look mentally incompetent so they could lock him down in a prison psych ward and keep him quiet with incapacitating drugs? He told me he sailed through the written and oral interviews. One of the psychologists laughed and told him he was "more stable" than the average Louisiana legislator.

By then Billy was war weary; the psychological scars from decades of battling the prison system were more pronounced. Housing him at the barracks was off the table. A newly appointed state police superintendent refused to let him return. In a payback rebuke of Billy's lawsuit against Paul Fontenot, state police superintendent Henry Whitehorn said he would never allow any inmate on the premises who had sued the state police. I wondered why Whitehorn didn't care about a man who blew the whistle on the pardons-for-sale scam instead of committing a crime.

Meanwhile, Billy's brother Dan successfully negotiated a deal with the department of corrections that would transfer Billy to the C. Paul Phelps Correctional Center, a medium-security prison near the Texas border. It was a relatively peaceful institution that housed young inmates with short sentences. He was assured there would be no more official harassment or retaliation if Billy stopped filing lawsuits and official complaints.

May 29, 2004

Dear Billy—

When you stop and think about it, Dan won. They came to the table and negotiated. And the offer was generous considering the circumstances. All they wanted in return was what you and I privately talked about in the months before you were transferred to Hunt—that we would do the rest of the time quietly with no more lawsuits and no more exposés of wrongdoing.

It says we scored some heavy points and it also says they know we can do some heavy damage if we choose. It's a good deal all the way around. Everybody gets something. A former prison official we know told me he had never heard of a deal like this.

I wrote you last week and told you we can't fight anymore from the low ground like the Confederates at Gettysburg and win. They fought with courage and great pride and valor, but they died by the hundreds in a futile cause. You wrote me back and said you'd rather die at Gettysburg.

Don't stay at Gettysburg. We won. Remember the last words of Stonewall Jackson as he lay dying after he was wounded at Chancellorsville, a battle that the Confederates won: "Those conflicts are over. Triumphant at last, The warrior may dream of the battle-fields past, And cry now in victory as bright visions please, Let us cross over the river and rest in the shade of the trees."

Billy agreed to the truce. In exchange, he was given an official guarantee that he would spend his remaining years in prison in peace. He dismissed all the lawsuits and official complaints he had filed and began preparing himself psychologically to reenter the general prison population for the first time since 1986.

He told me he wasn't afraid to be in general population at Phelps. But I wondered. Prison officials and federal law enforcement agents had made promises and then abandoned us again and again over the years. Did Billy's transfer to Phelps on June 7, 2004, send him to another hellhole where he would live in misery until 2011, when he would automatically discharge after serving half of his ninety-year sentence?

When *60 Minutes II* aired a story at the end of April about American abuse of Iraqi prisoners at Abu Ghraib, I burst out laughing as I watched members of Congress claim on TV the conduct was un-American. After twenty-three years as an American prisoner's wife, I knew abusing prisoners was as American as apple pie.

The *New York Times* reported that photographs of inmates at Abu Ghraib in November 2004 showed "detainees bound and cowering, or naked, hooded and forced into sexually humiliating poses." The Pentagon admitted twenty-five prisoners died in American custody in Iraq, according to *CBS News*. The photographs showed male prisoners "positioned to simulate sex with each other" while American guards were "laughing, posing, pointing or giving the camera a thumbs up."

Their treatment was identical to the abuse in a Georgia prison. In late May 2001, the *New York Times* reported that naked inmates there were forced to "to lift their genitals, to squat, to bend over and display themselves," tap-dance naked, and have their body cavities searched in front of others during a brutal shakedown.

The *Times* article ended with a scathing indictment of the US prison system. "The message with regard to the treatment of prisoners in the U.S. has been clear for years: Treat them any way you like. They're just animals."

When Billy was transferred to the Phelps Correctional Center, the torture he had endured at Hunt was over. The stories he told me about his reception from other inmates and officers at Phelps ended most of my fears.

Phelps was only 135 miles from Houston. Billy was closer to me than he had been in nearly twenty-four years. The long, exhausting trips that had tested my endurance for years were over.

Billy was almost sixty years old by then, and I was sixty-six. He had a heart murmur, high blood pressure, a stage-one heart block that reduced his heart rate, eyelids that were completely paralyzed, and growing paralysis of the eyes themselves. The medical staff at Phelps was concerned.

In August 2004, an assistant warden sent him to see an ophthalmologist in Lake Charles. The doctor told him his retinas needed daily light or they would stop functioning and he would go blind. He had almost no peripheral vision or lateral eye movement. He was already legally blind. Young inmates in his dormitory helped him tape his eye lids to his eyebrows every day so he could see. In November 2004, his "duty status" at Phelps was decreased, a change that showed prison officials at Phelps knew he was severely disabled.

In September, he was sent on several grueling trips to Charity Hospital in New Orleans as doctors there kept trying to diagnosis his condition. Guards at Phelps would wake him up at 1:00 a.m. to get dressed for the trip. An hour later, he was sent to the prison infirmary to put on an orange jumpsuit, required clothing for a hospital trip. He skipped breakfast to fight off the need to use the bathroom while he was shackled and manacled in the back of the prison van for the trip. It was a five-hour drive, and no pit stops were allowed. At Charity, he was locked in "the cage."

The cage for convict patients at the hospital was in a subbasement. It held about two dozen shackled inmates who waited anywhere from eight to twelve hours to see a doctor. The subbasement cage was filthy. Inmates who had to use the toilet were locked in an enclosure inside the cage before their restraints were removed. The smell of feces was overwhelming when they used the toilet.

The trips back to Phelps were harrowing. The officer driving the van routinely exceeded the speed limit to shorten the trip. Billy was shackled in the back, praying they wouldn't have a wreck. He knew there would be no surviving it.

On one trip to the hospital, the attending doctor said his EKG was defective. He was told to come back because the doctor suspected a heart block. How could a doctor, who thought an inmate had a heart block, send him back to prison? Why wasn't another EKG administered immediately? Kearns-Sayre syndrome was suspected in Billy's case. It can cause sudden cardiac arrest.

On October 5, I wrote Dr. Dwayne Thomas, the chief executive officer at Charity Hospital, to protest. I informed him, in case he had no idea, that trips from Phelps were grueling. Billy was in a "black box" for sixteen hours. The box covered keyholes in the handcuffs and forced prisoners to hold their arms in a parallel position. By the time he got back to Phelps, the cuffs and chains on his legs had rubbed his ankles raw, his legs were swollen, and he had temporarily lost most of the sensation in his hands.

My letter ended with a question. Why couldn't Billy stay at Charity until the hospital finished the tests needed to diagnose his condition? He was still slated to be examined by the neurology department and more blood tests were needed to check for several other conditions, including Refsum disease, a rare genetic condition that causes blindness. It was a waste of state money, I wrote the doctor, to schedule trip after trip. I sent copies of my letter to Richard Stalder and Bob Mann.

Since he was legally blind, Billy was essentially defenseless at Phelps. But a strange quirk of fate protected him. His autobiography, *A Life in the Balance: The Billy Wayne Sinclair Story,* was in big demand at the prison library. I had donated three copies to the library when Billy was sent to Phelps. Word that the "old man" had written a book spread quickly. It became the hottest item in the library. A three-page list of prisoners were waiting to read it. Most inmates at Phelps were young blacks from New Orleans. They didn't believe Billy was a snitch. When they read the book, they loved the way he had "taken on the system and kicked the shit out of it," as an eighteen-year-old inmate told Billy.

One day, a young inmate stopped Billy and asked to shake his hand.

"Mr. Sinclair, I heard about your book, but, you know, I can't read. My cellie read it to me, every night he read it to me. I respect you, man, and I respect your wife, too. You tell that woman I'm just, really, you know, a kid, but if I ever get me a wife, I hope she be half as strong as Jodie Sinclair, you know."

A couple of older inmates had done time with Billy at Angola.

They didn't regard Billy as a snitch either. Jerry Brown and Daryl Sylvester remembered him as a prison journalist trying to expose official corruption and a man who put his life on the line to integrate Angola when both men were held in segregated dormitories because they were black.

Brown worked in the garment factory at Phelps. When Billy was assigned to work there, Brown called all the inmates there together.

"I don't care what y'all may have heard about Billy Sinclair," Brown said. "I know the man. He was at Angola when the place was a bloody shithole. This man singlehandedly integrated the prison. He's paid his dues. I'm letting all of you know that I am standing with him. You got trouble with him, you got trouble with me. You know me, brothers, I don't want any shit. But I'm standing here to let all of you know I am with this man. He's good people. You do your thing and let him do his."

Daryl Sylvester was another inmate who put out the word that he and Billy were friends. Sylvester carried a lot of weight at Phelps. He made a point of walking the yard with Billy and sitting with him in the chow hall during Billy's first few weeks at Phelps to send a message to other prisoners.

The security staff didn't single Billy out for harsh treatment. The staff had a no-nonsense style of operation with one interest— keeping the prison safe. And Billy wasn't a threat. But there were exceptions: a visiting room guard and another young lieutenant.

Their dislike of me and Billy was apparent almost from the beginning. I wondered if the book had anything to do with their attitude. They seemed determined to humiliate us. I suspected they knew the prison library had a long list of inmates who wanted to read our book and that scores of prisoners already had. They no doubt knew the prison grapevine was full of admiring comments. That would easily make us targets of guards with an irresistible itch to put us in our places.

Early one Saturday morning, I got a frightening phone call from Billy.

"There's trouble, Jodie," Billy said in a whisper.

I sat straight up in bed, staring at the wall, trying to control my fear that he'd be hurt. I concentrated on the cross on my bedroom wall covered with a medieval pattern of flowers. There was no figure of Jesus on it. The shape was enough. It reminded me of how safe I felt as a child, kneeling between my grandparents at Mass.

Billy told me on the phone that an out-of-control lieutenant had started screaming orders at inmates lined up waiting for a weekend food sale. Prison authorities let inmate organizations hold the sales to raise money for recreational activities. Billy said the guard was yelling at the top of his lungs.

"You fucking vultures. The food's not ready yet. Get off the walk."

Two hundred inmates dutifully stepped off the walk near the prison's gym and into the prison yard, an open space where they were allowed to congregate, sun themselves, and talk. They were responding to notices posted on dormitory walls giving them official permission to gather for the sale. Suddenly, the door at the end of the walk flew open again. The same guard ran out screaming curses at inmates who had stepped into the yard.

"Okay motherfuckers, I want your IDs."

His eyes locked on Billy.

"Stay where you are," he demanded.

Inmates near Billy carefully stepped away from him. Others moved slowly toward the edges of the yard, hoping to get away without attracting the guard's attention. Billy stayed put. He'd been given a direct order. Any movement raised the possibility of being charged with disobeying an officer. The rampaging officer collected twenty to thirty prisoner IDs. Their owners sat with long faces waiting for the inevitable. The guard stormed back into the building with the cards.

When a guard took a prisoner's ID, a disciplinary write-up was on the way and perhaps a stint in lockdown. Guards targeted inmates they disliked to deliberately cost them "good time." Loss of good time lengthened their sentences by weeks or even months. There was no appeal. Prison disciplinary courts always believed a guard's claims no matter how specious or the number of inmate witnesses to the contrary. Billy had managed to call me as soon as he could. His voice had the quiet, ragged edge that I associated with trouble.

"Baby, don't come tomorrow if I don't call you back."

"What's wrong?"

"I could be in lockdown."

They were the words I dreaded. Lockdown cut inmate families off. Prisoners weren't allowed to call home for days, even weeks. Visiting privileges were terminated without notice. Families might travel hundreds of miles only to be barred from the prison when they arrived.

Prisoners in lockdown had no privileges. Their belongings were temporarily confiscated. They spent twenty-three hours a day in a cell for punishment. How was Billy going to manage without Band-Aids and help from young inmates to tape his eyes open every morning? I deposited money in his inmate account to pay for the Band-Aids and extra food to tide him over between the last meal of the day at 3:00 p.m. and breakfast the next morning at 5:00 a.m.

Would he sit in a cell for days with hunger pangs, unable to see without holding his eyes open with his fingers? I would have little information about him for weeks. Our lives, what we had of them, would be entirely disrupted.

Prisons are volatile places. Trouble frequently finds inmates who don't court it, like rogue waves that come from nowhere. Guards punish prisoners with psychological torture and verbal abuse for no reason. A bad mood could send an unstable guard out of control.

"Please Billy, just cut to the bottom line. Are you going to be locked up?"

"Can't tell. I just wanted to save you the trouble of making the trip tomorrow."

He had been at Phelps for ten months. There had been hints

of trouble from overbearing guards on a particular shift since Billy arrived. This was the first overt attack. It was something he had assiduously tried to avoid.

Wise to the ways of manipulative guards, Billy responded immediately to all orders with no retort. He gave the guards nothing to write him up for, no matter how abusive they got. But some persisted, unable to resist the temptation of goading a high-profile inmate into a write-up.

"I don't want you to make a 270-mile round trip to see me tomorrow for nothing. You know how this shift is, baby. It's targeting me. The first thing that guard did was run toward me. I haven't been in prison for forty years for nothing. I know the signs."

It was the same shift that ruined our previous visit. It was supposed to be a "picnic visit." They were reserved for inmates with good behavior records. Their visitors could bring in home-cooked food or specialties from restaurants. All the food and containers were searched. Picnic visits were restricted to a patio outside the prison's big visiting room unless the weather was bad. Then the inmates and their families were allowed to eat inside. The shift captain made the decision about the locale.

Inmates without good behavior records had "regular visits." The food they ate with their visitors came from vending machines in the visiting room. The arrangement was haphazard and arbitrary. It was never explained to visitors. Why shouldn't they be able to choose where they wanted to sit?

It was a question with no answer. Visitors who lodged complaints brought the guards' wrath down on the hapless inmate they were visiting. Sometimes the guard's vindictiveness lasted for weeks. Inmates were cursed at, yelled at, or otherwise goaded for no reason.

At chow: "I said go to the end of the line."

At pill call: "I said open your mouth wider."

Anytime: "Shut the fuck up."

The emphasis was on "fuck," a favorite one-syllable word among Southern rednecks.

A cool front had dropped the temperature in downtown Houston to forty-seven degrees the night before that visit. When I got to the prison at 10:30 that morning, a chilly breeze was blowing. Assuming all visits would take place indoors, I left my coat in the car. It was a mistake. The heat was on in the visiting room, but I was ordered outside. I addressed the guard politely.

"Sir, my husband may want to sit outside to eat what I've brought. But I'm not going to sit outside and eat. It's too chilly."

"You either eat outside, ma'am, or he doesn't get a picnic visit."

I rolled the cooler I had brought packed with Billy's favorite food back into the visiting room and sat down at a table. Billy sat down across from me.

"I won't eat without you, baby. It's too cold out there. I don't want you uncomfortable. That food doesn't mean that much to me."

But he had specifically ordered the fried chicken, barbecue wings, coleslaw, baked beans, and two little apple pies three days before, asking me to get them from a popular restaurant chain. I threw it all in the garbage when I got home. We ate candy from the vending machines instead.

"Jodie, I don't want any more picnic visits."

Billy decided to give up one of the few privileges to signal his contempt for that part of the system at Phelps. The prison was like a gossipy small town. When the guards noticed Billy had quit requesting picnic visits, even though he was eligible, we both knew it would bother them. They controlled inmates with carrots like picnic visits. But they didn't tempt Billy. I smiled, enjoying the prospect of the guards' discomfort.

"Baby, the captain and a couple of officers just showed up in the visiting room. They think you are going to complain about being told to sit outside. They'll say you were rude so they can terminate our visit."

I shifted my position at the table, deliberately turning my back on the captain and his officers, knowing they would get the drift. Prison is a place of interminable games. Billy and I played them better than most. We continued the visit on our terms, not theirs.

The phone call from Billy that morning, weeks after the picnic visit debacle, let me know trouble aimed at us could be rearing its ugly head.

"I'll try to call you back, Jodie. If I don't, I'm in lockdown."

We knew our conversation was being recorded. All prison phone systems record inmates. Prison officials maintained it was to prevent inmate scams. We used it to our advantage. It helped in situations like the "run-in" Billy was describing that morning. No doubt security guards were going to replay our conversation. Officers probably replayed all our conversations if there were incidents involving Billy.

Any disciplinary report they made would go straight to Johnny Creed's office. He had put Billy at Phelps. Guards at the prison would be questioned. Our comments on the tape would remind them of that. They would also be reminded how fast I could get the attention of the governor's office, several state legislators, and the media. I told Billy I would contact them right away if he was put in lockdown.

At 3:00 that afternoon, Billy called to tell me his ID had been returned and there was no write-up. That was atypical. Was the guard worried about "catching heat"? I crawled back in bed. The kind of sadism that delighted in hurting my husband made me sick to my stomach. I wondered how long I would have to keep thwarting the guards' nasty little games.

Worries about Billy's health never stopped plaguing me. After three months without a trip to Charity Hospital for a final diagnosis of Billy's condition, I wrote the president of the Louisiana senate begging for help. Dr. Donald Hines was a family physician. My January 18, 2005, letter explained Billy's medical condition, the potentially fatal outcomes I had been told were associated with it, and the need for further tests at Charity Hospital.

"All my life, Sir," I wrote the doctor, "I have had the great fortune of knowing physicians who rejoiced with me when they could help me and grieved with me when they could not. I have every reason to believe that you would be in that company."

The next day, I wrote Louisiana's new governor, Kathleen Blanco, the first woman in Louisiana history to be elected governor. Over her twenty-four years in state politics, she was known for "transparency, fairness and good government," according to *Louisiana Public Square,* a monthly Louisiana Public Broadcasting program.

I was deeply frightened. Some of the diseases Billy might have—myasthenia gravis and Kearns-Sayre syndrome—could cause sudden respiratory failure or cardiac arrest. Most of the tests he needed for a diagnosis had yet to be conducted. The corrections department was the only state agency that could schedule medical tests for inmates. But for three months, the department had done nothing.

The letters got results. Billy was quickly returned to Charity Hospital, where he spent almost a week undergoing test after test to determine why his eyes and eyelids were paralyzed and what the outcome might be. His condition was deemed inoperable.

I burst into tears when he told me. I wasn't going to let him die in prison or live there in misery until he was automatically released in 2011. The best medical care in the world was twenty blocks from my downtown Houston condo in a forty-acre medical park. The Texas Medical Center's hospitals, research centers, and offices and doctors were some of the best in the world. Billy doubted he would ever get to be treated there.

"The people that hate me have all the power," he said. "They've always had the power to decide things. I will never be paroled for that."

I contacted a Louisiana man I had heard was so powerful he had nothing to fear from the Baton Rouge clique opposing Billy's release. Senator Charles Jones was one of the most respected lawmakers in Louisiana. The votes the black legislator delivered from his constituency all over the state in 2003 had given Governor Blanco the winning margin in the governor's race.

He became her floor leader in the Louisiana senate. During the twenty-eight years he served in the legislature—from 1980 to 2008—his record of fighting for the poor and the disadvantaged was virtually unmatched. He was the powerhouse behind forty-three major pieces of legislation, over nearly three decades, that vastly improved the lot of the poor.

I turned to him for help after reading about another inmate Jones had represented successfully against daunting odds.

"He'll take the case, Billy. I have an appointment with him in Baton Rouge. If I have to crawl into his office on my hands and knees, I will. I just know he'll take the case."

The senator was a cordial man who greeted me with a smile and listened to me with growing concern when we met at his office at the state capitol. I gave him all the documents that were critical in Billy's case: medical assessments of Billy's condition, all the facts about his crime, his rehabilitation, the amount of time he had served, and the suppression of evidence at his trial. Jones told me he would take Billy's case on one condition.

"Mrs. Sinclair," he said, "I don't know why or how you came to me, but I feel God had a hand in it. I believe prayers brought you here and God is using me to answer them. I will take your case, but only after I personally meet with your husband. I want to get a sense of him as the man you've described and love."

Jones went to Phelps to see Billy in October 2004. The visit lasted three hours. He rose with a smile at the end and said Billy was indeed the man I had described. He agreed to represent Billy before the parole board. I paid him twenty-five thousand dollars to take the case, part of the money I had saved every month for years to help Billy when he came home.

When I got back to Houston, I contacted the Metropolitan Crime

Commission to thank its director, Rafael Goyeneche, for the group's continued support and to assure him the payment to Jones was a transparent, above-the-board fee with no illicit quid pro quo. There was no guarantee of a parole. But I knew with Jones we had the best shot.

The thought of Billy at home was overwhelming. My body had been in a tightly coiled, defensive "fight back" posture for too long. After twenty-five years, fear was a habit—maybe an addiction. Every light at the end of the tunnel had been a train. I wondered when and where the next attack was coming so I would be braced when it hit. It was better to focus on April 2011, when Billy would automatically be released on "good time" parole. But the logical mind said no. We stood a good chance with Jones. The blow might not be coming. I tried hard to banish my dread.

On an early spring morning in 2005, I wrote a note to myself to document forever a stunning moment in my life on an otherwise ordinary day that lifted fear from my soul and let me breathe in the joy of life again.

Houston, Texas
March 17, 2005

I met Billy Sinclair twenty-four years ago today. It's a Thursday morning with no extraordinary importance perhaps to anyone but me.

I am standing on a platform in the middle of Main Street waiting for a train that will take me to my office downtown. Another year has passed since I left my safe and promising world almost a quarter century ago when I met Billy Sinclair on St. Patrick's Day in the Death House at Angola.

I look east toward Sacred Heart Cathedral and begin a prayer. Only the Cross on its roof is visible above the buildings that stand between me, my mother's church, and the Catholic school she attended more than eighty years ago. It is my conscience.

I think of the victims' thirst for revenge and their crusade to keep my husband in prison. But no dark emotion wells up to cloud my thoughts. I have survived in spite of it. And so has he. Perhaps that is the lesson in our lives: The human spirit can endure in the face of implacable hatred. I end my prayer as the train arrives.

"... forgive us our trespasses as we forgive those who trespass against us..."

I step aboard and leave the victims in the care of the Cross. Love sings a hot song inside me. The train begins to move. I am traveling on a broad river, over the rocks, beyond the debris, lifted on its spray, wild and free.

Dear Billy... another letter to him starts in my head.

In January 2006, the new parole board under Governor Blanco granted Billy a hearing on Friday, April 21. Senator Jones represented us before the three-member panel. This time, I wasn't alone, bracing for another denial. Two of my sisters and my daughter were with me. We drove to Camp Beauregard, a minimum-security facility in central Louisiana, for the hearing.

We were searched before we were admitted to the prison. A guard escorted us to the chapel, where the panel was waiting at a table in front of the altar. My daughter sat behind me, her hand on my shoulder, knowing how much I would suffer if Billy was denied again after forty years in prison. Her love was my shield. While my daughter and my sons cherished the memories of their father, they still loved me, and they cared for Billy.

Chairs for the inmate congregants at Sunday service had been moved aside for the hearing. Members of the board faced the TV monitor where Billy would appear on a live feed from Phelps. A large group of the victim's family and friends were seated on one side of the chapel, staring at us. My sisters, my daughter, Senator Jones, and I were seated directly across from them on the other side. Everyone could see Billy on the monitor. Jones hadn't wanted him at the hearing. He feared it would become too emotional, possibly swaying the board to vote against him.

I told my sisters and my daughter not to react to the board's decision. If Billy was denied, I didn't want people who hated us to see us in tears. If he was paroled, I didn't think it was right to celebrate in front of them.

I stared at the panel, hoping for the best. Jim Wise was the panel's chair. He had been a deputy for eighteen years with the Calcasieu Parish sheriff's office and an investigator at Angola. Albert Mims Jr. was an outspoken crime victim's advocate. He was from Central City, a tough, low-income black neighborhood in New Orleans. His father had been murdered during an attempted robbery. The third member was Vedegra Scott, a prominent north Louisiana resident who had voted against a parole for Billy more than once.

The day of the hearing was dreary and overcast. Intermittent rain added to the gloom. Billy would later tell me that he felt a deep sense of dread. He didn't believe he would be paroled. He had been denied six times in fourteen years. The odds against him were overwhelming.

"The first thing I want to say," the victim's sister said, pulling an enlarged picture of J. C. Bodden from a bag as the hearing began, "is that my brother was not 'just a store clerk.' He was more than a 'convenience store clerk.' He was my brother, and he was a good husband. He was a friend to many people—and Billy Wayne Sinclair killed him."

Then Don Hooks stood up to speak. He was a prominent Baton Rouge businessman who was a high school friend of Bodden's. He spoke of the grief the family had suffered for years after Bodden's killing. The Baton Rouge district attorney's representative, Aaron Brooks—who had grossly and intentionally misrepresented facts to the board in previous hearings—spoke next.

In a quiet, measured tone, Brooks told the board the family was simply seeking justice. They felt the criminal justice system had betrayed them twice: first, when Billy's death sentence was vacated by the US Supreme Court and he was resentenced to life for shooting J. C. Bodden, and again when Governor Buddy Roemer commuted his life sentence to ninety years in 1992, making him parole eligible. Brooks begged the board not to betray the family a third time by granting Billy a parole.

Then, Gus Kinchen rose to speak on Billy's behalf. He was an unlikely but powerful ally. Kinchen played football at Louisiana State University with Billy Cannon, LSU's famous running back. From 1957 to 1960, Kinchen was a defensive end for the LSU Tigers. He was a member of LSU's famous 1958 National Championship team. His sons also played for LSU—one from 1984 to 1987 and another from 1989 to 1981.

Kinchen told the board he was surprised when a friend asked him to meet Billy Sinclair at the state police barracks where he was being held after exposing the pardons-for-sale scam. He said he had always thought Billy was a monster. But he said the man he met at the barracks was nothing like that. He asked the board to parole Billy.

Kinchen then greeted friends across the room who were opposing Billy's release, his LSU fans and longtime associates. He didn't ask them to change their positions. He said they would be always be his friends. But his strong plea for mercy, and his belief that Billy was a good man, must have been a surprise.

I stood up next to plead with the board for Billy's release. I had carefully vetted my remarks with Jones before the hearing.

"I have tried for twenty-five years to be the best possible wife I could be for my husband. He is desperately ill. I want to bring him home so I can get him the medical treatment he needs. I will bear the expense. The state of Louisiana should not have to pay for that. I love my husband and I have prepared a good home for him."

Jones then stood up calmly and moved gracefully to the center of the floor. He was confident and self-assured, a man in his element. He spoke about Billy's long, consistent history of rehabilitation, his role in exposing the pardon-selling scheme, and his support from the New Orleans Metropolitan Crime Commission.

Jones also told the board that Billy should have been convicted of manslaughter. He said Billy was given the death penalty because he didn't have competent counsel at his trial in 1966. He said Billy had served double the amount of time he would have served if he had been convicted of manslaughter.

"It is time for him to be released on parole," Jones said.

Brooks was on his feet immediately, raising an objection. But he waited politely for approval from the board before he began to speak. He accused Jones of misrepresenting the law and the facts in Billy's case. He said Billy was guilty of murder. He said the crime was entirely Billy's fault. It wasn't manslaughter. The victim shared none of the blame.

Senator Jones rose from his seat.

"I have been practicing law in the state of Louisiana for thirty years," he said, in a voice resonating with quiet dignity, "I have been a member of the state legislature for twenty-six years. I have never misrepresented the law or facts in any case."

Then he sat down. He had clearly won the moment.

Suddenly, a voice from Billy's opposition interrupted the hearing.

"My name's Gene Duke," a man said as he suddenly stood up.

The board's chairman interrupted him. Duke had been a crucial part of the Istrouma-based opposition in Billy's case for years. The chairman, Jim Wise, wasted no time addressing him.

"Excuse me," Wise said. "Our rules permit each side to have three speakers. This board has heard your three speakers. Please sit down."

I was astonished. It was the first time, at any of Billy's parole hearings, that a member of the opposition had been rebuked. Maybe this time the vote would be different.

"Mr. Sinclair," I heard the chairman say to Billy, "do you have any final remarks you want to make to the board?"

Billy's voice cracked as he began speaking.

"I've listened to the statements of both sides here today," he said. "And I am truly sorry for the pain that I have caused the Bodden family. I am the person responsible for what happened that night in December 1965—not J. C. Bodden." Then he bowed his head, braced for a denial.

The chairman announced it was time for the board to vote. I put my hands in my lap and squeezed them until the knuckles turned white. Vedegra Scott voted first. I expected her to deny Billy. But her vote surprised me.

"I vote for parole," she said. "But I want Mr. Sinclair to spend time in a halfway house before he is released." A staffer approached her and whispered in her ear. She withdrew her requirement for Billy to do time in a halfway house and reiterated her vote.

"I vote for parole," she said.

Albert Mims was next. I held my breath, waiting for a denial from a man whose father was murdered in New Orleans during a robbery.

"Billy Sinclair has served forty years," Mims said. "The police know who murdered my father. He's never served a day. I vote for parole."

Then it was the chairman's turn.

"I've seen a lot of cases like this in my day," Wise said. "I vote for parole."

There was dead silence in the room. Minutes went by. Then Brooks stood up.

"We are leaving," he said. "There is no justice here."

The victim's family and friends followed him out of the room without a word. Prison officials asked us to wait in the chapel until Billy's opponents had cleared the prison and left the parking lot, fearful that, stunned by the board's decision, they might confront us.

Billy didn't hear the vote. He sat without moving until a SWAT officer, assigned to guard him during the hearing, came up and told him he'd been paroled. He stood up in shock. When he stepped out of the witness room, a group of young gangbanger inmates from

New Orleans were waiting outside. They began to clap and high-five him.

"The old man made parole," they kept yelling, celebrating his release up and down the walk to the dormitory.

I could breathe at last. I drove from Camp Beauregard to Phelps to see Billy with my sisters and my daughter. We had been granted permission to visit him. We all talked and held hands. It all seemed unreal after a quarter of a century of waiting for Billy to be released. My daughter asked how long it would be before the system let him go.

"It generally takes five to six weeks for everything to be processed," Billy said.

"Not this time," I said. "Senator Jones is going to push for an immediate release. We need to get you out of here before something bad happens."

Could the system suddenly declare the vote invalid? Would the Istrouma network find a way to block the parole? Billy learned from a high-ranking prison official after we left that he would be released in forty-eight hours.

"Don't breathe a word to anyone, not even your wife," he said the prison official whispered to him. "We just got word from the secretary of corrections to have you ready for processing out on Monday. There's some people who want you out of the system now. I mean, like yesterday. Just be ready to go Monday morning."

On Monday April 24, 2006, twenty-five years after I met Billy in the death house at the Louisiana State Penitentiary at Angola, he was released on parole. An early afternoon call to my office in downtown Houston from one of Billy's brothers gave me the news I had waited a quarter of a century to hear.

I rushed out of my office and drove to the prison. I walked into the lobby and stopped dead in my tracks when I saw Billy. His jeans had holes in the knees and the legs. His shoes were so old, the soles flapped when he walked. He had given all his good clothes and belongings to young inmates in his dorm to thank them for helping him. He had on their threadbare clothes for the trip home.

We walked across the parking lot to my car, holding hands. We were alone for the first time in twenty-five years. I showed him how to belt himself in, turned the key in the ignition, and drove out of a prison parking lot in Louisiana for the last time, headed west to Texas with my husband.

We had believed in rehabilitation and honesty and had paid a terrible price. But the nightmare was over. We had a future together now, and it was smiling back at us.

IN HIS OWN WORDS: BILLY SINCLAIR'S FIRST DAY OF FREEDOM

NEARLY HALF A CENTURY IN prison ended for me without much fanfare on a quiet spring Monday afternoon. On the twenty-fourth of April, 2006, at 2:00 p.m., I was summoned to the control center. A security officer directed me toward an interview room where a classification officer sat behind a desk with a packet of documents.

"Billy," she said, "you've waited a long time for these. They're your release papers. Sign them and you are a free man."

I sat down and stared at her without moving.

"Billy," she repeated, "you are free when you sign these papers."

She smiled, lightly tapping the papers.

"Do you have someone to pick you up?"

"My wife in Houston," I said. "She's at work."

I hadn't expected to be released three days after the parole hearing. Normally, the process took weeks. I signed the documents and handed them back to her. She looked up, puzzled.

"Billy," she said gently, as though she were talking to a child. "You can get up and walk out of here this minute if you want. You are not a prisoner of Louisiana anymore."

I was sixty-one years old. I had served more than four decades in prison. Band-Aids held my eyelids up. The thought of being able to get up and walk out the front gate staggered me.

"I will call my brother in Sioux Falls and have him contact my wife," I said. "She can get here from Houston in about two hours."

I walked back to the prison dorm and, like a robot, dialed my brother's number.

"John, call Jodie at work," I said. "Tell her to come get me. I am free."

The gasp was audible.

"Thank God, brother. Thank God."

Jodie left to pick me up immediately. By 5:30, she had driven the 135 miles from Houston to the Phelps Correctional Center just outside DeQuincy, Louisiana. The warden escorted us through the lobby of the administration building. A photographer from a television station in Lake Charles was waiting at the front gate to film my release. We didn't stop for interviews.

I shook the warden's hand and walked out of the administration building across the parking lot with Jodie. We got into the car. She patted me on the shoulder and smiled. I sat there, worried that I would hear a siren and see flashing lights in the rearview mirror as we left. It was a long-buried reflex.

"How many miles to the state line?" I asked Jodie.

"Twenty or so," she said, smiling, and drove out of the prison.

I took my first real breath of freedom in Texas as Louisiana disappeared behind me forever. I was "headed for a better life" in the Lone Star State, listening to Keith Urban sing that song. I had asked Jodie to bring a tape of the song—I didn't know about CDs—so I could listen to it on the way home.

Four decades in prison hadn't prepared me for the free world. I had watched forty Super Bowls, the Vietnam War, political assassinations, moon landings, Watergate, the Gulf War, 9/11, and a succession of cultural revolutions on television. On the inside, I lived with the specter of death nearby, surviving a death sentence and an era of violence that once made Angola "the bloodiest prison in America." In a milieu of internal official corruption, racial hatred among inmates, and hopelessness, mental illness, sorrow, and suffering, I somehow managed to eke out a personal rehabilitation.

But "rehabilitation" is a penal concept—it impresses prison administrators, parole boards, and the general public. It is not, however, a social skill. It does not equip a long-term inmate with the skills to successfully reenter society. That reality stomped on all my expectations as Jodie and I drove home.

Jodie drove into Houston on the city's massive freeway system at sunset, circling around downtown before taking the exit to 2016 Main, our high-rise condo. She wanted me to see the lights of the mammoth buildings soaring into the sky downtown at night. It was awe-inspiring. Surges of nervous energy cascaded throughout my body. The lights, the speeding flow of traffic, the mind-boggling structures, and the incredible sounds nearly short-circuited my brain. I felt nervous. I didn't have the slightest idea of where we were going.

"We're almost home," Jodie said, sensing my concern.

"Home."

The word had an almost mythical sound to me. I had never had a "home"—not in the real sense of the word. I had known only places where I lived. Jodie and I had been married a quarter of a century. She had spent those twenty-five years creating a home for me. I had tried to imagine it. But I couldn't visualize it even with the pictures she had sent me over the years.

We left the freeway and drove a few blocks when Jodie suddenly made a right turn into the back of a dimly lit, twenty-six-story structure. It looked like a courthouse to me.

"Where are we?" I asked, confused.

"We're home," Jodie said, gently patting my knee. "This is the garage in our building."

She swiped a card to open the gates into the building.

"I'll get you your own swipe card, tomorrow," she said.

Our home was a condominium Jodie owned in one of the oldest, and most well-known, high-rise buildings in downtown Houston—2016 Main.

"You park in the building where you live?" I said, bewildered. I remembered driveways, carports, and front-yard parking. It was hard to fathom a place to live with an underground level of parking and four floors of parking above the street. Jodie expertly drove up and around three floors to our parking space.

"Each homeowner has his own parking space," she explained. She seemed so tuned to my feelings, almost anticipating each reaction, each question.

We walked up to a glass door. She used a "swipe" card to gain entry.

"First thing in the morning," Jodie said, squeezing my hand, "we will get you a card. You cannot get into this building without a swipe card. One of the reasons I bought this condo was because of the security."

Then she paused.

"If those crazy people in Baton Rouge ever decide to come over here to hurt you the way they said they would," she whispered fiercely, "they won't be able to get into this building. Too much security."

"Those people won't come, Jodie. They've gotten old like me," I said, thinking how ironic it was the prison term "security" was playing such a role in my first day of freedom.

I pulled her close to me as we waited for an elevator to take us up to the sixteenth floor. The building had four elevators. It would take weeks before I mastered the precise location of the sixteenth floor. I cursed myself each time I did not know instinctively where the button was located on the panel. While my lack of good vision played a role, it was only a small part. The panel itself intimidated me. Worst yet, knowing which way to automatically turn upon exiting the elevator proved even more difficult.

The elevator arrived. We stepped out on the sixteenth floor into a small foyer with tile flooring. Two long, carpeted hallways ran in separate directions. I followed Jodie to our unit. It was like walking through a luxurious hotel. As she inserted a key into 1613, she said, "We'll get you a key tomorrow morning." She opened the door.

"This is your home," she said, taking my hand and leading me inside.

I was like a child being led into an exotic, free-to-touch toy land. There were plants and indoor trees everywhere. Beautiful shelves were filled with books of every kind. A polished two-century-old armoire stood between the bookshelves. It was utterly majestic. The curtains were open. They revealed an amazing view of the lighted downtown Houston skyline at night. I sat down on a large white sofa. I could not speak. Tears welled up in my eyes.

I realized the sacrifices Jodie had made to make this a reality for me. It went far beyond the twenty-five thousand dollars she paid Jones to represent me and probably close to another $100,000 spent over the past quarter century for telephone calls, legal fees, court-filing fees, visiting trips, money she put in my account, FedEx bills, and trips to Kinko's to Xerox documents. And there were those trips she made to bookstores, antique shops, art shops, and a thousand other little places to select the right things to create the home that now overwhelmed me.

I sat on the sofa, reached out for Jodie as she stood before me, and pulled her between my legs. We could look each directly in the eyes.

"I love you, baby," I whispered. "It is . . . it is . . ."

I fought back tears.

"It is simply beautiful," I continued. "This is, and forever will be, the greatest moment in my life. It is so much more than you said, than you described—it is home."

She pulled my head against her chest.

"It is all yours, darling," she said, running her hand through my prison-shortened hair. "I made it for you—our home. Everything, every stitch, every book was put here with you in mind, with the love I have for you."

My arms encircled her small waist. I felt completely safe for the first time in my life. Forty years of living under virtual siege, in a state of perpetual heightened alert, drained away from me.

We toured the rest of our small, cozy home. Everything was neat, elegant, and utterly overwhelming.

"I must shower," I said.

The horrible sweat-smell of prison was torturing me. I wanted out of the ragged clothes I had on when we left Phelps. The shower was smaller than prison showers. The hot water felt good as I moved about trying to locate soap and shampoo. I nearly slipped, instinctively reaching for a towel rack on the wall. It broke loose. I was devastated. I had only been home for moments before breaking something. I could not, and would not, let it be an omen.

"It was just a stupid accident," I reassured myself.

Prison haunts the souls of those that survive it. Images of prison showers rushed back over me, like waves over the rocks. The curses, shouts, laughter, and crude grab-assing from prison showers reverberated around the corners in my brain.

"No more," I screamed silently to all the demons in cell blocks, dormitories, and solitary death cells. "You motherfuckers have no place in my world anymore ... fuck you, FUCK you!"

I pressed both hands against the white tile wall, letting the steaming hot water flow effortlessly down the back of my neck. "No more," I whispered as steam behind the shower curtain absorbed my tears.

Jodie had dinner ready by the time I got out of the shower. I don't remember what it was, but it was so good—a home-cooked meal. I ate slowly, sitting at our dining room table looking across our living room out the sliding glass windows at downtown Houston's skyline, amazed by its power and structure. The nation's fourth-largest city awaited me. I knew how to survive in prison. What would the power and pace of the free world demand of me?

Jodie led me to the bedroom, pulled a luxurious comforter back, patted the mattress, and told me to lie down on my side of our queen-sized four poster bed while she got ready for bed. I took off the white terry-cloth bathrobe she had bought for me. I never had a bathrobe before. Then I sank down into the mattress, pulled the comforter over me, and fell into a deep, peaceful sleep until the morning sun peeped through the curtains.

OUR REQUIEM

When Billy Sinclair and I pass away, I pray we will go together, me behind him in the saddle, nestled against his back, riding Destiny's horse into the clouds over the beautiful hills around us, the reins in his hands, my arms locked around his waist.

If I go first, I will wait for him at eternity's edge, as he would for me. Then, we will ride out of time together to face whatever awaits us.

Were we God's children or disciples of the Devil? A heavenly gift transformed Billy into the man of moral strength and character I loved.

Some might say it's a long shot. But I'm betting on Heaven.

Jodie Sinclair
The Texas Hill Country
May 2018

ACKNOWLEDGMENTS

Joyce Hooper Corrington

Joyce Corrington and I have been friends for sixty years. I am deeply grateful for her help with this book. Her vast experience in writing movies, books, and TV shows was an inspiration during the two years it took to write my memoir.

Joyce wrote scripts for six movies, including *The Omega Man* and *Boxcar Bertha.* She and her late husband, Bill Corrington, were head writers for daytime TV shows, including *Texas,* a series that was nominated twice for a Writers Guild of America award. They produced *Superior Court,* also nominated for an Emmy. After her husband's death, she coproduced *Decoration Day,* a 1990s Hallmark Hall of Fame TV show, which was also nominated for an Emmy.

She and her husband wrote four popular mystery novels. She wrote two more after his death. Before her retirement, she was the co-executive producer of eleven seasons of *The Real World,* an MTV series nominated for a People's Choice award.

BILLY SINCLAIR'S RECORD OF REHABILITATION

IN 1986, BILLY SINCLAIR WAS the only inmate who reported the notorious pardons-for-sale scam at Angola. Prisoners who paid the bribe were released after providing evidence in the case. Billy remained behind bars even though he exposed the scam. The prosecutor said he didn't provide enough evidence.

From 1979 to 1986, as co-editor of the *Angolite*—the nation's only uncensored prison magazine—he won the highest national honors for his articles: the George Polk Award, the Sidney Hillman Award, the American Bar Association's Silver Gavel, and the Robert F. Kennedy Award for Special Interest Journalism.

He traveled statewide without incident on overnight trips with an unarmed guard making speeches at Louisiana schools from 1980 to 1985. He was a model prisoner at the Louisiana state police barracks for eight years.